1991

THE ECONOMIC ORGANIZATION
OF THE HOUSEHOLD

The economic organization of the household

W. Keith Bryant
Consumer Economics and Housing, Cornell University

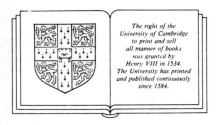

The right of the
University of Cambridge
to print and sell
all manner of books
was granted by
Henry VIII in 1534.
The University has printed
and published continuously
since 1584.

Cambridge University Press
Cambridge
New York   Port Chester   Melbourne   Sydney

Published by the Press Syndicate of the University of Cambridge
The Pitt Building, Trumpington Street, Cambridge CB2 1RP
40 West 20th Street, New York, NY 10011, USA
10 Stamford Road, Oakleigh, Melbourne 3166, Australia

First published 1990

Printed in the United States of America

Library of Congress Cataloging-in-Publication Data
Bryant, W. Keith (Wilfrid Keith), 1934–
The economic organization of the household / W. Keith Bryant.
p.   cm.
Includes bibliographical references (p.   ) and index.
ISBN 0-521-39187-3. – ISBN 0-521-39840-1
1. Consumption (Economics) – United States.   2. Income – United
States.   3. Households – United States.   4. Family – Economic aspects –
United States.   5. Consumption (Economics)   6. Income.
7. Households.   8. Family – Economic aspects.   I. Title.
HC110.C6B79   1990
339.2′2 – dc20   90-1910

British Library Cataloguing in Publication Data
Bryant, W. Keith
The economic organization of the household.
1. Household financial management
I. Title
640.42

ISBN 0–521–39187–3 hardback
ISBN 0–521–39840–1 paperback

to Frederick,
Andrew of Humpton, Wyoming,
Sunny, Abby, Vladimir, and Juan Valdes,
all of whom contributed so much
to the making of a family

CONTENTS

vii

Contents

x   **Contents**

TABLES AND FIGURES

xi

The economics of the family is a fairly new field of endeavor but its study is now widely dispersed in the curriculum among economics courses and courses on women's issues. To my knowledge, no attempt has been made to collect all the diverse threads of research and discussion, weave them together, and present them as whole cloth for either the undergraduate or the beginning graduate student. *Economics and Consumer Behavior* by Angus Deaton and John Muellbauer is the best treatment of demand theory and application for the advanced graduate student. Mark Killingworth's *Labor Supply* accomplishes the same task with respect to labor supply questions. T. W. Schultz's *The Economics of the Family* is the edited version of a collection of research papers on the family from two National Bureau of Economic Research conferences in the early 1970s. Gary Becker's *A Treatise on the Family* is what the title says it is and is not a textbook. None of these books covers the field from demand through labor supply and human capital to fertility and marriage and divorce. None is suitable as a text either at the undergraduate or at the first-year graduate level. None lays out the basic models of the household simply enough to serve as an introduction for family scholars from other social sciences who, nonetheless, need an introduction to the material. This book is my attempt to fill this need.

Consequently, this is a textbook on the economics of the family for students who have had as background a semester of introductory microeconomics. It is intended as a text for a junior–senior level semester-long course, but it can be used by first-year graduate students in economics programs, especially applied economics programs, and by students of the family in other social sciences who want a survey and introduction to the subject.

Comparative static analysis is used throughout and, with only minor exceptions, perfect foresight and certainty are assumed in the belief that a firm grounding in the basics is desirable. The discussion uses English, geometry, and algebra, with calculus relegated to mathematical notes following each chapter's notes. Indifference curve diagrams are used wherever possible to cement the basic hypothesis that family behavior arises out of attempts to maximize satisfaction subject to resource, legal, social, and technological constraints. Demand and supply diagrams are used periodically where appropriate.

The genesis of the book occurred in the late 1960s at the University of Minnesota when Vern Ruttan encouraged me to mount a consumption economics course. The subject matter of the course has evolved over time, first at Minnesota and since 1974 at Cornell University. The book has grown out of my experience in teaching the course and out of the reading and research that the course has stimulated.

The book shows the influence of my Cornell colleagues, Jenny Gerner, Scott Maynes, Jean Robinson, Katy Walker, and Peter Zorn. Almost daily discussions with them over the years and joint research with Jenny Gerner have provided much insight and given me great pleasure. Jean Robinson's detailed comments on the first draft were especially useful in making the material accessible to undergraduates. The first draft was written while on sabbatical in 1980 at the Landbouwhogelschool, Wageningen, Holland. I am indebted to Clio Presvelou for generously financing the sabbatical and for stimulating cricitism during the year in the Netherlands.

Past graduate students and now present colleagues Robin Douthitt, Loren Geistfeld, Jutta Joesch, Angela Mikalauskas, Pam Norum, Jan Pappalardo, Bill Putsis, Kay Stafford, Yan Wang, Rob Weagley, and Cathy Zick have all deepened my understanding of the subject and have stretched my capabilities. Fifteen years of questions and challenges from Cornell undergraduates have left their beneficial imprint on the text. One undergraduate, Seth Plattus, read the first draft and showed me ways to lighten the prose and to make clear what was not. I owe Cornell University a great debt for providing me access to such fine students.

The book's title is a variation of the title of one of T. W. Schultz's many books, *The Economic Organization of Agriculture.* His personal encouragement of my work at several points in my career has meant much.

Authors owe a great deal to their families for the space, peace, and time required to write and the encouragement to keep at it. My wife, Marty, and children, Frances and Mike, contributed so much more because they also served as sounding boards and critics for my ideas during innumerable dinnertime discussions as the children grew up. Furthermore, my children's behavior served as class examples. It is the penance paid for being the children of a family economist.

Without Patsy Sellen, my secretary for this project, the book would still be a muddle of documents on floppies gathering dust on my desk and shelves. Both she and I received much needed word processing advice from Pat Baker. Cathy Brashear transformed my sketches into camera-ready figures. I am indebted to them.

Matthew Hendryx, economics editor at Cambridge University Press, helped determine the final content of the manuscript. Russell Hahn guided me smoothly through the mysteries of book publication. A special thanks is due to Pam Bruton, my copy editor, for the care she took in preserving meaning while greatly improving clarity. Deep in my Canadian soul, however, I will continue to believe that *center* and *theater* are spelled with "re."

Ithaca, New York
November 1989

CHAPTER ONE

Introduction

The Economic Organization of the Household is an analysis of the economic behavior of the household. The easiest way to introduce the subject matter, its focus and limits, is to elaborate the meaning of each of the words in the title. We begin with the term *household*.

Household defined

Like all terms that do double duty in scholarly and common parlance, the term *household* has a multiplicity of meanings. In common speech, *household* means "those who dwell under the same roof and compose a family." [1] We seek, however, to explicate its meaning as used by economists.

In common with other social scientists, economists hold that a large part of human behavior is goal directed. Humans do not behave randomly nor are they pushed about like billiard balls having no control over their direction, velocity, and spin. By and large, humans attempt to control their lives so as to further their goals. An important part of human behavior is purposive.

Economists observe that humans tend to group themselves into larger units for the purpose of pursuing their goals. Of course, each group typically pursues several goals simultaneously. However, for the purposes of analysis economists have found it possible and useful to single out a few major goals – high-level goals, so to speak – and to distinguish among types of groups on the basis of the major goal pursued. Historically, economics identified and studied three types of groups and a fourth is gaining attention. The three are the satisfaction-seeking household, the profit-seeking firm, and the social welfare-seeking government. Economics is at present attempting to understand and explain the behavior of a fourth: the not-for-profit-seeking agency (e.g., foundations, churches, cooperatives, service clubs). We are here concerned with the behavior of the satisfaction-seeking household. The major criterion, therefore, by which economists distinguish households from other units in society is by the major goal they pursue, that of satisfaction seeking.

Satisfaction and *utility* are two terms economists commonly use to describe the overarching goal of households. *Well-being* is a term more commonly used by sociologists and home economists but it refers to the same goal. The critical

1

distinction that economists make is that although income generation and wealth accumulation may be the means to increased satisfaction, well-being, or utility, the maximization of wealth or of income is not a sufficient or even a necessary means to the maximization of satisfaction. If it were, households would behave much differently than they in fact do. Indeed, they would be identical with firms; the distinction between households and firms would collapse and with it half of the corpus of economic theory. Well-being or satisfaction certainly includes material well-being, but other factors, such as love, laughter, health, and nurture, also contribute importantly. The concept of satisfaction is cast broadly, then, rather than narrowly restricted to materialism. The view that economics is concerned only with dollars and cents or with greed is a gross misrepresentation.

That a group pursues satisfaction is not sufficient, however, to make it a household. In a large sense it is certainly the case that the people of the United States have banded together as citizens for the purpose of furthering their mutual well-being. But we do not call such a group a household. Therefore, another distinguishing feature of a household is that it is a *small constituent part of the larger society* and is not society itself. There is a continuum, of course, at one end of which is Robinson Crusoe, who was simultaneously a single-person household and a society, at least until Friday came along. At the other end of the continuum is the nation-state, or perhaps "Spaceship Earth" with its myriad of households, firms, governments, and agencies. We are concerned only with the smallest units of society that are formed for the purpose of increasing the well-being of their members.

Two other characteristics of households are important. One is that the unit must have *resources* with which satisfaction may be pursued and that these resources must be *shared* among the members. The other is that the group must have alternative ways of improving its well-being so that *choice* exists. Without resources a household is not viable and dissolves, the members perishing or joining other households that do have resources. Without the sharing of resources among household members, those with the least resources die or leave to join other households where resources are shared. Without choice, the unit cannot pursue its own well-being and, therefore, cannot be said to be goal seeking.

The attributes just discussed – pursuing the well-being or utility of its members, being small, possessing and sharing resources, and having alternatives – are all rather abstract. How do households typically pursue members' well-being? Household resources are rented or sold to obtain the income with which to purchase goods, services, and environment that increase satisfaction, and resources are used within the household to produce the goods, services, and environment that contribute to the well-being of its members: food, clothing, shelter, basic health services, socialization, nurture, love, leisure, and so on.

Thus, households do and provide those things that we usually think of families as doing and providing. But families (which we define as parents and children, with perhaps some other blood relatives, living together) are not the only entities that have these attributes and perform these tasks. Consequently, our concept of household must be broad enough to include single persons living alone, couples, and other groups of people that have the same attributes and perform the same functions – for example, communes of the kibbutz type in Israel and the various communal groups and communities that exist in the United States.

There are other characteristics of households that, although typical, are not universal. The goods, services, and social and physical environments that are provided to members of households are provided through nonmarket transactions among household members. The term *nonmarket* means that money is not exchanged in return for the things provided. The transactions are typically of a one-way nature or have an implicit barter exchange nature. There is reciprocity in the sense that members do things for each other but the reciprocity need not take place simultaneously and no strict or formal accounting is made of the balance of payments among members. It is further the case that typically most of the resources in a household are regarded as common property and are allocated in common.

The U.S. Bureau of the Census defines a household as "all persons who occupy . . . separate living quarters. . . . A household includes related family members and all the unrelated persons who share the separate living quarters" (1982, p. 4). Although this definition includes groups of unrelated individuals who share an apartment and no other resources (e.g., students) and, thus, is somewhat broader than we intend, it is the best current empirical definition of a household.

Households so defined have changed in number and in type over the recent past, the changes bearing witness to the dynamic nature of households. Some of these changes are documented in Table 1.1, which shows the numbers and types of households in the United States in both 1950 and 1980. Over the thirty-year period from 1950 to 1980, the number of households increased by 85 percent from 43.6 million to 80.8 million. The increase in the population and rising affluence are two of the important factors underlying this increase.[2] More fascinating is the changing importance of the several types of households. Family households became less important, dropping from 89 percent of the total in 1950 to 74 percent in 1980, and nonfamily households became more important. Within both family and nonfamily households, those headed by women became much more important. The average sizes of both households and families fell over the thirty-year period: household size by 18 percent; family size by 7 percent. Average household size (including family and nonfamily households) fell because family size and the importance of families declined. Family size fell because of declining birthrates and because the propor-

Table 1.1 *Number, type, and size of households in the United States: 1950 and 1980*

| | 1950 | | 1980 | |
Type of household	Number[a]	%	Number[a]	%
Total households	43,554	100	80,776	100
Family households	38,838	89	59,550	74
Married couples	34,075	78	49,112	61
Male headed (without spouse)	1,169	3	1,733	2
Female headed (without spouse)	3,594	8	8,705	11
Nonfamily households	4,716	11	21,226	26
Male	1,668	4	8,807	11
Female	3,048	7	12,419	15
Average household size	3.37		2.76	
Average family size	3.54		3.29	

[a] In thousands.
Source: U.S. Bureau of the Census 1982, Table 60, p. 43.

tion of families with only one spouse rose. Later chapters will return to these trends and seek explanations.

A household, then, may be one person or a small group of people who share resources for the purpose of pursuing their mutual well-being. It possesses resources that are shared among household members and has several alternative ways of using them to gain its ends.

Household economic organization

Economics conceives groups in society – households, firms, governments, and agencies – as deploying the resources at their disposal among activities the outcomes of which they expect to further their goals. Firms, for instance, use labor, land, and capital in processes from which they expect to reap profits. Likewise, households allocate their resources among several activities with the expectation that the outcomes will be found to be satisfying; that is, the outcomes will enhance the well-being of household members.

Conditions both inside and outside the household determine the amounts and kinds of resources possessed by the household, the productivities of each resource in the activities pursued, and the satisfaction the household receives from the activities. As these conditions change, some activities will yield more satisfaction and others less. As this happens, incentives are created for the household to reduce or terminate the activities yielding less satisfaction and to initiate or expand the activities yielding more. Likewise, resource productivity in each activity will alter as conditions change. The gaps between actual and potential resource productivity serve as incentives for the household to shift some resources out of those activities in which they are less productive and into those activities in which they are more. Thus, as the conditions inside and outside the household change, the *patterns of resource use and of activities* pursued by the household change. These patterns are part of what is meant by the economic organization of the household.

Three other attributes complete what is meant by the term. These are the *size, composition,* and *structure* of the household. How so? It has been noted that to an economist, the salient features of the household are the resources it possesses and what (the activities) it does with them to improve its well-being. A two-person household has more labor resources than a one-person household. Clearly then, the size of the household importantly affects the quantity of resources at the household's disposal. A two-person household composed of an adult and a child has fewer resources than a two-person household made up of two adults. Equally clearly then, the composition of the household importantly affects the quantity of its resources.

The structure of a household, too, affects the resources possessed by the household. Compare, for instance, two otherwise-identical couples, one married and the other not. The resources of a household include both present resources and future, expected resources. Because of the marriage commitment and the costs of divorce, the future of the married couple is more certain than the future of the unmarried one. Consequently, the future, expected resources of the married household are greater than those of the unmarried one. The structure of the household, therefore, importantly affects household resources.

It is also the case that the size, composition, and structure of the household are attributes of activities that yield satisfaction independently of the satisfaction indirectly produced by the resources implicit in these three attributes. Rearing children affects the size and the composition of the household, but it also is an important activity of the household that may yield satisfaction. The arrival of a baby increases family size and it alters family well-being: (perhaps) improving it if children are planned and (perhaps) reducing it if children are not. Finally, it is unnecessary to dwell on the fact that marriage and divorce are activities that profoundly affect the structure and well-being of the households involved.

By economic organization of the household, then, is meant the size, structure, and composition of the household as well as the patterns of resource use and of activities pursued by the household.

The resource–activity–satisfaction schema elaborated

Both resources and activities can be analyzed so as to flesh out the schema that has been presented and give it greater meaning. These classification schemes also serve to organize the analysis and discussion of future chapters. We begin with resources.

Household resources

The resources of the household can be broken down into *human* and *physical* resources. Each of these can be further divided. *Human resources* include the time, skills, and energy of each member of the household. The time of each member is unique and nonrenewable. Although there are ways to prolong life and certainly many to shorten it, in each day each individual has twenty-four hours – no more and no less – and they must be used in some fashion. Along with the time of each household member necessarily comes the individual's skills and energy. The skills may be physical, like strength, agility, grace, and the ability to perform certain physical activities. Or the skills may be mental capacities of various sorts, like memory, logic, insight, and adeptness at personal relations. The skills may be general in that they may be applied in a wide variety of contexts, or they may be specific and be capable of being applied in only one context or in a very narrow range of contexts. The energy an individual possesses can be physical or mental. In contrast to an individual's time, skills and energy can be developed or dissipated and, thus, are renewable within bounds.

Physical resources include financial resources and can be arranged along any number of continua, each one stressing a different attribute of the resources. One continuum refers to the ease with which resources can be changed into other forms – how liquid they are. Along this continuum, cash is the most liquid. One's credit line, savings accounts, stocks, and bonds are somewhat less liquid, and cars, houses, and land are even less so. Perhaps, household goods like furniture and appliances are least liquid, there being exceedingly poorly developed markets for such secondhand articles. Another continuum refers to the physical asset's durability; that is, its length of useful life. Along such a continuum perishable food owned by the household has a very short life whereas land is long-lived. The length of life of cash depends, of course, on the rate of inflation, a high rate depreciating the value of a dollar very quickly.

The usefulness of the particular continuum employed to classify resources depends on the problem being analyzed. Different continua will be used in this book as different problems are analyzed. The distinction between *time* and *income* as representing a human and a physical resource will be employed extensively.

Household activities

Household activities involve the use of resources, human and physical, and have attributes from which the household derives satisfaction either directly or indirectly. Whether satisfaction is derived directly or indirectly forms the basis for one major classification of activities. Work is an example of an activity from which satisfaction is derived indirectly. Consumption and leisure activities are examples of activities from which satisfaction is derived directly. Another major classification arises out of the fact that some activities involve the transfer of resources from one period to another whereas others do not. Saving and borrowing are examples of activities that transfer resources between periods. Consumption, work, and leisure activities do not. A third classification of activities is based on whether the activities involve one- or two-way transfers of resources either within the household or between households.

Some activities involve the transformation of particular resources into forms more highly valued by the household. These are called *work* activities. The most obvious example is, perhaps, the process whereby an individual sells his or her skills and time in return for cash income. Less often the work involves exchanging one's skills and time for goods and services, as when a student does housework and child care for a family in return for room and board. Work activities are usually divided into *market work* and *nonmarket work* (also called *household work*) activities. This distinction is based on whether the work activities take place in the context of an employer–employee relationship (i.e., in the labor market) or take place in the worker's household, where the goods and services produced are also consumed.

One of the distinctions between *work* and *nonwork,* or *leisure,* activities is that the household derives satisfaction directly from the latter activities but only indirectly from the former. This is not entirely true, because many of us derive much pleasure from work. The person who is in love with his or her job and the avid weekend gardener both derive much pleasure directly from these activities, as well as income, vegetables, and flowers. The distinction is really a relative one: those activities performed primarily for the money or the goods and services produced are called work; those performed primarily for pleasure are called nonwork. To simplify discussion, for many of the topics addressed in this book we will not consider the satisfaction yielded by work activities or the income or goods and services yielded by the nonwork activities. This simplification will not much affect the validity of the analyses or the conclusions reached.

A distinction is also made between activities from which utility is derived immediately and activities from which utility is derived in some future period.

Another way of looking at this distinction is to note that some activities simply transfer resources from one period to another and other activities use resources in the current period for the purpose of immediate satisfaction. The former are called *saving* or *investment* activities. The latter are called *consumption* activities.

The essence of saving is the postponement of consumption and, thus, present pleasure. Again, we must note that some people do derive satisfaction directly from the process of saving in addition to any satisfaction yielded in future periods when savings are used. The mythical King Midas is an extreme example of such a person. Generally, any present satisfaction from saving is of secondary importance and is ignored by economists to simplify analysis without seriously invalidating the conclusions reached.

Activities yielding satisfaction directly and immediately are either *consumption* or *leisure* activities. The former term is employed when the goods and services used in the process are stressed. The latter is employed when the time used in the process is stressed. In reality it is very difficult to think of consumption activities that do not also require time or leisure activities that do not also require goods and services.

A final set of activities can be identified. These activities transfer resources from the household to other groups in society or transfer resources to the household from other households and groups in society. They are called *transfer* activities. Taxation, government welfare programs, gift giving and receiving, and volunteer work are all examples. The essence of such activities is that they are one-way and not exchanges. Households engage in transfers either for the satisfaction they yield or because of coercion. The coercion is typically legal; the most obvious example is the Sixteenth Amendment, which requires households to pay federal income taxes. The satisfaction yielded via the receipt and giving of gifts is obvious.

Constraints on the system

If the resource–activity–satisfaction schema were all that governed household behavior, we could conclude that households attempt to maximize satisfaction or well-being (why would they not?) and that they are successful in doing so. The resulting economic organization would be determined entirely by the household's goals (i.e., preferences) and would change only in the event that household goals changed. In fact and in theory, each of the elements – resources, activities, satisfaction – are constrained so that households can only attempt to maximize satisfaction *subject to constraints*. Thus, the economic organization of the household is importantly affected by the constraints as well as by household goals. An understanding of the types of constraints, how they limit behavior, and the interaction among them is, consequently, crucial to an understanding of the economic organization of the household.

The constraints that impinge on the household are of four types: economic, technical, legal, and sociocultural. Each is introduced in turn.

Resource, or economic, constraints

Household resources are not limitless, and thus, household behavior and the resulting economic organization of the household are importantly affected by the types and amounts of resources available to it. People have only so many skills. They are mortal and have only their own lifetimes in which to pursue their goals. Time is bound by the clock and each day has but twenty-four hours. The household has only so much income, so many assets, and only so much credit. It is with these resources and these alone that it pursues its goals. Resource, or economic, constraints, therefore, figure importantly in what households do, how they do it, and with what results.

Historically, economics has emphasized the resource constraint and has studied its effects on household behavior. Consequently, resource constraints are also called the economic constraints. The neoclassical theory of the consumer postulated that a household derives satisfaction from the consumption of goods and services and uses its limited resources to gain access to them. Consumer behavior was conceived, therefore, as the behavioral consequence of the conflict between what the household wanted to consume and what its income allowed it to consume.

Increasingly in the 1950s and 1960s economists recognized the importance of time as a constraint on behavior.[3] Because consumption takes time as well as goods and services, it was realized that households confront a double squeeze of limited income and limited time. Furthermore, the resources of time and money are intimately related because much of household income arises out of the time resource: households trade off their time for wages and salaries in the labor market. Too, in the past thirty years the relationships between the skills humans possess and their income and wealth have been revealed.[4]

Technical constraints

Resources do not produce well-being magically. They are simply inputs into productive processes that are technical in nature. *Technical* in this context refers to the fact that the processes obey the laws of biology, chemistry, and physics. The gestation period in humans is nine months, and thus, the addition of one person to the family via childbirth takes a minimum of nine months. Synthetic fibers are altered in specific ways when washed in very hot water, whereas cotton fibers are not. Different types of food preparation techniques alter the color, taste, consistency, and nutrients contained in raw foods in specific ways. We are slowly learning the technical processes involved in child development.

With current technology there are narrow limits to what is possible in the heating of dwellings and maintaining them at specific temperatures. Household behavior, therefore, and the household's resulting economic organization are determined in part by technical constraints. Although home economists have long recognized the importance of household technology, it was not dealt with systematically until the 1960s.[5]

Legal constraints

Household behavior is also importantly circumscribed and, thus, in part determined and directed by the laws and regulations of the political entities in which the household participates. The laws forbid some activities, limit the conditions under which others may be performed, forbid the use of some resources, and prevent their use in some activities by some types of people. Laws also importantly alter the prices at which some resources may be bought and sold. Examples are manifold. Cars may not be driven by children. Prescription drugs may be bought only by those whom doctors have certified as needing them. Many goods and services may not be sold on Sundays as a consequence of "blue laws." Murder and robbery are outlawed. Sales tax laws raise the prices of many goods and services while income tax laws reduce the wage rates at which people work. Medical malpractice laws increase the fees of doctors. An important determinant of the economic organization of the household will be missed, if legal constraints are ignored.

Sociocultural constraints

Finally, social and cultural norms and mores importantly affect the resources, the activities, and the satisfaction received by the household. The violation of accepted patterns of speech, manners, and dress provokes intense pressure to conform. Also, our ideas of well-being and satisfaction are in part determined by social norms and customs. Americans think baseball fun and cricket a bore whereas the British believe the reverse. Hunting, an almost universal activity among American men fifty years ago, is now frowned on by large numbers of Americans as a savage, inhumane activity.

Relative and absolute constraints

It is important to note that of the four types of constraints – resource, technical, legal, and sociocultural – the first two are absolute in the sense that they cannot be disregarded at a given point in time. The latter two, however, are relative and can be ignored by the household. American men can, and some do, wear skirts. Some "perverse" Americans do enjoy cricket. Marijuana, although illegal, is widely smoked. The national crime rate is evidence of the fact that laws can be broken. Thus, if the household is willing to pay the social cost of being different or risk the consequences of breaking the law, then the sociocultural and legal constraints need not be constraints at all.[6] The resource and technical constraints cannot be ignored no matter how much we may wish to. We have only so much time, so much income, so much available credit. Once these resources are depleted, they are gone. And to think of violating the laws of chemistry, biology, and physics is to enter the realm of fantasy.

Yet, although the resource and technical constraints cannot be overlooked at any point in time, they can be altered in future periods by purposeful behavior in the present. Investment activities can augment both human and physical resources. Formal education, for instance, is the most prominent way we invest in children so as to enhance their worth as citizens, workers, and human beings when they reach adulthood. Research and development activities alter the technology. Indeed, investment and research and development have importantly altered the resource and technical constraints facing households and have been important transformers of the economic organization of the household.[7]

Of the four constraints, the resource, technical, and legal constraints will be treated most extensively in this book, with the sociocultural constraints commanding less attention. This is in large part a reflection that this is a text in economics and the economic organization of the household and not on family sociology.

Organization of the book

Geometric and algebraic versions of the basic economic model of the household are developed in Chapter 2 utilizing the consumption activities of the household as examples. Chapter 3 contains an analysis of the household's consumption activities and how income and price changes affect them. Chapter 4 analyzes the household's saving, borrowing, and lending activities. The household's work and leisure activities are analyzed in Chapter 5. A special set of household activities, those that increase the household's stock of human capital, are analyzed in Chapter 6. Chapter 7 deals with the household's fertility behavior; that is, the demand for children. Chapter 8 discusses the economics of marriage and divorce.

CHAPTER TWO

Household equilibrium

Introduction

We are now ready to begin the economic analysis of the household. This chapter is devoted to developing the basic economic model of the household that underlies the remaining discussion. The model is set up to analyze the household's demand for goods and services and so prepare for the discussion in Chapter 3. The model abstracts from the many household attributes and environmental factors that were introduced in Chapter 1, concentrating on two important attributes: (1) the set of goods and services the household can afford, given its income and market prices; and (2) the goals of the household expressed in terms of the preferences it has for goods. The former attribute – what the household can have – is described by the household's *budget constraint;* the latter – its goals – is described by the household's *preference map* and *utility function.* We discuss each in turn. To add concreteness to the analysis we will use food as an example. Hence, we are interested in developing a model of the household that will allow us to analyze the demand for food. By the household's demand for food we mean the quantity of food the household is willing and able to purchase and (presumably) consume in a given time period, say per year. The analysis will be general, however, and applicable to the demand for any good.

The budget constraint

In each period (say, a year) we suppose the household to enter the marketplace to purchase those quantities of food and other goods and services that will maximize the family's satisfaction. In doing so it faces market prices for food and other things along with the limited income it possesses. Its choices are made in the light of these facts of necessity. We can gain great insight into the choice environment faced by the household by organizing and representing these facts both algebraically and geometrically. We do the algebraic representation first.

Let the market price at which a unit of food may be purchased during the time period under consideration be p_f dollars per unit of food. Likewise, let

12

p_o be the price at which units of the composite good "all other goods" may be purchased. Similarly, let the quantities of food and "all other goods" purchasable per period by the family be q_f and q_o respectively.[1] And let the family's total income per period be Y.

There is no reason to suppose that the family will not use all of its income, because, as we will see subsequently, using all of its income is the only way it can achieve greatest satisfaction or well-being. Thus, the family spends all of its income on the two composite goods, food and "all other goods."[2] This fact can be represented as

$$p_f q_f + p_o q_o = Y. \tag{2.1}$$

This equation is called the budget constraint.

Definition: The budget constraint represents all the possible combinations of food and "all other goods" purchasable by the family, if it uses all of its income in the period of analysis.

By setting q_f at 0, the maximum quantity of "all other goods" purchasable by the family can be found. Denoting the maximum quantity of "all other goods" purchasable by the family by q_o^m,

$$q_o^m = Y/p_o. \tag{2.2}$$

Likewise, the maximum quantity of food purchasable by the family, q_f^m, is

$$q_f^m = Y/p_f. \tag{2.3}$$

Consequently, the family's budget constraint says that the family is able to purchase quantities of food between 0 and q_f^m and quantities of "all other goods" between 0 and q_o^m with its income of Y in the time period under study.

A geometric representation of the budget constraint can be obtained by solving equation (2.1) for q_o and plotting the resulting line on a graph with q_o measured along the vertical axis and q_f measured along the horizontal axis. The resulting equation is

$$q_o = Y/p_o - (p_f/p_o)q_f. \tag{2.4}$$

The shape of equation (2.4) can be seen by taking an example. Suppose $Y = \$40$, $p_f = \$8/$unit, and $p_o = \$4/$unit. Then, we can use equation (2.4) to find the various quantities of food and "all other goods" that are possible for the household to purchase. In this case equation (2.4) is

$$q_o = 40/4 - (8/4)q_f = 10 - 2q_f.$$

The following tabulation gives the possible combinations open to the family:

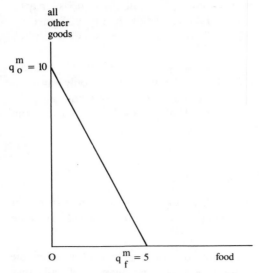

Figure 2.1 The budget line when $Y = \$40$, $p_f = \$8/\text{unit}$, and $p_o = \$4/\text{unit}$; i.e., $q_o = 10 - 2q_f$

q_f	q_o
0	10
1	8
2	6
3	4
4	2
5	0

These combinations are plotted in Figure 2.1 with the points joined to show the budget line. The line has as its vertical intercept the point $(q_o^m, 0)$, which represents the maximum quantity of "all other goods" purchasable by the family (i.e., 10 units) and the zero quantity of food it can purchase as a consequence. The line's horizontal intercept is at point $(0, q_f^m)$, representing the maximum quantity of food purchasable (i.e., 5 units) with the family's income of $40 and the consequent zero quantity of "all other goods."

Definition: The budget line, as $q_o^m q_f^m$ is called, represents all the possible combinations of food and "all other goods" purchasable by the family if it exhausts its income, Y.

The budget line has two properties: its slope and its location. Each has economic meaning and is discussed in turn.

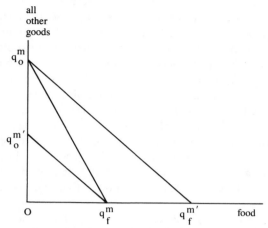

Figure 2.2 The slope of the budget line, $-(p_f/p_o)$

Relative prices. The slope is the gradient of the line, its steepness. The equation for any straight line is represented as $y = b + mx$ where y is the variable plotted on the vertical axis, x is the variable plotted on the horizontal axis, b is the line's vertical intercept, and m is the line's slope. In equation (2.4), $b = Y/p_o$ is the intercept and $-(p_f/p_o) = m$ is its slope. The slope can also be found by dividing the "rise" (i.e., vertical intercept) by the "run" (i.e., horizontal intercept) of the line. Hence, $-(p_f/p_o) = -(Y/p_o)/(Y/p_f)$.

What economic concepts does the slope represent? The slope is the relative price of food in terms of "all other goods." The lower the relative price of food, the gentler the slope of the budget line; the higher the relative price of food, the steeper the budget line. Figure 2.2 shows three budget lines of varying steepness, or slope. The relative price of food in the budget line $q_o^m q_f^{m'}$ is lower than in $q_o^m q_f^m$ since the slope of the former is less than that of the latter.

The slope also represents the market exchange rate between food and "all other goods"; that is, the rate at which "all other goods" must be given in exchange for food. In the above numeric example, $p_f = \$8/$ unit of food and $p_o = \$4/$ unit of "all other goods"; therefore, $(p_f/p_o) = 2$, and 2 units of "all other goods" can be exchanged in the marketplace for 1 unit of food. Conversely, 1 unit of food can be exchanged for 2 units of "all other goods." If, however, $p_f = \$4/$ unit and $p_o = \$4/$ unit, then the household would be able to exchange 1 unit of food for 1 unit of "all other goods" in the marketplace. *The slope, therefore, represents the rate at which the household can exchange food for "all other goods" in the marketplace.*

16   **Household equilibrium**

Changes in prices. Take note of another feature of Figure 2.2. The vertical intercepts of two budget lines ($q_o^m q_o^f$ and $q_o^m q_o^{f'}$) are the same, q_o^m. Since the vertical intercept represents Y/p_o, this ratio must be the same for each of the two budget lines (see equation [2.4]). Furthermore, since only the horizontal intercepts of the two budget lines are different and, thence, the slopes differ, the only feature of the two budget lines that differs must be p_f. Consequently, these two budget lines in Figure 2.2 represent the change in a family's budget line if p_f changes, Y and p_o remaining the same. Likewise, budget lines $q_o^m q_o^f$ and $q_o^{m'} q_o^f$ in Figure 2.2 represent the budget lines facing a household before and after a change in p_o, family income and the price of food remaining unchanged. A change from $q_o^m q_o^f$ to $q_o^{m'} q_o^f$ in Figure 2.2, thus, represents an increase in the price of "all other goods," Y and p_f held constant, whereas a change from $q_o^{m'} q_o^f$ to $q_o^m q_o^f$ in Figure 2.2 represents a decrease in the price of "all other goods," Y and p_f remaining unchanged.

Finally, note that budget line $q_o^m q_o^{f'}$ is longer than line $q_o^m q_o^f$ in Figure 2.2. Recall, also, that the former line represents a situation in which p_f is lower than in the latter, p_o being the same in both circumstances. Each point on $q_o^m q_o^{f'}$ represents a combination of food and "all other goods" available to the consumer if all of his income is spent. Consequently, the longer the budget line, the more choice afforded the consumer.[3] A drop in the price of food with the prices of "all other goods" remaining unchanged, therefore, expands the choices open to consumers; the lower the p_f, the more food and "all other goods" purchasable by the household.

Size of income. The location of the budget line is the distance of the budget line from the origin. Its location represents the quantity of resources available to the family during the time period; that is, its income, Y. The further from the origin, the greater the income; the closer, the more meager the income. This, too, is illustrated in Figure 2.2. The budget line $q_o^{m'} q_o^f$ represents half the family income represented by $q_o^m q_o^{f'}$. This is so because the distances $O q_o^{m'}$ and $q_o^{m'} q_o^m$ are equal, as are $O q_o^f$ and $q_o^f q_o^{f'}$, indicating that the family can purchase twice as much food and "all other goods" if its situation is represented by $q_o^m q_o^{f'}$ rather than by $q_o^{m'} q_o^f$.

Notice, also, that the slopes of the two budget lines $q_o^m q_o^{f'}$ and $q_o^{m'} q_o^f$ are equal in Figure 2.2, indicating that the price of food relative to "all other goods" is the same in each case. Consequently, the two budget lines differ only in the size of family income. Indeed, the shift from $q_o^{m'} q_o^f$ to $q_o^m q_o^{f'}$ represents a doubling of income, p_o and p_f being unchanged, because the latter budget line is twice as far from the origin as the former. Again, note that $q_o^m q_o^{f'}$ is much longer than $q_o^{m'} q_o^f$, indicating that a larger income affords more choices to the household than smaller incomes. Such a change in the budget line, it should be noted, could also take place if all prices, p_o and p_f, declined by half, with family income, Y, remaining unchanged. This, of course, is the opposite of inflation; that is, deflation.

An algebraic example of the effect of a change in income, with prices remaining unchanged, is if Y changes from \$40 to \$80 in the earlier example. The result of this change is to change the budget line from $q_o = 10 - 2q_f$ to $q_o = 20 - 2q_f$. An example of deflation is when p_f falls from \$8/unit to \$4/unit and p_o falls from \$4/unit to \$2/unit. The resulting budget equation with $Y = \$40$ is $q_o = 40/2 - (4/2)q_f = 20 - 2q_f$, the same as if income had doubled.

The location and slope of the household's budget line, therefore, represent the amount of real resources possessed by the household and relative market prices, respectively. Changes in income, prices remaining constant, can be represented by parallel shifts in the budget line. Changes in relative prices can be represented by changes in the slope starting from either the vertical or the horizontal intercept, depending on which of the two prices changes.

Preferences

In order to complete the simple model of the household for the purpose of analyzing its demand behavior, the household's preferences must be represented as well as its budget constraint. The household's preferences reflect its likes and dislikes, its views as to what will increase and what will decrease its well-being, its goals if you will. The inclusion of the household's preferences in our model of household demand behavior is crucial because the household's demands for goods and services are the result of the interaction between its preferences and its possibilities, the latter being represented by the budget constraint.

To begin with, economists are much less interested in the details of a household's preferences than with the structure of those preferences. If the structure of preferences does not differ from household to household, then economists can say quite a lot about their demand and consumption behavior even though the details of households' preferences are very different. What do we mean by the structure of a household's preferences? By structure we mean whether preferences follow certain logical rules, regardless of what the preferences are about or how strongly they are held. Let us be more specific.

With respect to any two combinations of goods – say, food and "all other goods" – assume that the household can tell us which of the two it prefers or whether it prefers each of the combinations equally. In short, we assume that *households can rank all the possible combinations of food and "all other goods."*

Next, it is assumed that *the household prefers more to less:* more food or more "all other goods" or more of both. You may wish to argue with this assumption, correctly pointing out that there are many things, including food in amounts greater than some limit, that the family prefers less to more. Rather than invalidating the model we are building, we can make a distinction between things that are economic "goods" and those that are economic "bads." Economic bads are things that reduce well-being (like garbage, for instance) whereas economic goods increase well-being. We can redefine economic bads to be goods simply by taking their negative. Thus, less garbage is a good as are less pollution and less sickness. Consequently, assuming that more is preferred to less is not an unduly restrictive assumption.[4]

The household is also presumed to be consistent in its preferences. If it prefers combination A to combination B, and combination B to combination C, then it cannot prefer combination C to A. In mathematical terms consistent preferences are transitive preferences.

In sum, the structure of household preferences refers to these three properties that we assume for each household: (1) the household can rank each combination of goods or services, (2) the household is consistent in its preference ranking of goods and services, and (3) the household prefers more goods to fewer.

We can summarize the household's preferences for goods algebraically with a *preference,* or *utility, function.* In particular, the utility function describing its preferences for food and "all other goods" would look like

$$U = u(q_f, q_o) \tag{2.5}$$

where U represents the amount of satisfaction gained from a particular combination of q_f and q_o (see mathematical note 1). The term *amount* need not be taken literally if one doubts that satisfaction or well-being can be measured cardinally. The variable U can merely be taken as a ranking or ordinal measure of the comparative satisfaction derived from combinations of q_f and q_o that the household prefers more and from combinations of q_f and q_o that it prefers less.[5] In words, then, equation (2.5) says that the household's satisfaction or well-being depends on the amounts of food and of "all other goods" that it purchases and consumes.

The household's utility function and the assumptions about the structure of preferences can be understood more easily and clearly geometrically than algebraically. Consequently, in Figure 2.3 we have, again, plotted q_o up the vertical axis and q_f along the horizontal axis. Any point within Figure 2.3, then, represents a particular combination of q_o and q_f. Take point A, for instance. It represents q_o^a of "all other goods" and q_f^a of food.

Consider combinations A, B, and C, where B contains the same quantity of q_o as A but more q_f, and it contains the same quantity of q_f as C but more q_o. The assumption that the household prefers more to less simply means that B is preferred to both A and C. Combinations represented by points farther away from the origin in the northeasterly direction are always preferred to combinations represented by points closer to the origin in the southwesterly direction. Thus, the household prefers D to A, B, and C; and B to A and C. As yet we have no basis for telling whether it prefers A to C or C to A or likes A and C equally well.

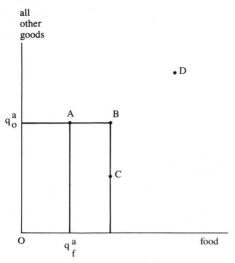

Figure 2.3 The household's preference for combinations *A, B, C,* and *D*

To tell whether the family prefers *A* to *C* or *C* to *A* or likes them equally well, we must introduce the geometrical concept of the indifference curve.

Definition: An indifference curve is the locus of points representing all the combinations the household prefers equally well (see mathematical note 2).

We know that indifference curves must be negatively sloped. Why? If one was positively sloped, of every two combinations joined, one would contain more of both q_f and q_o than the other. But this would violate the assumption that households always prefer more goods to less. Thus, indifference curves cannot be positively sloped. Neither can indifference curves be horizontal or vertical. A glance at Figure 2.3 will confirm this. Combinations *B* and *A* cannot be on the same indifference curve since *B* contains more q_f than *A* and the same amount of q_o. Consequently, *B* must be preferred to *A*. An analogous set of statements can be made about *B* and *C* (see mathematical note 3). Indifference curves have negative slope, therefore.

Figure 2.4 is a household's preference map on which several indifference curves are shown. Each is negatively sloped as argued above. Recognize that the indifference curves in Figure 2.4 are simply a few of the many that could be drawn. Indeed, one must think of each point in Figure 2.4, each representing a combination of q_o and q_f, as having an indifference curve passing through it.

The assumption that the household prefers more to less means that indifference curves farther away from the origin represent greater well-being or utility than ones closer to the origin. Consequently, the location of indifference curves represents the extent of the satisfaction obtained by the household: indiffer-

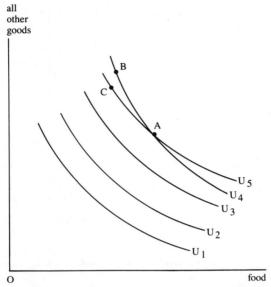

all
other
goods

B

C

A

U 5
U 4
U 3

U 2

U 1

O   food

Figure 2.4 The household's preference map: indifference curves

ence curve U_3 in Figure 2.4 represents more satisfaction than U_2. The household's preference map, therefore, appears more as a "hill of satisfaction," with its foot at the origin and its peak off the page somewhere in a northeasterly direction. Each indifference curve, then, is analogous to an isoaltitude line on a contour map.

Another characteristic of indifference curves is that they cannot intersect one another. Figure 2.4 also makes this clear. Indifference curves U_4 and U_5 intersect in this figure at point A. In this picture A and B are located on U_4, which means that they are equally preferred by the household. Similarly, A and C are on U_5 and are also, therefore, both equally preferred. But B is farther to the northeast than C and, thus, is preferred to C. But, since B is as well liked as A and A is as well liked as C, then B must not be preferred to C. Intersecting indifference curves imply, therefore, that the household simultaneously likes two combinations equally well and also prefers one of them over the other. This is a most inconsistent state of affairs and contrary to the assumptions made earlier.

Thus far it has been established that indifference curves are negatively sloped and do not intersect one another. Furthermore, we have established that their locations (i.e., their distances from the origin) represent levels of satisfaction or well-being. We now must discuss the economic interpretation of their slopes. The indifference curves in Figure 2.4 have all been drawn convex to the origin; this is their usual shape. Not only are indifference curves negatively sloped,

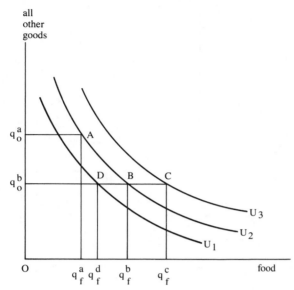

Figure 2.5 The marginal rate of substitution of food for "all other goods"

almost all are convex to the origin. Two limiting cases (one in which the indifference curve is a downward-sloping straight line and one in which it has the shape of a right angle) will be discussed later. Here we discuss the economic meaning of the convexity of indifference curves.

The marginal rate of substitution

Definition: The slope at any point on an indifference curve represents the rate at which the household is willing to exchange food for "all other goods" (or vice versa), holding satisfaction constant. This "preferential" rate of exchange is called the marginal rate of substitution of food for "all other goods" (see mathematical note 4).

Figure 2.5 illustrates the marginal rate of substitution. Begin at point A on the indifference curve and consider whether the household would willingly give up $q_o^a q_o^b$ quantity of "all other goods" in exchange for $q_f^a q_f^d$ additional food. The answer is no because the household would be less well off at point D than at point A, D being on a lower indifference curve than A. Consider, again, whether the household would willingly give up $q_o^a q_o^b$ in order to get $q_f^a q_f^c$ additional food. The answer is yes. Since C is on a higher indifference curve than A, the exchange would make the household better off. Finally, consider whether the household

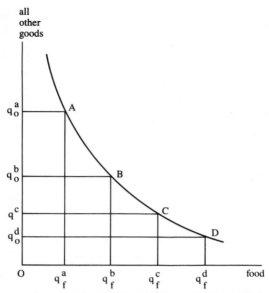

Figure 2.6 The decline in the marginal rate of substitution of food for "all other goods" as more food is substituted for "all other goods"

would exchange $q_o^a q_o^b$ for $q_f^a q_f^b$ added food. The answer is that the family would be indifferent because combination A and combination B provide it with the same level of satisfaction.

Thus, the household would be willing to exchange $q_o^a q_o^b$ "all other goods" for $q_f^a q_f^b$ more food *and still be as satisfied as it was before.* Now move point B along the indifference curve closer and closer to point A. In the limit, as B approaches A, the ratio of the amounts the household would be willing to exchange and be equally satisfied equals the slope of the indifference curve at point A. The slope at any point on an indifference curve, therefore, represents the rate at which the household would willingly exchange "all other goods" for food and be as satisfied after as before the exchange.

Since any indifference curve changes slope throughout its length, the marginal rate of substitution is different at each point along its length. In fact, the marginal rate of substitution declines as the amount of food increases. This is illustrated in Figure 2.6. It is constructed so that $q_f^a q_f^b$, $q_f^b q_f^c$, and $q_f^c q_f^d$ are all of equal length, each representing a "unit" of food. Points A, B, C, and D are all on the same indifference curve. Begin at point A and note that the family is willing to give up $q_o^a q_o^b$ units of "all other goods" in order to get an added unit of food, $q_f^a q_f^b$. At B the household is willing to give up $q_o^b q_o^c$ units of "all other goods" in

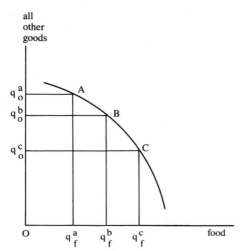

Figure 2.7 An indifference curve exhibiting increasing marginal rate of substitution

order to get another unit of food, $q_f^b q_f^c$. Note that the quantity of "all other goods" the household is willing to give up at B for an added unit of food was less than at point A. At C it is willing to give up $q_o^c q_o^d$ units of "all other goods" for yet another unit of food, $q_f^c q_f^d$. Again, the quantity of "all other goods" the family is willing to give up for an added unit of food is less at point C than at point B. Indeed, the smaller the quantity of "all other goods" the family possesses, the less it is willing to give up even more "all other goods" for an added unit of food: the marginal rate of substitution of food for "all other goods" declines.

A declining marginal rate of substitution is a property of indifference curves that are convex to the origin. Declining marginal rates of substitution reflect *relative satiation*. Relative satiation means that the more of something a family possesses relative to other goods, the less of other goods it will give up in order to acquire even more of the already abundant good. Alternatively, the more of something the family possesses relative to other goods, the more of that good it will be willing to give up in exchange for a good it has less of.

Economists believe that the preferences of typical households exhibit relative satiation, and therefore, indifference curves that are convex to the origin are very representative of families in general. It is useful, however, to consider the implications of indifference curves that are concave to the origin as a contrast to the ones that are convex to the origin.

Figure 2.7 illustrates an indifference curve concave to the origin. Again, the figure has been constructed so that $q_f^a q_f^b$ and $q_f^b q_f^c$ are equal, representing equal

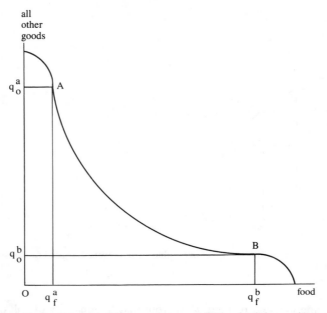

Figure 2.8 An indifference curve exhibiting both increasing and decreasing marginal rates of substitution

units of food. As the household moves from A to B and from B to C along the indifference curve, it is clear from Figure 2.7 that it is willing to give up increasing quantities of "all other goods" in order to acquire additional units of food, holding utility constant.

Preferences represented by indifference curves concave to the origin exhibit increasing marginal rates of substitution. Such preferences are pathological, at least if carried to the extreme. They imply that the more one has of a good relative to other things, the more of other things one is willing to give up in order to acquire even more of the good in question. This is like the mythical King Midas, who sacrificed everything, even his daughter, for more gold: the more gold he got, the more willing he was to give up other things for yet more gold. Typical households do not possess such preferences.

Typical families may, however, have segments of their preferences that do exhibit increasing marginal rates of substitution. Figure 2.8 illustrates such a case. Here, the indifference curve is concave to the origin near the axes, where points represent combinations of very little of one good and a lot of the other. This may be more representative of reality. When we have very little food relative to other things (less than q_f^a), we may be willing to give up increasing

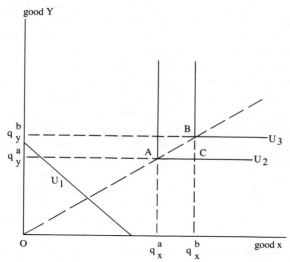

Figure 2.9 Indifference curves for perfect substitutes and perfect complements

quantities of other things for additional quantities of food within a small range. Once we possess a "minimally adequate" quantity of food relative to other things (at point A), then diminishing marginal rates of substitution take over.

The reverse occurs when we have very little of anything except food (less than q_x^b). In such a case we are adequately fed but may have grossly inadequate housing and few if any clothes. Hence, we might be willing to give up increasing amounts of food for additional units of, say, housing and clothing. But when a "minimally adequate" quantity of other things is possessed (at point B), then diminishing marginal rates of substitution once again become the rule. The typical American family, consuming at least "minimally adequate" quantities of all goods, will exhibit preferences with diminishing marginal rates of substitution between points A and B.

Substitutes and complements

There are two other cases of nonconvex indifference curves worth discussing. One is the downward-sloping, *straight-line indifference curve* and the other is the *right-angled indifference curve*. These are illustrated in Figure 2.9.

Consider the straight-line indifference curve, U_1, first. Indifference curve U_1 exhibits constant marginal rates of substitution throughout its length: regardless of how much good Y the household possesses, it is always willing to give up the same amount of it in order to acquire an added unit of good X. Reflection on this situation will convince you that such goods must be perfect substitutes for one another. Goods that are substitutes for each other tend to be used by the household for the same purpose. A push lawn mower, a power lawn mower, and a scythe are all substitutes for each other since each can be used to cut grass. The scythe is an inferior substitute for a push lawn mower. Similarly, the push lawn mower is an inferior substitute for a power lawn mower. Two identical mowers, however, are perfect substitutes for each other. The reason is that the household would be willing to give up one for the other at the rate of one-for-one, and the marginal rate of substitution would remain constant. Another example is regular and extrastrength aspirin tablets. They are perfect substitutes for each other even though the former has 325 mg of aspirin per tablet and the latter has 500 mg per tablet. The marginal rate of substitution of extrastrength for regular aspirin is $325/500 = 0.65$ and is constant. That is, 0.65 of an extrastrength aspirin is a perfect substitute for 1 regular aspirin.

At the other extreme are the right-angled indifference curves: U_2 and U_3 in Figure 2.9. Note that the points of the right-angled indifference curves lie along the straight line, OAB, emanating from the origin. Points along this line represent combinations of goods Y and X with the same proportions of Y to X. The family obtains the same satisfaction from $q_y^a q_x^a$ as it does from $q_y^c q_x^b$ (i.e., at C) or from $q_y^b q_x^a$. Adding $q_y^b q_y^a$ of Y to $q_y^a q_x^a$ of Y and X adds no satisfaction. Neither does adding $q_x^b q_x^a$ of X to $q_y^a q_x^a$ of X and Y augment utility. The only way the household is better off is if the quantities of Y and X are increased in the same proportion: $q_y^b q_y^a / q_x^b q_x^a$. Clearly, goods X and Y not only complement each other, they are perfect complements. They are used together for the same purpose. Examples are coffee and cream for those who like cream in their coffee, left and right shoes for those with two feet, and tires and cars if the household wishes the car to provide transportation.

Most goods are neither perfect substitutes for each other nor perfect complements. Consequently, the indifference curves describing the preferences for most goods will be neither downward sloping straight lines nor right angles. Instead, they will be downward sloping and convex to the origin, representing diminishing marginal rates of substitution. The greater the convexity the indifference curves possess, the less satisfactory are the goods as substitutes for each other; the less convex, the better are the goods as substitutes for each other.

If we are to know the shapes and locations of the indifference curves of any particular household, we must ask the household many detailed questions about its preferences. Our purpose, however, is to explain and predict the economic behavior of households on the average, not the behavior of any particular household. For this limited purpose it is sufficient simply to know that household indifference curves exhibit diminishing marginal rates of substitution. A detailed knowledge of households' preference maps is not necessary.[6]

We have discussed the household's budget constraint as if it were the only constraint facing the household. Yet, previously, we mentioned legal, technical, and sociocultural constraints. In this simple model of consumer behavior the sociocultural norms regarding the use of food and "all other goods" have already been taken into account by the household in forming its preferences. Likewise, it is presumed that the technical constraints governing the use of food and "all other goods" by the household also have been taken into account by the indifference curves of the household. Also, the composite goods (food and "all other goods") do not include any illegal commodities, such as absinthe or marijuana. In short, we presume that the legal, technical, and sociocultural constraints upon the household's behavior have already been taken into account and have affected the shapes and slopes of the indifference curves. These constraints can be dealt with separately in more complex models, as we will see subsequently. But in this simple beginning model, they have been built into the household's preferences.

Putting the parts together: consumer equilibrium

The budget constraint, equation (2.1), and the utility function, equation (2.5), constitute two of the three elements of the algebraic model of the consumer aspects of a household. Likewise, the budget line and the indifference curves constitute two of the three geometric elements of the same model. It is left to put them together. This is done with the third element of the model, a *behavioral assumption*, or *hypothesis*. The hypothesis has been mentioned before (it is, indeed, the major economic hypothesis about the way households behave): in any period of time households attempt to maximize satisfaction or well-being, subject to the resource, legal, technical, and sociocultural constraints on their behavior. Simply stated, among the choices open to it, the household will choose that alternative that most furthers its goals. That is, among all the possible combinations of goods available to the household, it will choose the combination that makes it better off or more satisfied than any other combination. As was pointed out in Chapter 1, such behavior is part and parcel of being goal directed, the behavioral assumption shared by all the social sciences.

The satisfaction-maximizing combination of food and "all other goods" can be found by putting the household's indifference curves together in the same figure as its budget line. Obviously, the satisfaction-maximizing combination of "all other goods" and food will be somewhere on the budget line. The fact that households prefer more to less ensures that there are combinations on the budget line the family prefers to any given point to the southwest of the budget line. Combinations to the northeast of the budget line are unattainable given the household's income and the market prices of food and "all other goods." The combination that maximizes satisfaction, therefore, will be represented by that point on the budget line that rests on the highest indifference curve touching the budget line. The purchase and consumption of no other combination of food and "all other goods" will bring the household as much satisfaction.

These points are illustrated in Figure 2.10, in which a household's indifference curves have been superimposed over its budget line. Which combination of food and "all other goods" will maximize this household's satisfaction? The question may be approached by supposing the household initially is at point a at the intersection of AC and U_1. Suppose the household experiments with other combinations of food and "all other goods" by trying combinations with less food and more "all other goods" than at point a. By doing so it will reach lower and lower indifference curves, signifying that it gets less and less satisfaction from such substitutions. Consequently, it will at least return to the combination of food and "all other goods" represented by point a.

Now suppose it experiments in the opposite direction, choosing instead combinations along the budget line to the right of point a. Say it moves to point b, where it consumes q_o^b of "all other goods" and q_f^b of food. Since point b is on U_2 and point a is on U_1, the household will be more satisfied with combination b than with combination a.

Given that it increased its satisfaction (i.e., came closer to achieving its goals) by substituting food for "all other goods," assume that it continues to experiment by increasing its purchases of food at the expense of "all other goods," moving to point c on the budget line. Again, it is more satisfied at c than it was at b.

If it again tries to substitute more food for "all other goods" and moves to, say, point d, it finds that it has moved to a combination of food and "all other goods" that is not as satisfying as the combination at point c. Inspecttion of Figure 2.10 reveals that no point between d and c or between b and c will yield as much satisfaction as the combination at point c – all of them except c being on indifference curves inferior to U_3. The combination of food and "all other goods" represented by point c is unique: of those attainable by the household, no other point makes the household as satisfied. The combination represented by point c, therefore, is the combination that maximizes the household's satisfaction and will be the combination chosen by the household.

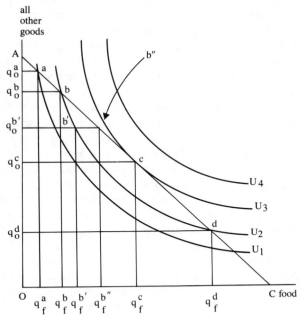

Figure 2.10 Maximization of satisfaction at point *c*

Geometrically, point *c* is the *point of tangency* between the budget line and the highest attainable indifference curve, U_3. At point *c* the household's marginal rate of substitution of food for "all other goods" (represented by the slope of U_3 at point *c*) equals the rate at which food and "all other goods" exchange for each other in the marketplace (represented by the slope of the budget line). Recall that the marginal rate of substitution is the rate at which the household *is willing* to exchange "all other goods" for food. Recall also that the exchange rate between food and "all other goods" in the marketplace represents the rate at which the household *is able* to exchange "all other goods" for food. At point *c*, then, the rate at which the household is willing to exchange "all other goods" for food equals the rate at which it is able to exchange these two goods. At point *c* and at no other point are these two rates equal.

If the rate at which the household is willing to exchange and the rate at which it is able to exchange goods are not equal, then the household is not maximizing satisfaction and could be "doing better" at some other point. If the rate at which it is willing to substitute food for "all other goods" is greater than the rate at which it is able to in the marketplace, then surely it pays the household in terms of satisfaction to substitute food for "all other goods." This is so because the rate at which a family is willing to exchange "all other goods" for food is the maximum price that it is willing to pay for more food, whereas the rate at which it is able to exchange "all other goods" for food is the market price for food. If the price it is willing to pay for food is greater than the market price of food, food can be said to be "a good buy" and the household will increase its satisfaction by buying more food and less "all other goods."

This idea is represented in Figure 2.10 by the fact that at points a and b (and at any points on the budget line northwest of point c) the slopes of the indifference curves are greater than the slopes of the budget line. Look at point b in particular. By substituting $q_f^b q_f^{b'}$ of food for $q_o^b q_o^{b'}$, it can remain as satisfied as it was before. But by exchanging the same quantity of "all other goods," $q_o^b q_o^{b'}$, for food in the marketplace, it can get $q_f^b q_f^{b''}$ food, $q_f^{b'} q_f^{b''}$ more food than the $q_f^b q_f^{b'}$ it would be willing to take. At point b, therefore, food is priced more cheaply than it is worth to the household, and the household will increase its satisfaction by purchasing more food and less of "all other goods."

The opposite situation exists at point d (and all other points on the budget line to the southeast of point c). At point d the slope of the indifference curve is less than the slope of the budget line. This indicates that at point d the relative market price of food in terms of "all other goods" is higher than the food is worth to the household, again, in terms of "all other goods." Alternatively, at point d the market price of "all other goods" (as shown by the slope of the budget line) is lower than the maximum price the household is willing to pay for more "all other goods" (as shown by the inverse of the slope of the indifference curve). "All other goods" are a good buy in terms of food, therefore, and the household could increase its well-being if it bought more of "all other goods" and less of food. This is represented in the diagram by moving along the budget line from d in the direction of point c. At point c, the price it is willing to pay for food in terms of "all other goods" is equal to the market price of food in terms of "all other goods," providing no incentive for the household to buy either more food or more of "all other goods."

When the household purchases and consumes the combinations of goods and services that maximizes its satisfaction (i.e., allows it most nearly to achieve its goals), the household is said to be in equilibrium.

Definition: A household is in equilibrium when it has no incentive to change its purchase pattern.

Clearly, this is the case at point c because to change its purchase pattern and move to any other point would lead to a reduction in its satisfaction. The household will continue its purchase pattern of q_o^c of "all other goods" and q_f^c of food per period so long as the market price of food in terms of "all other goods" remains equal to the price of food in terms of "all other goods" that it is willing to pay. These two prices will remain equal so long as its preferences, its income, and market prices remain unchanged.

There is another useful way to interpret equilibrium. At point c

$$MU_f/p_f = MU_o/p_o \tag{2.6}$$

holds (see mathematical note 5). In equation (2.6) MU_f represents the *marginal utility of food* and MU_o denotes the *marginal utility of "all other goods."*

Definition: The marginal utility of any good is the added utility that a household can obtain from purchasing and consuming an added unit of the good, holding the consumption of all other goods constant.

Thus, the marginal utility of food is the added satisfaction the household can obtain from purchasing an added unit of food, holding the consumption of "all other goods" constant.

What, then, does equation (2.6) say? The ratio of the marginal utility of a good to its price is the marginal utility of an added dollar spent on that good. Equation (2.6) can be read, then, as follows: in equilibrium an added dollar spent by the household on any good (in this case, on food or on "all other goods") must yield the same added satisfaction. On reflection this must be so for suppose

$$MU_f/p_f > MU_o/p_o; \tag{2.7}$$

that is, an added dollar spent on food yields more satisfaction than an added dollar spent on "all other goods." Then the household would be more satisfied if it shifted its purchase pattern by spending a dollar less on "all other goods" and by spending it instead on more food. If that were the case, the household would have the incentive to do so and, in consequence, cannot be said to be in equilibrium. Equilibrium, recall, is when the household has no incentive to alter its purchase pattern in any way.

Figure 2.10 illustrates a kind of equilibrium in which the household demands some food and some of "all other goods." This kind of equilibrium is called an *interior solution* because equilibrium occurs somewhere on the budget line rather than at either end. Another kind of equilibrium exists in circumstances in which the household demands none of the good being analyzed. This kind of equilibrium is called a *corner solution.* When this occurs, the marginal rate of substitution is less than the market rate of exchange between the good being analyzed and "all other goods."

Figure 2.11 illustrates a corner solution equilibrium. Suppose we are interested in the household's demand for, say, VCRs. Some people own VCRs and some don't. Figure 2.11 has the quantity of VCRs plotted on the horizontal axis

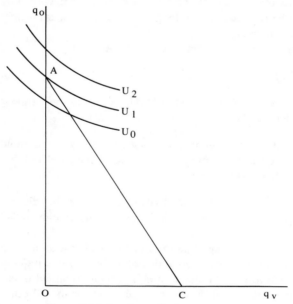

Figure 2.11 A corner solution

and "all other goods" plotted on the vertical axis. Line AC is a particular household's budget line. The slope of AC is the ratio of the price of VCRs to the price of "all other goods," p_v/p_o. U_0, U_1, and U_2 are three of the household's indifference curves representing its preferences for VCRs and "all other goods." Given the household's budget line, the highest indifference curve it can reach is at point A, representing the situation in which the household spends all its income on "all other goods" and buys no VCRs. Point A is the point of maximum satisfaction. It is an equilibrium position because no other point on AC would be more satisfying to the household, and therefore, the household has no incentive to move from point A. But note: at point A equation (2.6) does not hold. Instead,

$$\mathrm{MU}_v/\mathrm{MU}_o < p_v/p_o \tag{2.8}$$

holds (see mathematical note 6).

At point A the slope of the indifference curve U_1 is less than the slope of the budget line. This represents the fact that the price the household is willing to pay for one VCR (in terms of the quantity of "all other goods" it would be willing to give up in order to get a VCR and be as satisfied as it was before) is less than the market price of VCRs. Consequently, although it is able to buy a VCR, it is not willing to. Its demand for VCRs is zero and the household is in equilibrium. All households who do not purchase particular goods are at a corner solution with respect to those goods. Since all households do not buy all goods in any given year, all households are at a corner solution with respect to some goods all the time. Corner solutions, therefore, are ubiquitous.[7]

Summary

If the family's preference map were known by the economist to be as pictured by the indifference curves in Figure 2.10, and if the economist knew that the household's income in conjunction with the market prices of food and "all other goods" would result in a budget line as pictured in Figure 2.10, then the economist would predict that the family's purchase pattern was q_o^c of "all other goods" and q_f^c of food. If that were not the family's purchase pattern, the economist would predict that it soon would be, because the family would be in *disequilibrium* and would have the incentive to change it to q_f^c of food and q_o^c of "all other goods." Figure 2.10 (or Figure 2.11), consequently, answers the first of two major questions asked by the economist:

(1) What is the household's purchase pattern?
(2) How would it change if other things change?

The first question is often phrased a little differently and is focused on the particular good under study, in this case food. The alternative way of asking the first question is:

(1) What is the household's demand for food?

The answer provided by Figure 2.10 is:

The quantity of food demanded by the household is q_f^c, given its income is Y and the market prices of food and "all other goods" are p_f and p_o, respectively.

The answer to the analogous question about the demand for VCRs provided by Figure 2.11 is:

The number of VCRs demanded by the household is zero, given its income and the market prices of VCRs and "all other goods" represented by the budget line AC.

These answers, however, pertain to a particular household given a knowledge of its preferences, its income, and market prices. Economists don't often know enough about a particular family's preferences to be able to make such a prediction. Of what use is the model, then? The usefulness comes in being able to predict the economic behavior, not of the individual household, but rather of the representative or average household. And more important, the usefulness comes in being able to predict whether the average household will increase or decrease its purchases of food, VCRs, or other goods or activities being analyzed in response to changes in prices, incomes, or preferences via changes in the technical, legal, or sociocultural constraints facing households. Typically, it is sufficient to know far less about preferences to explain the behavior of the representative household than is required to explain the behavior of any particular household. The answers to these questions are addressed in the next chapter.

CHAPTER THREE

The analysis of consumer demand

Introduction

This chapter is concerned with the analysis of consumer demand. The model of the household developed in Chapter 2 is used to examine the effects of several types of changes in the household's economic environment on the household's demand for a good. The discussion is suggestive rather than exhaustive, the possibilities for analysis and application being very large. Beginning with an analysis of income effects, the chapter progresses to a discussion of price effects and then to analyses of several applications depicting several different price schemes with which consumers are commonly faced. Finally, the effects of family size and composition on demand are treated.

The discussion is couched in terms of hypothetical experiments. The model of the household is observed in equilibrium given an initial set of conditions (i.e., income, prices, and preferences). Then a change in one of these conditions (for instance, income) is introduced and the model altered to include the change. The model's new equilibrium is found and compared with the initial equilibrium. The comparison of the prechange and postchange equilibria leads to conclusions about how the change affected the equilibrium combinations of goods demanded by the modeled household. The conclusions become hypotheses as to how typical households' demands for the goods in question would change given a change in the factor (i.e., income, price, etc.) being analyzed. Finally, the findings from a few empirical economic studies are reported to give the flavor of the actual demand behavior of households in response to the changes in the conditions discussed. This type of analysis is called *comparative statics* and is the analytical technique used throughout the chapter.

Before beginning the analysis it is useful to get an intuitive notion of the dimensions of consumer demand in the United States. Table 3.1 provides a picture as of 1987. Personal disposable income (PDI) is the dollars people in the United States have available to them for spending and saving after income, estate, gift, and property taxes have been paid. PDI was $3,209.7 billion (American billion) in 1987 (i.e., $35,871 per household). Of this, 2.9 percent went to pay interest on outstanding debts, 3.2 percent was saved, and 93.8 percent was

Table 3.1. *Use of personal disposable income in the United States: 1987*

Item	Billions of dollars	Percentage of personal disposable income
Personal disposable income	3,209.7	100.0
Interest paid on outstanding debt	92.1	2.9
Net personal transfers to foreigners	1.3	0.0
Personal saving	104.2	3.2
Personal consumption expenditures	3,012.1	93.8
Food and tobacco	562.1	17.5
Clothing, shoes, accessories, and jewelry	221.5	6.9
Personal care	44.4	1.4
Housing	467.7	14.6
Household operation	362.3	11.3
Furniture, furnishings, cleaning and polishing supplies	77.5	2.4
Household utilities	169.6	5.3
Electricity	63.3	2.0
Gas	25.5	0.8
Water and sanitary services	20.4	0.6
Telephone and telegraph	44.3	1.4
Medical care	403.2	12.6
Personal business	215.5	6.7
Transportation	378.9	11.8
User-operated transportation	346.5	10.8
Purchased local transportation	8.0	0.2
Purchased intercity transportation	24.5	0.8
Recreation	223.3	7.0
Private education and research	51.3	1.6
Religious and welfare activities	68.1	2.1

Source: U.S. Bureau of the Census 1989, Table 693.

spent on consumption goods and services. The focus of this chapter is the analysis of the demands for consumption goods and services.

Consumption goods and services can be broken down into the categories included in Table 3.1. As of 1987, 17.5 percent of PDI was spent on food, 6.9 percent on clothing, 25.9 percent on housing and household operation, 12.6 percent on medical care, 11.8 percent on transportation, and smaller amounts on personal care, recreation, private education and research, and religious and welfare activities.

Another way to classify goods and services is to classify them into the three categories of durables, nondurables, and services. Durables according to the U.S. Department of Commerce are goods with lives of over three years (U.S.

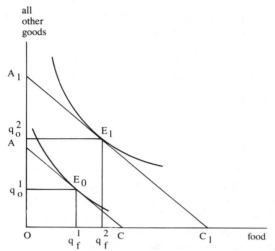

Figure 3.1 The effect of an increase in income on the family's purchase pattern

Bureau of Economic Analysis 1986). Examples are cars, car parts, furniture, and appliances. Nondurables are goods with lives of less than three years (food, clothing and shoes, gasoline and oil, etc.). Services include the rental value of owner-occupied housing, house rents, household operation expenses (e.g., electricity and domestic service), financial services (banking and insurance), transportation, health care, recreation, and private education.

From 1980 to 1988, consumption (as opposed to expenditures) of durables per household rose 13.3 percent, the consumption of nondurables per household rose 5.4 percent, and the consumption of services per household rose 12.8 percent (U.S. Bureau of the Census 1989, Tables 58 and 694). Clearly, American consumption patterns changed importantly during the 1980s. Relatively speaking, Americans consumed more durables and services and fewer nondurables at the end of the 1980s than they did at the beginning.

Income effects

We begin our discussion with the model of the household developed in the last chapter, which focused on the household's food demand and consumption behavior. Because of the focus on food, all other goods demanded by the household were collapsed into one composite good called "all other goods." This example will be used again.

In Figure 3.1 the typical household is represented by its indifference curves and its budget line, which takes into account its annual cash income, Y_1, and the market prices for food and "all other goods," p_f^1 and p_o^1, respectively. Its initial equilibrium is at E_0. At E_0 it purchases q_f^1 amount of food and q_o^1 amount of "all other goods" per year. In so doing, it is as well off as it can be given its income and market prices.

Suppose, now, that the household experiences an increase in income from Y_1 to Y_2 per year. This increase in income causes the budget line to change from

$$q_o = (Y_1/p_o^1) - (p_f^1/p_o^1)q_f \tag{3.1}$$

to

$$q_o = (Y_2/p_o^1) - (p_f^1/p_o^1)q_f. \tag{3.2}$$

Note that the only difference between the two equations is in the intercept: before the change it was (Y_1/p_o^1); after the change it is (Y_2/p_o^1), the latter intercept being bigger. The slopes of the two budget lines, $-(p_f^1/p_o^1)$, are the same.

This change is represented in Figure 3.1 by the shift in the budget line from AC to A_1C_1. Faced with the expansion of its opportunities, the household responds by choosing to purchase and consume more of both food and "all other goods." Given the higher income, the family reaches its new equilibrium at E_1, purchasing and consuming q_f^2 amount of food and q_o^2 amount of "all other goods." The effect of the change in income, $Y_2 - Y_1$, on the annual demand for food has been an increase of $q_f^2 - q_f^1$ units. Likewise, the effect of the increase in income on the demand for "all other goods" has been an increase of $q_o^2 - q_o^1$ units (see mathematical note 1).

It is important to note that since income is the only element of the household's environment that changed, the changes in the demands for food and for "all other goods" are solely attributable to the change in income. In particular, note that the household's preference did not change, because the shape and location of the indifference curve remained unchanged. All that the increase in income did was to expand the family's consumption opportunities. Given the expanded opportunities, the household took advantage of them for its own betterment, reestablishing equilibrium at E_1.[1]

Both preferences and market prices can modify the effects of income on demand. One would expect that a \$100 increase in income would affect a family's demand for food differently if food were cheap relative to "all other goods" than if it were expensive. If food were relatively cheap, then the budget lines facing families would be relatively flat (compared with the slopes of budget lines if food were relatively expensive). Being flat, food would tend to bulk large in the equilibrium purchase patterns of typical families. Given the concept of relative satiety (i.e., diminishing marginal rates of substitution of food for other things), an increase in income might affect the demand for food less than if food were relatively expensive.

Likewise, even though the "average" family may increase its demand for

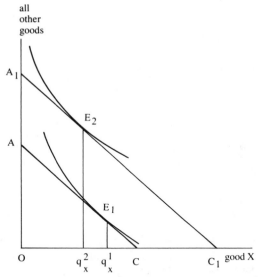

Figure 3.2 Budget lines and indifference curves for an inferior good

food by X amount in the face of a $100 increase in annual income, the response of individual families, all with Y_1 initially and all experiencing a $100 increase in annual income, can be expected to vary because each family's preferences differ in major or minor ways from others'.

Figure 3.1 depicts a situation in which an increase in income has increased the demands for both food and "all other goods." However, if the family had begun with Y_2 income and then experienced a decline in income to Y_1, then Figure 3.1 also shows that its demand for food will decline from q_f^2 to q_f^1. Thus, the income effect is positive: an increase in income increases food demand whereas a decline in income occasions a decline in the demand for food.

Definition: Any good the demand for which increases as income increases and decreases as income decreases, prices and preferences held constant, is called a normal good.

A positive effect of income on the quantity demanded, however, is not necessary. Figure 3.2 illustrates a case in which the demand for good X declines as income increases. In Figure 3.2 the family's preferences are such that as income rises, expanding its consumption alternatives from AC to A_1C_1, the demand for good X actually declines; the income effect on its demand is negative: as income increases, demand for X falls. Carbohydrate-rich food products are examples of inferior goods. As income increases, holding prices constant, we know that

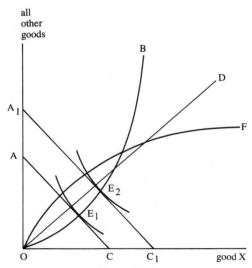

Figure 3.3 Three income–consumption lines

people demand more protein in their diets and less carbohydrates (Adrian and Daniel 1976). Protein is, therefore, a normal good. Goods like carbohydrates, however, with negative income effects are called inferior goods.

Definition: Any good the demand for which decreases as income increases and increases when income decreases, prices and preferences held constant, is called an inferior good.

The income–consumption line

Up to the present two circumstances have been compared, the only difference between them being a difference in income. It is possible, however, to imagine an experiment in which a family with given preferences and facing given relative prices initially has zero income and then is exposed to increasing income. At each income level, the family would establish an equilibrium purchase pattern defined by the tangency between the budget line and an indifference curve. If the points representing each of these equilibrium purchase patterns are joined, the line so formed is called the income–consumption line.

Definition: The income–consumption line is the locus of all points representing equilibrium purchase patterns as income changes, holding preferences and relative prices constant.

Figure 3.3 displays three income–consumption lines: *OB, OD,* and *OF*. Budget lines AC and A_1C_1 are two of the many budget lines underlying income–consumption lines OB, OD, and OF. Equilibrium points E_1 and E_2 are two of the many equilibrium purchase patterns on OB. These three income–consumption lines illustrate some of the possible shapes that income–consumption lines can take. All of these begin at the origin, indicating that with no income, neither good X nor "all other goods" are demanded. For luxury goods the income-consumption line would intersect the "all other goods" axis, indicating that at low incomes good X would not be purchased at all.

Engel curves

The income–consumption line shows the relationship between equilibrium purchase patterns and income. Usually, however, the analyst is particularly interested in the relationship between the demand for a specific good and income. Although this relationship can be seen with an income–consumption line, an Engel curve is a simpler representation of the relationship.

Definition: An Engel curve is the locus of all points representing the quantities demanded of the good at various levels of income, prices and preferences held constant.

Figure 3.4 illustrates an Engel curve for food and shows how it is derived from the indifference curve diagram. In panel A of Figure 3.4 is an indifference curve diagram representing the equilibrium purchase patterns of a family at two levels of income. Y_1 and Y_2, holding the family's preferences and relative prices constant. E_1E_2 is the income–consumption line arising from these purchase patterns.

In panel B is a diagram with income, Y, on the vertical axis and the quantity of food demanded, q_f, on the horizontal axis. Panels A and B are lined up so that the quantities of food demanded in the equilibrium purchase patterns in the upper panel can be projected down to the lower panel. The incomes, Y_1 and Y_2, are represented by the budget lines, AC and A_1C_1, respectively. E_1E_2 is the income–consumption line and F_1F_2 is the analogous Engel curve. Theoretically, Engel curves begin at the origin or intersect the income axis. With zero income, the quantity demanded must be zero since the household can afford no purchases.[2] At very low incomes, however, the demand for particular goods may also be zero.[3]

Panel B of Figure 3.4 illustrates the *money income* Engel curve since Y is plotted on the vertical axis. A *real income* Engel curve can be derived directly on the indifference curve diagram. Real income is the purchasing power represented by the money income and, of course, purchasing power depends upon prices. Expressed in terms of the quantity of "all other goods" the household's income could purchase, real income is Y/p_o. Alternatively, in terms of the amount of

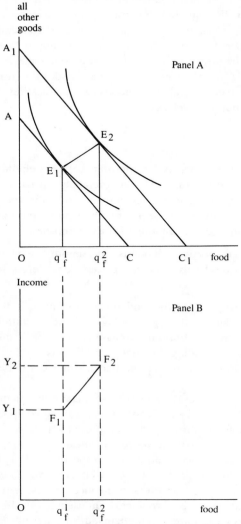

Figure 3.4 Deriving the Engel curve from the income–consumption line

food the household's income could purchase, the household's real income is Y/p_f. These, of course, can be read directly off the vertical and horizontal axes of an indifference curve diagram.

Consider Figure 3.5, which again shows the equilibrium purchase patterns of the household at two income levels, holding preferences and relative prices

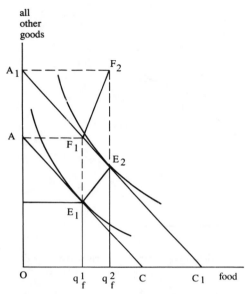

Figure 3.5 Derivation of the real income Engel curve for food from the income–consumption line. Real income is measured in terms of the amount of "all other goods" money income can buy, Y/p_o.

constant. With money income equal to Y_1, real income measured in terms of the amount of "all other goods" it could buy is the distance OA (i.e., $Y_1/p_o = q_o^m$). Likewise, with money income equal to Y_2, real income in terms of the amount of "all other goods" it could buy is OA_1 (i.e., q_o^{m1}). The point F_1 (where the horizontal from A and the vertical from E_1 intersect), therefore, represents the quantity of food demanded, q_f^1, when the family has real income Y_1/p_o. Likewise, point F_2 (i.e., the intersection of the horizontal from A_1 and the vertical from E_2) represents the quantity demanded of food, q_f^2, when the family has real income Y_2/p_o. Joining all points like F_1 and F_2 results in the real income Engel curve. Of course, a real income Engel curve for "all other goods" can be plotted by measuring real income in terms of the amount of food that money income can buy, Y/p_f.

The income elasticity of demand

Three income–consumption lines were shown in Figure 3.3, each representing possible different responses of a household to changes in its income. With respect to some goods, the household responds to an increase in its income with a large increase in the quantities demanded. With respect to others, the re-

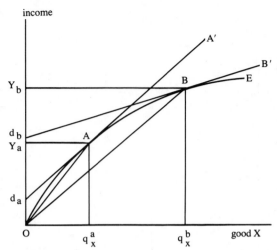

Figure 3.6 The income elasticity of demand for X derived from the Engel curve for X

sponse in their quantities demanded is quite small. The magnitude of the response in demand to changes in income is frequently measured by the income elasticity of demand. Since the income elasticity is measured in percentage terms, the response in demand for one good to changes in income can be compared with the responses in the demands for others.

Definition: The income elasticity of demand for a good is the percentage change in the quantity demanded due to a 1 percent change in income, holding preferences and relative prices constant.

In general, the formula is

$$N_x = (\Delta q_x/q_x) \cdot 100/(\Delta Y/Y) \cdot 100 = (\Delta q_x/\Delta Y)(Y/q_x) \tag{3.3}$$

where Δq_x is the change in the quantity demanded of good X due to the change in income, ΔY is the change in income, and q_x and Y are the prechange values of the quantity of X demanded and income, respectively.

There are two computing formulas for the income elasticity: the *point* and the *arc* income elasticity. The former formula is used to compute the income elasticity at a specific point on an Engel curve, and the latter is used when the change in income is large. The differences between point and arc elasticities can be more easily understood when discussed in terms of a diagram.

Figure 3.6 illustrates the Engel curve OE for good X. Consider the income elasticity at point A, where the household demands q_x^a amount of good X when its income is Y_a. The slope of the Engel curve at point A represents the change in income, ΔY, divided by the change in q_x, Δq_x; that is, $\Delta Y / \Delta q_x$. It can be found by taking the slope of the tangent to the Engel curve at A. Straight line $d_a A A'$ is the tangent to OE at point A. Suppose the equation for the tangent is

$$Y = d_a + n_a q_x. \tag{3.4}$$

d_a is the vertical intercept of $d_a A A'$ and n_a is the slope, $\Delta Y / \Delta q_x$, at A. Now, draw a straight line from point A to the origin; that is OA. It has slope Y_a / q_x^a. The point income elasticity of demand for X at point A can, then, be phrased in terms of the slopes of these two lines:

$$N_x^a = \frac{\text{slope of the straight line from } A \text{ to the origin}}{\text{slope of the tangent to the Engel curve at } A} \tag{3.5}$$

or

$$N_x^a = (Y_a / q_x^a) / n_a = (Y_a / q_x^a) / (\Delta Y / \Delta q_x) = (\Delta q_x / \Delta Y)(Y_a / q_x^a). \tag{3.6}$$

Likewise, the point income elasticity of demand for X at point B is

$$N_x^b = (Y_b / q_x^b) / n_b = (Y_b / q_x^b) / (\Delta Y / \Delta q_x) = (\Delta q_x / \Delta Y)(Y_b / q_x^b) \tag{3.7}$$

where n_b is the slope of $d_b B B'$, which is tangent to the Engel curve at B and Y_b / q_x^b is the slope of OB.

Suppose, instead, one does not know the Engel curve for X but only has the following facts: when income is Y_a, the quantity of X demanded is q_x^a, and when income is Y_b, the quantity of X demanded is q_x^b. In other words, there is no knowledge of the slope of the Engel curve either at point A or at point B. The income elasticity can still be computed but it will be an approximation. There are three approximation formulas: one at point A, one at point B, and one at the average of the two points, at income $(Y_a + Y_b)/2$ and quantity $(q_x^a + q_x^b)/2$.

The approximate measure of the point elasticity of demand at point A is

$$N_x^a = [(q_x^b - q_x^a) / (Y_b - Y_a)](Y_a / q_x^a).$$

Likewise, the approximate measure of the point income elasticity at point B is

$$N_x^b = [(q_x^b - q_x^a) / (Y_b - Y_a)](Y_b / q_x^b).$$

The approximation made at the average of the two points is called an *arc elasticity* (the arc between points A and B). To compute it, take the change in quantity as $q_x^b - q_x^a$ and the income change as $Y_b - Y_a$. The arc income elasticity formula is

$$N_x = [(q_x^b - q_x^a) / (Y_b - Y_a)][(Y_a + Y_b) / (q_x^a + q_x^b)]. \tag{3.8}$$

The arc elasticity will lie between the point elasticities at A and B.

An example

An example of the use of these formulas is as follows. Suppose that with an income over the school year of $4,200 after tuition and fees are paid, Doug purchases ten books per school year. After his school-year income rose to $5,000 per school year, he purchased twelve books per year. His income elasticity of demand for books at the lower income was

$$N_b^l = [(12 - 10)/(5,000 - 4,200)](4,200/10) = 1.05.$$

This means that when his income rose by 1 percent, he increased his demand for books by 1.05 percent. His income elasticity of demand for books at the higher income is

$$N_b^h = [(12 - 10)/(5,000 - 4,200)](5000/12) = 1.042.$$

This means that when his income rose by 1 percent, he increased his demand for books by 1.042 percent. Finally, his arc income elasticity of demand for books is

$$Arc\ N_b = [(12 - 10)/(5,000 - 4,200)](9200/22) = 1.045.$$

Translated, as Doug's income rose by 1 percent, he increased his demand for textbooks by 1.045 percent. Note that these are all approximations of Doug's income elasticity of demand for books and that the arc income elasticity does fall between the two point elasticities.

The geometry of income elasticities

It is possible to deduce the relative size of the income elasticity from the shape of the Engel curve. For normal goods, the income elasticity will be positive. Consider Figure 3.7 and take any point, A, on the Engel curve OE. Draw the tangent to the curve at point A, DAA', and also draw the straight line from the origin through A, OA. Now the income elasticity at point A is

$$N_x^a = \text{(slope of } OA)/\text{(slope of tangent of Engel curve to } OE \text{ at } A)$$
$$= (AB/OB)/(AC/OB) = AB/AC.$$

Since $AB > AC$, the ratio must be greater than 1 and $N_x^a > 1$.

This can be generalized. Note carefully that $AB/AC > 1$ and, thus, $N_x^a > 1$, because the slope of DAA' is less than the slope of OA. This happens only when DAA' intersects the income axis. Consequently, the income elasticity of demand at a point on an Engel curve is greater than 1 if the tangent to the Engel curve at the point intersects the income axis.

An income elasticity of demand greater than 1 indicates that the percentage response in the demand for X is greater than the percentage change in income. This indicates great responsiveness and such goods are said to be *income elastic*.

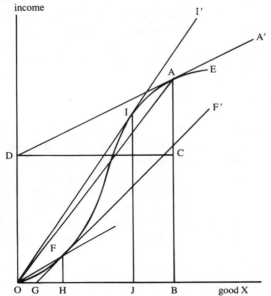

Figure 3.7 The geometry of income elasticities of demand

Income elastic goods are also sometimes called luxury goods, for obvious reasons.

Examples of income elastic goods include food consumed away from home ($N = 1.2$) and motor vehicles ($N = 2.7$).[4]

Now consider the income elasticity at point F on Engel curve OE in Figure 3.7. Draw the straight line from it to the origin as well as the tangent to the curve at F, GFF'. Now the income elasticity at point F is

$$N^i_x = (FH/OH)/(FH/GH) = GH/OH.$$

Since $GH < OH$, the ratio must be less than 1 and $N^i_x < 1$.

Again, this can be generalized. $GH < OH$ only because the slope of the tangent to the Engel curve at point F is greater than the slope of OF. This happens only when the tangent to the Engel curve at point F intersects the goods axis. Thus, the income elasticity of demand at a point on an Engel curve is less than 1 if the tangent to the Engel curve at the point intersects the goods axis.

An income elasticity of demand for a good less than 1 indicates that the percentage response in the demand is less than the percentage change in income. This indicates that the demand for the good is not very responsive to changes in income and such goods are said to be *income inelastic*. Income inelastic goods are sometimes called necessities, again, for obvious reasons.

Examples of income inelastic goods are food eaten at home ($N = 0.4$) (Tyrrell & Mount 1987), furniture and household equipment ($N = 0.69$), clothing and shoes ($N = 0.69$), as well as all services ($N = 0.67$) (Bryant & Wang 1990a).

Finally, consider point I on Engel curve OE in Figure 3.7. The line drawn through point I to the origin and the tangent to OE at point I coincide and are each OII'. Thus, the income elasticity at I is

$$N_x^i = (IJ/OJ)/(IJ/OJ) = 1.$$

At I the income elasticity of demand for X is unitary: a 1 percent increase in income engenders a 1 percent increase in the demand for good X. Suppose the straight line through the origin, OI, were an Engel curve. The income elasticity of demand at any point along it would be unitary because the slope of the line from any point on OI to the origin and the slope of the tangent to any point on OI are the same. Thus, the income elasticity of goods with Engel curves that are straight lines through the origin have unitary income elasticity and are said to be *unitary income elastic*. For such goods, the demand changes in the same proportion as income changes.

There are, perhaps, no goods the demands for which are exactly unitary income elastic. The demand for "other durables" (i.e., durable toys, sports equipment, boats and motors, yard and garden equipment, home repair equipment) in the United States, however, has been estimated recently at 1.05 (Bryant & Wang 1990a). Thus, a 1 percent increase in consumer income increases the demand for "other durables" in the United States by about 1 percent.

Uses of income elasticities

Income elasticities of demand are used by corporations to predict changes in the demands for the consumer products they produce as consumer incomes rise and fall. Governmental policy agencies use income elasticities of demand to predict how different industries producing different consumer goods and services will be affected by changes in consumer incomes. Income elasticities are also used to predict how families eligible for particular types of governmental income subsidies will change their demands when the income subsidy is altered. For instance, the income elasticity of demand for food is frequently used to predict the change in the demand for food by recipients of food stamps when a program change alters the amount of food stamps they receive. Likewise, the income elasticity of demand for housing is useful in calculating the changes in the demand for low-income housing resulting from changes in welfare benefits from, say, the Aid to Families with Dependent Children Program.

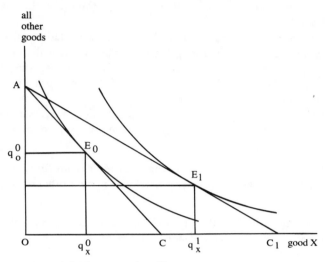

Figure 3.8 The own-price effect

Price effects

As with income effects, we analyze price effects in the absence of any other change that would affect the purchase pattern of the household. There are two prices in our simple model of demand, the price of good X and the price of "all other goods." Either price could change and affect the demand for X. The effect of a change in the price of a good on the demand for the same good is called the own-price effect. The effect of a change in the price of a good on the demand for another good is called a cross-price effect. We will discuss the own-price effect first.

The own-price effect

As before, the analysis begins by assuming that a household is in equilibrium given its income, the relative prices at which goods can be purchased, and its preferences. Then the price of one of the goods is changed (raised or lowered) and the household's response to that change is observed. The difference between the equilibrium quantities demanded of the good whose price changed is the own-price effect. This is illustrated in Figure 3.8.

Figure 3.8 depicts a typical household's purchase pattern involving good X and "all other goods." Good X is plotted on the horizontal axis. Prior to any change in p_x the household is in equilibrium at E_0, purchasing and consuming q_x^0

of good X and q_o^0 of "all other goods." The price of X then falls, shifting the budget line from AC to AC_1.

The decline in the price of X does two things. It lowers the relative price of X, making X cheaper relative to "all other goods." The falling price also expands choice, making possible many more purchase pattern alternatives than were open to the household before the price change. Of course, a price increase would reverse each of these two phenomena.

After the fall in p_x, the household maximizes satisfaction at E_1, purchasing and consuming q_x^1 of X and q_o^1 of "all other goods." Clearly, the own-price effect on the demand for X is $q_x^1 - q_x^0$.

Definition: The own-price effect is the change in the demand for a good in response to a change in that good's own price, holding income, other prices, and preferences constant.

The own-price effect of p_x on the demand for X is negative: as p_x falls, the demand for X rises. This is the almost-universal response.

The price–consumption line

A price–consumption line can be formed by joining the points representing the equilibrium purchase patterns given different prices of X. Such a line provides a picture of the own-price response of the household. In Figure 3.8 the price-consumption line is formed by joining points E_0 and E_1.

Definition: The price–consumption line is the locus of all equilibrium purchase patterns as p_x varies, holding household income, the price of "all other goods," and household preferences constant.

Of course, each household's own-price response will differ from those of other households since preferences can be expected to differ among households. The three panels of Figure 3.9 illustrate three differently shaped price–consumption lines representing the own-price responses of three households with different preferences but with the same income. In panel A the household's own-price response is "small" relative to the own-price response depicted in panel C. The price–consumption line in panel B is intermediate between the other two.

Real income as well as preferences can alter the household's own-price effect. It is reasonable that a change in the price of food might affect a poor family's demand for food differently than that of a rich family. Indeed, the response of a poor family's demand for food to a decline in the price of food might be expected to be larger than the response of a rich family. The reason is that the rich family will already be relatively sated with food whereas the poor family will not.

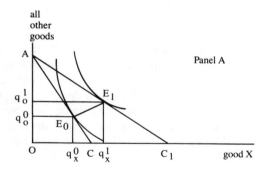

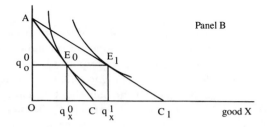

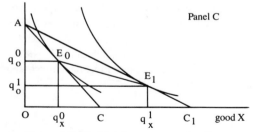

Figure 3.9 Three price–consumption lines

The own-price elasticity of demand

Just as the income effect was measured by the income elasticity, the own-price response is measured by the own-price elasticity. The elasticity measurement is useful because elasticities of different goods can be compared because they are measured in percentages.

Definition: The own-price elasticity of demand for a good is the absolute value of the percentage change in the quantity demanded of the good due to a 1 percent change in its price, holding other prices, income, and preferences constant.

Algebraically the own-price elasticity of demand can be stated as

$$E_x = |(\Delta q_x/q_x) \cdot 100/(\Delta p_x/p_x) \cdot 100| = |(\Delta q_x/\Delta p_x)(p_x/q_x)| \qquad (3.9)$$

where Δq_x is the change in the quantity of X demanded in response to the change in price, Δp_x. Even though the own-price response is almost universally negative, there may the very odd case in which the own-price response is positive.[5] In order to allow for this possibility, the own-price elasticity is defined to be positive; that is, the negative sign is ignored. In reporting estimates of own-price elasticities of demand for particular goods, we will always include the negative sign as a reminder that as the price of a good rises, the demand for it falls and vice versa.

The geometry of price–consumption lines

The shape of the price–consumption line is an indicator of the own-price elasticity of demand. That is, the shape of the price–consumption line can indicate the degree to which the demand for the good is own-price responsive.

Consider the price–consumption line in panel B of Figure 3.9. It is a horizontal straight line. That it is horizontal implies that the household demands the same quantity of "all other goods" before and after the fall in p_x. Because the price of "all other goods" did not change, the horizontal price–consumption line also implies that expenditures on "all other goods," $p_o q_o$, remained unchanged despite the fall in p_x. Because the household's total expenditures exhaust its income, $p_o q_o + p_x q_x = Y$, before and after the fall in p_x, the horizontal price–consumption line implies, finally, that the expenditures on X remained unchanged also. If expenditures on X, $p_x q_x$, remain unchanged in the face of a fall in the price of X, then the quantity of X demanded must have increased by an amount just sufficient to offset the fall in p_x.

It is the case that

$$\Delta(p_x q_x) = p_x \Delta q_x + q_x \Delta p_x; \qquad (3.10)$$

that is, the change in expenditures on X equals the prechange price of X times the change in the quantity of X plus the prechange quantity of X times the change in the price of X (see mathematical note 2). In the case of a horizontal price–consumption line, $\Delta(p_x q_x)$ is 0; that is,

$$0 = p_x \Delta q_x + q_x \Delta p_x, \qquad \text{or} \qquad p_x \Delta q_x = -q_x \Delta p_x,$$

and taking the absolute value,

$$|(p_x \Delta q_x)/(q_x \Delta p_x)| = |(\Delta q_x/\Delta p_x)(p_x/q_x)| = E_x = 1. \qquad (3.11)$$

Thus, the own-price elasticity of demand for X is 1 if the price–consumption line is a horizontal straight line.

Put differently, for expenditures on a good to remain constant in the face of changes in its price, the demand for the good must change by the same percentage as the percentage change in price. Such goods have an own-price elasticity of 1 and are said to be *unitary price elastic*. A price–consumption line that is horizontal, then, indicates that the demand for the good on the horizontal axis is unitary price elastic.

In panel A of Figure 3.9 the price–consumption line is positively sloped, indicating that the demand for "all other goods" rises as the price of X falls. Since p_o is unchanged, expenditures on "all other goods" must have increased. Consequently, expenditures on X must have fallen in the face of the drop in p_x if total expenditures are to equal household income before and after the price change. If the fall in p_x results in a fall in expenditures on X, then in terms of equation (3.11),

$$0 > p_x\Delta q_x + q_x\Delta p_x, \qquad \text{or} \qquad p_x\Delta q_x < -q_x\Delta p_x,$$

and taking the absolute value,

$$|(p_x\Delta q_x)/(q_x\Delta p_x)| = |(\Delta q_x/\Delta p_x)(p_x/q_x)| = E_x < 1. \tag{3.12}$$

Thus, a price–consumption line that is positively sloped with respect to the horizontal axis indicates that the good measured along the horizontal axis has an own-price elasticity less than 1. Goods whose own-price elasticity is less than 1 are said to be *own-price inelastic*. The demands for such goods are not very responsive to changes in their prices.

A positively sloped price–consumption line means that the rise in the demand for X in response to the fall in p_x was insufficient to prevent expenditures on X from falling. If a 1 percent increase in q_x exactly offsets a 1 percent fall in p_x and leaves p_xq_x unchanged (see panel B of Figure 3.9), then a fall in p_xq_x in response to a 1 percent decline in p_x must mean that q_x rose by less than 1 percent. Consequently, the own-price elasticity of demand for X must be less than 1; that is, $E_x < 1$.

Although the demands for few, if any, goods are exactly unitary price elastic, there are many that are price inelastic. The demand for all food is very price inelastic, about -0.17, although individual foods like beef are less price inelastic (Mann & St. George 1978). Other price inelastic goods are housing (-0.65) and clothing (-0.55) (Eastwood & Craven 1981) and electricity in the short run (-0.11) (Beierlein, Dunn, & McCornon 1981).

Finally, consider panel C of Figure 3.9. Here, the price–consumption line is negatively sloped, indicating that the demand for "all other goods" falls as the price of X falls. Since p_o is unchanged, expenditures on "all other goods" must fall, and consequently, expenditures on X, p_xq_x, must rise in response to a fall in p_x. For expenditures on X to rise due to a 1 percent fall in p_x, the increase in the demand for X must have been greater than 1 percent. The own-price elasticity of demand for X in such a case, therefore, is greater than 1, $E_x > 1$. Goods possessing own-price elasticities of demand greater than 1 are said to be *price elastic*.

This is easily shown using equation (3.11) again. If the fall in price results in an increase in expenditures on X, then the change in expenditures on X, $\Delta(p_x q_x)$ is positive, and therefore,

$$0 < p_x \Delta q_x + q_x \Delta p_x, \quad \text{or} \quad p_x \Delta q_x > -q_x \Delta p_x,$$

or taking the absolute value,

$$|(p_x \Delta q_x)/(q_x \Delta p_x)| = |(\Delta q_x/\Delta p_x)(p_x/q_x)| = E_x > 1. \tag{3.13}$$

Price elastic goods show great responsiveness to price. Some examples are hamburger (-1.5) (Capps & Havlicek 1987), electricity in the long run (-1.2) (Taylor 1975), women's hats (-3.00), and movies (-3.70) (Houthakker & Taylor 1970).

The formula for the own-price elasticity of demand for a good,

$$E_x = |(\Delta q_x/\Delta p_x)(p_x/q_x)|, \tag{3.14}$$

is definitionally correct, but computing formulas are needed when one is confronted with real data. Suppose that we know that the demand for good X is q_x^a when the price is p_x^a and the demand for X is q_x^b when the price is p_x^b. One can estimate the own-price elasticity either at point A or at point B with a *point own-price elasticity formula*.

The point own-price elasticity at A can be estimated by

$$E_x^a = |[(q_x^b - q_x^a)/(p_x^b - p_x^a)](p_x^a/q_x^a)|.$$

Likewise, the point own-price elasticity or demand for X at point B is estimated by

$$E_x^b = |[(q_x^b - q_x^a)/(p_x^b - p_x^a)](p_x^b/q_x^b)|.$$

If the price change is large or if an average price elasticity is desired between points A and B, then the *arc own-price elasticity* is relevant. The formula for the arc price elasticity is

$$\text{Arc } E_x = |[(q_x^b - q_x^a)/(p_x^b - p_x^a)][(p_x^a + p_x^b)/(q_x^a + q_x^b)]|.$$

An example

Suppose that at a price for apartments in Collegetown of $1.25 per square foot per month, Doug and his two friends rent an apartment with 700 square feet (three bedrooms of 10 feet $\times$ 10 feet each, a kitchen of 10 feet $\times$ 10 feet, and living room, bathroom, and hallway space equal to another 300 square feet).

Then, suppose the price of Collegetown apartments rises to \$1.50 per square foot per month. At the higher price Doug and his friends move to an apartment with 600 square feet of space. Their point price elasticity measured at the lower price is

$$E_h^1 = |[(700 - 600)/(1.25 - 1.50)](1.25/700)| = 0.71.$$

Their price elasticity of demand for housing at the higher price is

$$E_h^2 = |[(700 - 600)/(1.25 - 1.50)](1.50/600)| = 1.00.$$

Their arc price elasticity of demand is

$$\text{Arc } E_h = |[(700 - 600)/(1.25 - 1.50)](2.75/1,300)| = 0.85.$$

As with point and arc income elasticities, the arc own-price elasticity lies between the two point elasticities. Not knowing Doug's responses to price changes smaller than from \$1.25 to \$1.50 per square foot, the arc own-price elasticity is, perhaps, the better estimate to use. Using it, the demand for housing by Doug and his friends is, therefore, own-price inelastic. For each 1 percent increase in the price of Collegetown housing, Doug and his friends will reduce their demand for housing by 0.85 percent. This means that Collegetown landlords can increase their gross profits from renting to Doug and his friends by raising rents. If their demand for Collegetown housing had been own-price elastic, however, Collegetown landlords would be able to increase gross profits from renting by lowering rents.

The household's demand curve

Usually, the relationship between the price of a good and the quantity demanded is studied and graphed directly rather than studied in the context of the household's indifference diagram. This relationship between the quantity of X demanded and the price of X is called the *demand curve for X*. It is derived from the household indifference diagram in Figure 3.10.

In the top panel of Figure 3.10 three equilibrium purchase patterns are depicted at three different prices for X, with income, other prices, and preferences held constant. In the bottom panel is a diagram with the price of X plotted on the vertical axis and the quantity of X demanded plotted along the horizontal axis such that quantities of X in the equilibrium purchase patterns in the top panel can be dropped vertically down the horizontal axis on the bottom panel. As the price of X falls from p_x^0 to p_x^1 to p_x^2, the demand for X increases from q_x^0 to q_x^1 to q_x^2. The curve so mapped out is the demand curve for X.

Definition: The demand curve for a good is the schedule of quantities the con-

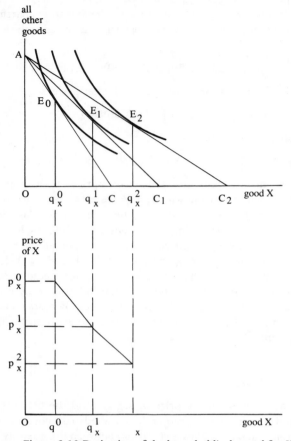

Figure 3.10 Derivation of the household's demand for X

sumer is willing and able to consume at different prices, holding income, other prices, and consumer preferences constant.

Note that the slope at any point on the demand curve in the bottom panel of Figure 3.10 is

$$(\Delta p_x / \Delta q_x);$$

that is, the rise over the run. Note also that if one were to draw a line from the point on the demand curve to the origin, the slope of that line would be

$$(p_x / q_x).$$

Since the own-price elasticity of demand has been defined as $E_x = |(\Delta q_x/\Delta p_x)(p_x/q_x)|$ (equation [3.14]), it is clear that the own-price elasticity of demand can be estimated from the demand curve as

$$E_x = |(p_x/q_x)/(\Delta p_x/\Delta q_x)| = |(\Delta q_x/\Delta p_x)(p_x/q_x)|;$$

that is,

$$E_x = \frac{\text{slope of the line from the origin to the point on the demand curve}}{\text{slope of the demand curve at the point}}$$

Income and substitution effects

It was stated previously that a price change evokes two different changes in the environment of a household. It makes the good whose price has changed more or less expensive relative to other goods. And it alters the alternatives open to the household: reducing choice if the price increases, and increasing choice if it falls. Not surprisingly, then, the own-price effect of any price change can be decomposed into two effects: the one due to the relative price change and the other due to the change in the choices open to the household. The part due to changing relative prices is called the *substitution effect*, and the part due to changing alternatives induced by the price change is called the *income effect*.

The substitution effect can be explained in the following way. Suppose the price of good X falls. Even if the household were neither more nor less satisfied after the price change than before, the fact that the price of X has fallen relative to the prices of all other things creates an incentive for the household to substitute the now cheaper X for some of the now relatively more expensive "all other goods" that it had been buying. That is to say, at the prechange equilibrium purchase pattern, the price that the household is willing to pay for X is more than the new, lowered price of X. Consequently, it will buy more of X and less of "all other goods."

Definition: The substitution effect of a price change is the effect of a change in a good's price on the demand for that good, holding satisfaction constant.

The income effect is quite simple. The decrease in the price of X opens up consumption alternatives not available at the old price. This is exactly what an increase in real income does, and the household responds in the same way: by increasing its consumption of both X and "all other goods" (so long as both are normal goods).

Definition: The income effect of a price change is the effect on the demand for X of the change in "income" brought about by the change in the price of X.

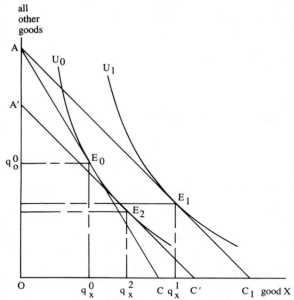

Figure 3.11 Decomposing the own-price effect

The geometry of income and substitution effects

Figure 3.11 illustrates the geometry of income and substitution effects. The household's pre-price-change budget line is AC, and given its preferences, its equilibrium purchase pattern of X and "all other goods" is E_0. Now suppose p_x falls, the new budget line being AC_1. The postchange demand for X is q_x^1, so that the own-price effect is $q_x^1 - q_x^0$.

Now suppose, instead, that at the same time p_x fell, sufficient income was (hypothetically) taken away from the household so that it was no better and no worse off at the new, lower price of X than it was before the price fell. If the household is no better and no worse off at the new relative price of X than it was at the old relative price, it must be on the same indifference curve. If the household faces the new price of X rather than the old, and if it is no better off than before, its budget line must be tangent to the same indifference curve it was on before the price fell and some of its income had been taken away. This budget line is $A'C'$ in Figure 3.11. It has been drawn *parallel to AC_1,* reflecting the new relative price of X, and *tangent to U_0,* reflecting the fact that the household is no better and no worse off than it was before. At the pre-price-decline equilibrium, E_0, the slope of U_0 (i.e., the [marginal rate of substitution]$_{x0}$) is greater than the slope of $A'C'$, indicating that the relative price the household is willing to pay for X is higher than the new market price of X. Consequently, the household alters its purchase pattern by substituting X for "all other goods" until it reaches E_2, where the marginal rate of substitution of X for "all other goods" is equal to the relative market price of X. The substitution effect of the fall in p_x is, therefore, an increase of $q_x^2 - q_x^0$ in the amount of X demanded.

Note that so long as the indifference curve is convex to the origin, the substitution effect is negative: the quantity demanded of X rising as its price falls and vice versa. Since indifference curves are usually convex to the origin, we will assume that the substitution effect is always negative.

Having identified the substitution effect, we can now return to the household the income we (hypothetically) took away from it. Returning the income is equivalent to expanding the household's alternatives, shifting the budget line from $A'C'$ to AC_1. With the increase in real income the household maximizes its satisfaction on AC_1 at E_1, where q_x^1 is demanded. The income effect of the price change, therefore, is $q_x^1 - q_x^2$. This is the effect (measured at the new relative price of X) of the expanded alternatives opened to the household due to the fall in p_x.

Notice that so long as good X is a normal good, the income effect and the substitution effect augment each other, making for a larger own-price effect. If, however, good X is an inferior good (i.e., the income effect is negative), then the substitution effect and the income effect of the price change tend to offset each other, making the total price effect smaller.

The own-price effect is equal to the sum of the substitution effect and the income effect. This can be expressed algebraically as[6]

$$\Delta q_x/\Delta p_x = [(\Delta q_x/\Delta p_x)|_{u=c}] - [q_x(\Delta q_x/\Delta Y)|_{p_x=p_k}] \tag{3.15}$$

where

$\Delta q_x/\Delta p_x =$ the own-price effect,

$(\Delta q_x/\Delta p_x)|_{u=c} =$ the own-substitution effect,

$-q_x(\Delta q_x/\Delta Y)|_{p_x=p_k} =$ the income effect of the price change.

The minus sign on the income effect adjusts the income effect for the direction of the price change. A price increase reduces real income, whereas a price decline increases real income.

Several propositions follow from the decomposition of the own-price effect into its substitution and income effect components.

Proposition 1: The more and better substitutes good X has, the larger the substitution effect of any own-price effect and, ceteris paribus, the larger the own-price effect.

Proposition 1 relates to the own-substitution effect in equation (3.15). The more and better substitutes good X has (and, therefore, the larger the own-substitution effect), the easier it will be for the household to substitute other goods for X if p_x rises, holding satisfaction constant. Likewise, the better a substitute X is for other goods, the easier it will be for the household to increase its consumption of X at the expense of other things should p_x fall. Thus, the bigger the own-substitution effect, the larger the own-price effect.

As an example, compare the price elasticities of hamburger and of food (about -1.5 and $-.17$, respectively) (Mann & St. George 1978; Capps & Havlicek 1987). Hamburger has many good substitutes (e.g., chicken, pork, fish, beans, tofu), whereas all food does not. One might be able to substitute some clothing and housing for a little food in order to burn fewer calories staying warm, but the scope for substitution is quite narrow. Consequently, the demand for hamburger will be more price elastic than the demand for all food.

The geometry of the proposition is straightforward. Recall from Chapter 2 that the extent of the curvature of the indifference curves reflects the substitutability of X for other things: the shallower the indifference curve, the better X substitutes for other things. Finding the substitution effects with indifference curves of different curvature will readily establish that the shallower the indifference curve, the greater the substitution effect, thus illustrating Proposition 1.

Proposition 2: The more responsive to income is the demand for a good, the larger the income effect of any price change and the larger the total price effect.

This proposition deals with the $(\Delta q_x/\Delta Y)|_{p_x=p_x}$ part of the term representing the income effect in equation (3.15). Suppose p_x^1 falls. The household no longer has to use as much of its income as it did before to buy the same quantity of X. The "extra" income it has is an approximate measure of the increase in real income brought about by the fall in p_x. The consumer will respond to this increase in income in the same fashion as if income had increased through any other means, and the extent of the response will depend on the income effect: the larger the income effect, the larger the own-price effect.

Examples are easy to find. Take hamburger and pork, for instance. The income and own-price elasticities of these two meats are as follows (Capps & Havlicek 1987):

	Income elasticity	Own-price elasticity
Hamburger	1.38	−1.58
Pork	1.11	−1.30

The demand for hamburger is more own-price elastic than the demand for pork in part because it is more income elastic, in accordance with Proposition 2.

Proposition 3: The more X is demanded prior to the change in its price, the larger the change in income caused by any price change, and the larger the own-price effect.

This proposition relates to the $-q_x$ part of the income effect, $-q_x(\Delta q_x/\Delta Y)|_{p_x-p_x'}$, in equation (3.15). The point is roughly this. Consider a \$0.05/unit fall in the price of X. If the consumer had purchased 100 units of X prior to the price decline, the same 100 units would cost \$5.00 less after the price drop than before. The extra \$5.00 could be spent on more X or more "all other goods." If, however, only 50 units of X were consumed prior to the price decline, the price drop would yield only \$2.50 of additional real income. Given that the income effect, $\Delta q_x/\Delta Y$, is on a per dollar basis, the greater the increase in real income brought about by the price decline, the greater its income effect and, in turn, the greater the own-price effect.

One implication of Proposition 3 is that because rich people demand more of most goods and services than poor people (because most goods and services are normal goods), rich people's demands for goods and services will have larger own-price effects than poor people's, ceteris paribus. We, therefore, might expect rich people "to take advantage" of sales more than poor people.[7]

Some examples: bringing theory closer to reality

The circumstances and changes that have been discussed have been simplifications of reality, the simplifications being made for the purposes of exposition. If the discussion were left here, one might be able to accuse the theory of not being able to handle the complexities of the real world. In this section several examples are discussed in an attempt to show the scope and power of simple demand theory.

Quantity discounts: the laundry detergent case

Anyone entering a modern supermarket must be impressed with the myriad products for sale, the variety of package sizes in which most products come, and the price variability among package sizes. In most, but not all cases, larger packages have lower unit prices than smaller packages; in short, quantity discounts abound.[8] Here we present an example of quantity discounts, what they do to consumer choice, and what typical consumer responses are.

Suppose laundry detergent is priced in the following way. The price per quart (qt.), p_d, is \$5.00 if no more than 5 qt. are purchased. But if more than 5 qt. are purchased, $p_d = \$2.50/\text{qt}$. Suppose the consumer has budgeted $Y = \$40$ to be spent in the store and suppose, for simplicity, that the price of "other things" in the store, p_o, is \$1.00/unit.

This type of quantity discount has a startling effect on the budget line con-

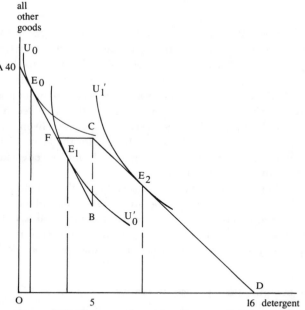

Figure 3.12 The case of quantity discounts on laundry detergent.

fronting the consumer. Figure 3.12 illustrates it. The AB part of the budget line is found in the following way. If no detergent is purchased, then $Y/p_o = 40/1 = 40$ units of other things can be purchased. This is point A in the diagram. If 5 qt. of detergent are purchased, then $p_d q_d = 5 \times 5 = \$25$ is spent on detergent, leaving $15 to be spent on other things, which, since $p_o = \$1.00$/unit, comes to 15 units. This is represented by B in Figure 3.12. AB is, then, the budget line facing consumers who buy no more than 5 qt. of detergent.

The CD portion of the budget line is found as follows. If all that the consumer buys is detergent, then it can be purchased most cheaply in the large size at $2.50/qt. and $Y/p_d = 40/2.50 = 16$ qt. of detergent can be purchased. This is point D. Finally, suppose (contrary to fact) that the consumer can buy 5 qt. of detergent at $2.50/unit; then if $12.50 is spent on detergent, $27.50 can be spent on other things (27.5 units of other things). This point (27.5, 5) is point C in Figure 3.12. Although point C does not represent an option available to the consumer, because the $2.50/qt. price applies only to quantities greater than 5, it does represent the lower limit of what can be attained at the discounted price. After all, the consumer could conceivably buy 5.01 qt. and so gain the $2.50/qt. price. CD, then, is the budget line if the consumer buys more than 5 qt. of detergent.

Two different consumers are illustrated in Figure 3.12, both of whom face budget line $ABCD$, consumer 0 with indifference curve U_0 and consumer 1 with indifference curves U_0' and U_1'. Consumer 0 has a very small demand for detergent and maximizes satisfaction at E_0, demanding less than 5 qt. of detergent. For consumer 0 to maximize satisfaction on the AB part of the budget line, the indifference curve to which AB is tangent must pass above point C; otherwise, buying more than 5 qt. would bring greater satisfaction.

This is the situation in which consumer 1 finds himself. AB is tangent to indifference curve U_0' at E_1, but maximum satisfaction is attained at point E_2 on the higher U_1', at which consumer 1 buys more than 9 qt. and, hence, can take advantage of the quantity discount.

Notice how the vertical part of the budget line, BC, "shades" the FB portion of AB. It is shaded in the sense that there are points on CD that dominate any point on FB. For the same income (i.e., \$40) the consumer can buy more detergent and the same amount of "all other goods" at points on CD than he can on FB. Because more is preferred to less, no consumer will be in equilibrium on FB. Thus, no consumer will buy quantities of detergent between 2.5 and 5 qt. To do so would place them in the FB portion of the AB budget line. This is precisely the situation of consumer 1. If there had been no quantity discount, consumer 1 would have maximized satisfaction at E_1. With the quantity discount, however, consumer 1 finds it in his own best interest to demand 9 qt. of detergent at E_2.

Quantity discounts, then, spur the demand for the discounted product in a fashion not simply the result of a conventional price effect: the discontinuity in the budget line caused by the quantity discount is an additional inducement. Such discontinuities and the effect they have in making uneconomic the purchase of quantities slightly smaller than the quantity at which the discount begins may be part of the reason for odd package sizes. An equally cogent reason is that odd package sizes tend to confuse the consumer to the store's benefit.

Another way of looking at the quantity discount is that it is a species of *price discrimination* practiced by manufacturers and stores: the higher price for small sizes being the advantage the store takes of the consumer with the small demand. Perhaps the consumer with the small demand is a single person living in an apartment with no laundry facilities. To buy the large size would mean that the large and heavy container would have to be carried to the laundromat. Paying the higher price for the smaller container is, therefore, the price paid for more convenience. Or the consumer with the small demand might be the poor consumer for whom other demands on income force purchasing many items in quantities too small to be able to exploit quantity discounts. The quantity discount strategy of the manufacturer (store) is specifically designed to exploit such consumers.

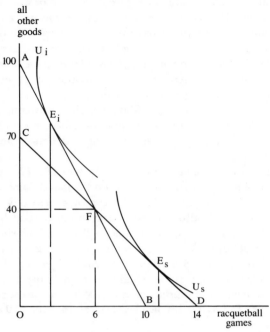

Figure 3.13 The case of a racquetball club's annual membership fees and lower hourly court rent

Two-part prices: the racquetball club racket

Racquetball, tennis, and fitness have all become quite popular in recent years. Typically, the individual interested in such activity has the following alternatives. One can "pay-as-you-play" by renting courts or exercise equipment by the hour. Alternatively, by joining a club, one is able to pay lower fees for the use of courts. Joining a club, however, involves paying an annual membership fee.

Suppose for example, that an individual has an income of $100/yr. and can play racquetball on pay-as-you-play courts at the rate of $10/hr. Or he or she can join a racquetball club at an annual membership fee of $30/yr. and play on the club's courts at the rate of $5.00/hr. Again for convenience, suppose that the price of "other things" is $p_o = \$1.00/\text{unit}$. We need to plot and compare the budget lines.

The pay-as-you-play budget line is line AB in Figure 3.13. If no racquetball is played, 100 units of other things can be purchased, hence, point A. If the consumer does nothing but play racquetball on pay-as-you-play courts, $Y/p_r = 100/10 = 10$ hr. can be played. This is point B. Membership in the club with no racquetball played allows the individual to buy $100 - 30 = 70$ units of other things, point C. Belonging to the club and doing nothing but playing racquetball allows the consumer to play racquetball for $(100 - 30)/5 = 14$ hr., point D. Line AB is the pay-as-you-play consumer's budget line, whereas ACD is the racquetball club member's budget line.

The pay-as-you-play budget line lies above the club member's budget line in the AF region. The reverse is true in the FD region. Point F, the point of intersection, is at $(40, 6)$. It is not in the best interests of the individual to join the club unless that person plans to play at least 6 hr. of racquetball per year. The implication for consumer behavior, of course, is that only serious racquetball players (e.g., the possessor of indifference curve U_s) will join a club, whereas infrequent players (the individual represented by U_i, e.g.) will pay as they play. Serious players are induced to play more racquetball than if club membership was unavailable. Infrequent players play less often than if the lower hourly court rentals available only with membership were available.

Electricity rates: block rate pricing

With respect to electricity the typical household faces what is called "block rate pricing." The particular scheme depends on the particular utility company supplying the electricity. Here, a simple imaginary block rate pricing structure will be discussed that has attributes most rate structures possess.

For the purposes of discussion suppose a household has an annual income of $100 and that the price of "other things" is $p_o = \$1.00/$unit. With respect to electricity suppose that the household must pay a flat annual hookup charge of $10, even if it uses no electricity at all during the year. For any electricity used under 500 kilowatt-hours (kWh) the household pays a price of $p_e^0 = \$0.10/$kWh. Finally, the household pays $p_e^1 = \$0.05/$kWh for all kilowatt-hours used greater than 500 kWh.

The budget line is illustrated in Figure 3.14 and arises as follows. If the household chooses to consume no electricity and is not hooked up, it can spend $100 on other things. This is point A in Figure 3.14. If the consumer is hooked up but uses no electricity during the year, the consumer pays the hookup annual fee of $10, leaving $90 to be spent on other things. This is point B. If the household uses exactly 500 kWh during the year, it spends $10 on the annual hookup fee plus $0.10 \times 500 = \$10 + \$50 = \$60$ on electricity, leaving $40 to be spent on other things. This is point C. Finally, if the household buys electricity and nothing else, it consumes 500 kWh $+ (100 - 10 - 50)/0.05 = 500 + 800 = 1,300$ kWh per year. This is point D in Figure 3.14. The budget line is, then, $ABCD$.

Clearly, the small demander of electricity (consumers like the one possessing indifference curve U_0) pay higher per kilowatt-hour prices for electricity and,

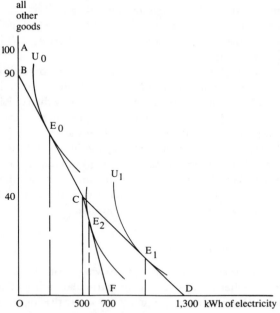

Figure 3.14 Block rate pricing

partly in consequence, are induced to consume less electricity than they would if the price were lower. Big users of electricity (like the one possessing indifference curve U_1) pay lower prices for the electricity they use and, again partly in consequence, consume more electricity than they otherwise would.

Given the impetus to save electricity in the past fifteen years, especially that produced with high-priced foreign oil, this price structure for electricity has been severely criticized on both efficiency and equity grounds. Large electricity consumers are rewarded by the declining nature of the block rate structure while small electricity consumers are penalized for their small consumption. In order to induce conservation, the critics argue, consumers should be rewarded for consuming small amounts and penalized for consuming large amounts of electricity. This would be achieved if, say, the price for electricity use above 500 kWh were $0.20/kWh rather than $0.05. If it was $0.20/kWh, the budget line would be $ABCF$ instead of $ABCD$ and the large electricity consumer would be induced to consume less, at E_2, rather than at E_1. Equity would also be achieved because small electricity consumers tend to have small incomes and large users tend to have high incomes, electricity being a normal good.

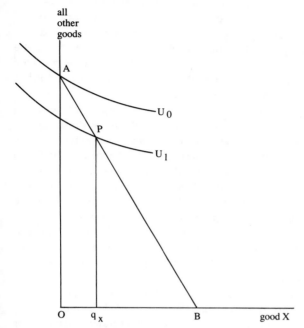

Figure 3.15 The zero purchase solution

Purchase versus nonpurchase behavior

Most textbook indifference curve diagrams are drawn with "interior solutions" in mind. That is, the illustrated situation is one in which some of each good X and all other goods are consumed. But at any point in time, some households are purchasers of good X and others are not. Since no household purchases every good in every period, the "corner solution" illustrated in Figure 3.15 is representative of every household for some goods. For the consumer depicted in Figure 3.15, satisfaction is maximized at point A and good X is not purchased.[9]

Consider Figure 3.15 in more detail. The slope of the indifference curve through A (i.e., the slope of U_0 at A) is less than the slope of the budget line at A; that is,

$$\text{MU}_x/\text{MU}_o|_A = \text{MU}_x/\text{MU}_o|q_x = 0 < p_x/p_o,$$

where MU_x = marginal utility of X, MU_o = marginal utility of "all other goods," the $|_A$ notation means "at point A," and $|q_x = 0$ means "at $q_x = 0$." The ratio p_x/p_o is, of course, the market price of good X in terms of "all other goods." Recall that the slope of any indifference curve reflects the real price the consumer is willing to pay for more X, holding satisfaction constant. Recall, too, that the slope of the budget line is the real price the consumer must pay for the good in the marketplace.[10] At a price of $MU_x/MU_o|_A$ the consumer is indifferent between zero consumption of X and a little X. $MU_x/MU_o|_A$ is called the consumer's *reservation price* of X. Because the consumer's reservation price for X is less than the market price of X, given the consumer's income and other prices, there is no incentive for the consumer to buy any of X at all.

Now consider the firms selling good X. They are, of course, interested in changing the nonpurchaser into a purchaser of X if it can be done cheaply enough. The indifference curve diagram isolates the various options firms have to influence consumer behavior and, thus, presents a clear picture of the firms' marketing problem and the several ways of solving it. The options are to (1) raise the consumer's income if X is a normal good, (2) raise the price of other goods and so make X relatively cheaper, (3) lower the price of X below the consumer's reservation price, and (4) raise the consumer's reservation price above the market price by changing preferences or by redefining the good. Neither raising consumer income nor raising other prices is feasible for individual firms. This leaves lowering the price of X or raising the consumer's reservation price as possible alternatives.

An obvious method is to reduce the price of X below the consumer's reservation price so as to draw the consumer into the market. A knowledge of the reservation prices of nonbuyers would tell firms how many added consumers of X would result from any given price decline. Although firms lack knowledge of the reservation prices of individual consumers, they do have quite accurate general knowledge of the distribution of reservation prices of nonpurchasers. For example, through experience, car dealers know roughly how many added cars they will sell if they allow their salespeople to bargain with customers at lower prices. Part of the bargaining process employed by salespeople is intended to discover the individual consumer's reservation price and how it might be manipulated. Again, through experience, department stores know reasonably accurately how much extra merchandise they will sell during a sale at which prices are slashed by a given amount. In both cases, a knowledge of the distribution of consumers' reservation prices allows firms to predict the effectiveness of price declines of different magnitudes.

The other common way of turning nonpurchasers into purchasers is to raise the reservation prices of consumers; that is, to make consumers more willing to buy the good than before. Advertising is an important means of changing consumer preferences so as to raise reservation prices. Geometrically, advertising good X rotates consumers' indifference curves clockwise and, therefore, steepens the slope of the indifference curve through point A. Marketing departments of firms seek information that will indicate how many added purchases a given expenditure on advertising will yield. The cost of changing customer preferences can then be balanced against the projected added sales revenue to be generated to determine the level of the advertising campaign.

A final way to raise the reservation price is to redefine the good being offered for sale. Instead of selling a box of breakfast cereal at price p_x, for instance, the firm will offer at the same price a box of breakfast cereal plus a magic decoder ring used to decode messages from Mars. The consumer's reservation price, thereby, changes from

$$MU_1/MU_3|q_1 = 0$$

where MU_1 = marginal utility of the box of cereal and MU_3 = marginal utility of all other goods, to

$$(MU_1 + MU_2)/MU_3|q_1 = 0 \text{ and } q_2 = 0$$

where MU_1 and MU_3 are defined as before and MU_2 = the marginal utility of the magic decoder ring (see mathematical note 5). So long as the consumer gets some positive utility from the magic decoder ring, the consumer's reservation price for the "tied sale" is higher than the reservation price for the box of cereal alone. If MU_2 is high enough (and that depends upon the pressure the consumer's five-year-old son puts on him or her!), the consumer's reservation price may rise enough so that it exceeds the market price and the consumer will become a purchaser. The firm must balance the cost of the magic decoder ring against the added revenue generated by the tied sale.[11]

Cross-price effects

Just as a change in the price of good X induces changes in the demand for X, so does a change in the price of a good other than X. The effect of a change in the price of another good, say p_y, on the demand for X, holding p_x, income, and preferences constant, is called the cross-price effect of p_y on the demand for X.

Two illustrations will be given. In the first, the price of "all other goods" changes and the effect on good X is observed; in the second, there are more than two goods, and when the price of one of them changes, its effect on the demand for X is observed.

The first case is pictured in Figure 3.16, in which the household is at equilibrium at point E_0 at prechange prices and income, demanding q_x^0. Then the price of "all other goods," p_o, falls, reducing the price of "all other goods" relative to X and expanding the purchase pattern alternatives open to the household. These changes are seen by comparing the initial budget line, AC, with the postchange budget line, A_1C. At the new prices and assuming the household to possess indifference curves U_0 and U_1, the household responds by demanding more X than before: q_x^1 rather than q_x^0. The total cross-price effect of the decline in p_o on X is $q_x^1 - q_x^0$, an increase in the demand for X.

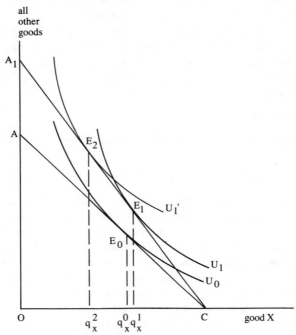

Figure 3.16 The cross-price effect of a decline in the price of "all other goods" on the demand for X

The cross-price effect on the demand for X need not be negative, however; that is, a fall in p_o inducing a rise in q_x. The total cross-price effect can just as easily be positive; that is, a fall in p_o inducing a fall in the demand for X. If the household possessed indifference curves U_0 and U_1', the decline in p_o would lead the family to reestablish equilibrium at E_2 rather than at E_1. In this case, the family's demand for X falls from q_x^0 to q_x^2 in response to the fall in p_o. Here, then, the total cross-price effect is positive.

Figure 3.16 is an accurate representation of the effect on the demand for X when the prices of all goods other than X change (and in the same proportion). What if the price of one of the many goods and services available to the household changed? How would it effect the demand for X?

To analyze this situation, one must leave the indifference curve diagram, for it allows consideration of just two goods: X and "all other goods" combined. Instead, we must conduct the analysis in terms of a demand diagram. Figure 3.17 pictures the demand curve for X and the effect changes in the price of another good, Z, have on the demand for X. Line DD represents the quantities

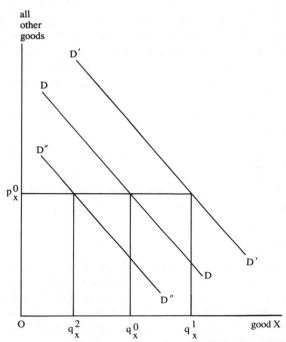

Figure 3.17 The cross-price effect of p_z on the demand for X when X and Z are substitutes and complements

demanded of X at various possible prices of X, p_x, holding all other prices, family income, and preferences constant. Suppose the price of X is p_x^0. Then, at p_x^0 the household demands q_x^0 of X.

Now suppose that the price of good Z, p_z, falls. The fall in p_z will induce an increase in the quantity of Z demanded. What will be its effect on the demand for X? Its effect will differ depending on whether X and Z are substitutes or complements. Suppose they are substitutes for each other and, in consequence, tend to be alternative ways of satisfying a particular want. As p_z falls, Z becomes cheaper relative to X than before, and because they are substitutes, the household will substitute added use of Z for some of its use of X. The demand for X will, therefore, fall. Consequently, the household's demand curve for X will shift to the left in Figure 3.17 to $D''D''$, indicating that regardless of the price of X, a fall in the price of Z will induce the family to demand less X than before. In particular, with the price of X at p_x^0, the fall in p_z leads to a fall in the quantity of X demanded from q_x^0 to q_x^2.

In contrast, suppose that X and Z are complements. That is, X and Z tend to be used in conjunction with each other to meet the same need. Then, as p_z falls and the quantity demanded of Z rises, the demand for X will also rise, because the two are complements of each other. Consequently, the family's demand curve for X will shift to the right in response to a fall in p_z, say to $D'D'$, indicating that the quantity demanded of X is larger as p_z falls, regardless of the price of X. In particular, at a price of X equal to p_x^0 the quantity of X demanded rises from q_x^0 to q_x^1 with a fall in p_z.

Substitutes and complements, then, can be defined in terms of the signs of their cross-price effects.

Definition: Two goods are substitutes if a rise in the price of one of the goods increases the demand for the other good.

Definition: Two goods are complements if a rise in the price of one of the goods reduces the demand for the other good.[12]

Cross-price elasticities

Cross-price effects can be measured in terms of elasticities just as can own-price effects. The advantage is the same; cross-price effects can be compared in elasticity terms because elasticities are defined in terms of percentage changes that are comparable across commodities. In contrast, cross-price effects, being defined in terms of the units in which the goods are sold, are not comparable, because the units are not commensurable.

Definition: The cross-price elasticity of demand for X with respect to the price of Z is the percentage change in the demand for X given a 1 percent change in the price of Z, holding other prices, income, and preferences constant.

The algebraic formula is

$$E_{xz} = (\Delta q_x / \Delta p_z)(p_z / q_x).$$

The formula is for the point cross-price elasticity. The arc cross-price elasticity is analogous to the arc price and income elasticities:

$$\text{Arc } E_{xz} = (\Delta q_x / \Delta p_z)(p_z^0 + p_z^1)/(q_x^0 + q_x^1),$$

where the superscripts 0 and 1 denote the prechange and postchange price levels, respectively. Computing formulas for point and arc cross-price elasticities are analogous to those for own-price elasticities and need not be given.

Empirical estimates of cross-price elasticities tend to be smaller than the estimates of the own-price elasticities for the same good. Eastwood and Craven (1981), for instance, estimate the own-price elasticity of demand for food eaten at home to be -0.23, whereas the cross-price elasticity of demand for food with respect to clothing prices is about -0.10, with respect to housing prices about

− 0.1041, and with respect to the prices of durable goods about − 0.16. Clearly, these broad categories of goods are all substitutes for each other: a decline in the price of one increases the demands for the others. For instance, a 10 percent decline in the price of clothing can be expected to raise the demand for food by about 1 percent.

Another example of changes in the price of one good on the demands for other goods is the effect of the price of women's time on the household's purchase pattern. As the price of women's time has risen, married women increasingly have entered the labor market and, in consequence, have reduced the household work they do. Also in response, households have increased their demands for some goods and services and reduced their demands for others. Recent estimates indicate that the cross-price elasticity between the price of women's time (i.e., female wage rate) and the demand for housing is 0.29; for gasoline and motor oil, − 0.62; for electricity and natural gas, − 0.40; and for transportation services, − 0.33 (Bryant & Wang 1990a). As female wage rates have risen and continue to rise, the demand for housing rises while the demands for gasoline and oil, electricity and natural gas, and transportation services all fall due to cross-price effects.

Family size and composition effects

Changes in prices and income are not the only things affecting the demand for goods and services by families. Perhaps the two most powerful factors explaining differences in the demands for goods and services among families are family size and composition. This section discusses these effects and reports some illustrative empirical estimates of such effects.

Differences in family size and composition have different effects on demand depending on the good or service in question. Furthermore, a change in family composition may affect family size. The addition of a baby simultaneously changes the family's size as well as its composition. The aging of the baby, however, changes only the family's composition. Adding a baby to a family increases the family's demand for baby clothes, baby foods, baby furniture, and the like, whereas the arrival of a grandparent affects the demands for none of these goods and services but will affect the demands for others, like medical services and food and perhaps television and telephone service. Adding either increases the family's demand for housing but to different degrees.

The essential thing that a change in family size or composition does is alter the family's preferences for goods and services. Geometrically this means that the shapes of the family's indifference curves are altered. Another way to put it is that such changes alter the family's marginal rates of substitution between goods and services. Prior to the arrival of a baby the family would be quite unwilling to give up any other good or service in order to increase its consump-

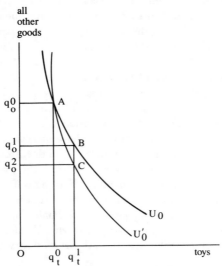

Figure 3.18 The effect of the arrival of a child on the family's preference map with respect to children's toys

tion of, say, diapers. The arrival of a baby changes this: the marginal rate of substitution of diapers for "all other goods" increases precipitously. Upon arrival of the baby, the family is much more willing to give up some other things in order to acquire diapers, holding satisfaction constant.

In a diagram with toys, say, on the horizontal axis and "all other goods" on the vertical, a new baby alters the indifference curves so that they are steeper. This is illustrated in Figure 3.18. Indifference curve U_0 is one of the family's indifference curves between toys and "all other goods" prior to the arrival of a child. Assume that $q_t^1 - q_t^0$ measures one unit of toys. At point A on indifference curve U_0, then, the household would willingly give up $q_o^0 - q_o^1$ units of "all other goods" in exchange for an added unit of toys, holding satisfaction constant. In other words, points A and B are on U_0. When a child is added to the family, however, the family's preferences change. Now, it is willing to give up more of "all other goods" in exchange for another unit of toys and still be as satisfied as it was before. Where before at point A it would have given up $q_o^0 - q_o^1$ for an added unit of toys, now it will give up $q_o^0 - q_o^2$ and still be as satisfied as it was before. If so, then, point C rather than B must now be on the same indifference curve as point A. Thus, the arrival of the child into the household served "to rotate" the family's indifference curves counterclockwise and make them steeper at point A.

The effect of the child-induced shift in preferences on the demand for toys is

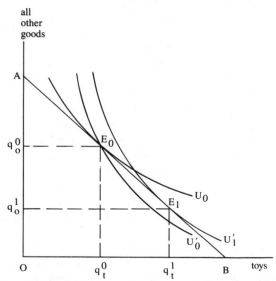

Figure 3.19 The effect of the arrival of a child on the family's demand for toys

illustrated in Figure 3.19. Prior to the arrival of the child, the family's demand for toys was q_t^0, given prices and its income represented by the budget line AB, and given preferences represented by indifference curve U_0. The arrival of a child increases the marginal rate of substitution of toys for other things, shifting the indifference curves to U_0' and U_1'. At the prechild equilibrium purchase pattern, E_0, the family is now willing to pay a higher than market price for toys relative to other things; that is, the marginal rate of substitution at point E_0 (i.e., the slope of U_0') is now steeper than the budget line. Consequently, in order to maximize satisfaction the family increases its demand for toys and reduces its demand for "all other goods" until it reaches E_1, at which it demands q_t^1 of toys and q_o^1 of "all other goods."

Note that neither relative market prices nor the family's income altered and, therefore, the budget line remained unchanged. Instead, the family's preferences changed with the arrival of the child and, in consequence, altered the family's purchase pattern of goods and services. In order to buy more toys for the child, the family had to reduce its demand for other things. This occurred because before and after the child arrived, the family's expenditures exhausted its income. Something had to make way for the added toys in the family's purchase pattern.

As the child grows, the needs and wants of the child (and of the parents for the child and for themselves) will change, and these, too, will alter the family's preference map. The marginal rates of substitution between some goods will increase while others will reduce. As they do, the family's demands for the individual goods and services will increase or decrease. These are family composition effects because family size remains constant.

The arrival of a child in the family (or some other individual, such as an older adult) has both size and composition effects. The two effects are difficult to separate empirically.

An example of family size and composition effects on demand is the change in demand for clothing. Hager and Bryant (1977) studied the family size and composition effects on the demand for clothing by poor rural families in the early 1970s. They estimated that family clothing expenditures rose by $17.00 per quarter (i.e., per three-month period) with the arrival of each new baby. An added female teenager increased family clothing expenditures by $23.00 per quarter; an added male teenager, by about $11.00. Increases in family size, then, increase the demand for clothing, the amount depending on how family size increases.

Changes in family composition also change family clothing demands, as is suggested by the discussion of the effects of family size. For instance, clothing expenditures on the same child change as it grows up. The same clothing study revealed that as boys grew from babies into toddlers, clothing expenditures for them declined by about $4.00 per quarter. Another decline of about $4.00 per quarter occurred when they became school-aged. Then, when they entered their teenage years, clothing expenditures rose again by about $11.00 per quarter.

Summary

Four of the major determinants of household consumption patterns are prices, income, family size, and family composition. As the real income of the consumer changes, more or fewer consumption alternatives become available depending on the direction of the real income change. In response, consumers alter their consumption patterns: increasing their demands for normal goods and reducing their demands for inferior goods with income increases. As some prices change relative to others, some consumer goods become cheaper and others more expensive. The price changes set up incentives for consumers to demand more of the cheaper goods and less of the more expensive ones. The price changes also alter the household's real income, inducing income effects as well.

Neither price nor income changes are hypothesized to alter consumers' preference patterns; that is, the shapes and locations of their indifference curves. Changes in household size and composition, however, do shift people's preferences. A change in either household size or composition alters the prices consumers are willing to pay for goods and services; that is, their marginal rates of substitution between goods. These changes in preferences, operating against a background of constant market prices and real income, lead the household to change its purchase pattern: in favor of those goods for which the marginal rates of substitution have risen and away from those goods for which the marginal rates of substitution have fallen.

CHAPTER FOUR

Consumption and saving

Introduction

In Chapters 2 and 3 a simple one-period model was developed and was used to analyze household demands for goods and services at any point in time: per month or per year, say. In such a model the household has no memory and no foresight; it lives only in the present. Although terribly simple, the model is very helpful in understanding how families allocate their current income among the competing current demands for those resources.

But households are not so myopic as to confine their decision making to the present. They recognize that today is not a capsule with no yesterday and no tomorrow. Rather, today's decisions must be made in recognition of what went on before and what is expected to occur in the future. Commitments made in previous periods are honored in the present. Furthermore, not only do they expect to demand goods and services tomorrow, but households also expect to have added resources in the future. Consequently, one can expect that households will behave today in the light of their yesterdays and what they expect of their tomorrows.

That the consumption behavior of families has a past is reflected in the fact that families have debts from the past that they must pay off at least in part in the present and that they have resources from the past (financial assets like bank accounts, stocks, and bonds and physical assets like owned homes, cars, durables, and the like) that can be used to augment present consumption. That families' consumption behavior anticipates a future is reflected in the fact that families typically do save and do not consume all their assets in the present.

These facts are well reflected in the national data on consumption and saving for the United States shown in Table 4.1. In 1970 $640 billion was spent on consumption, $58 billion was saved, and $17 billion was used to pay the interest on consumer debt. These amounts accounted for 89.4 percent, 8.1 percent, and 2.4 percent of personal disposable income (PDI), respectively. By 1987 American consumers were consuming much more, saving much more, and paying much more interest on consumer debt absolutely. But the percentages of PDI show that by 1987, Americans were consuming more, paying more interest on consumer debt, and saving less relative to PDI than they did in 1970.

Table 4.1. *Income, consumption, saving, and interest payments in the United States: 1970–87*

	Billions of dollars			Percentage of PDI		
Item	1970	1980	1987	1970	1980	1987
Personal disposable income (PDI)	716	1,918	3,210	100	100	100
Personal consumption expenditures	640	1,733	3,012	89.4	90.4	93.8
Personal saving	58	137	104	8.1	7.1	3.2
Interest paid by consumers	17	47	92	2.4	2.5	2.9

Source: U.S. Bureau of the Census 1989, Table 695, p. 428.

In each year, however, the saving was done with the view to consumption in the future, and the interest payments were made by consumers on debts incurred in the past in order to expand past consumption. Clearly, the past, present, and future are reflected in these patterns.

Making present decisions in the light of the past and the expected future is characteristic of all household economic behavior. In this, our first examination of the consequences of decision making over time, we will concentrate on the household's aggregate consumption and saving decisions: how much of current resources is devoted to present consumption and how much is used to pay for either past or future consumption. Consequently, both borrowing and lending will be analyzed since they are the principal ways by which households are able to transfer resources from one period to another. In brief, each household must decide what fraction of its current resources it will consume and what fraction it will save.

But what is consumption and what is saving? We need accurate definitions of these two concepts and a better understanding of how each is carried out.

Definition: Consumption is an activity in which goods are purchased and yield satisfaction in the current period.

Food purchased and consumed today is consumption. The purchase and use of a theater ticket or electricity today is consumption. What about purchases and use of cassette tapes or clothing today? Certainly, consumption is involved because resources are being expended today that yield satisfaction today. But since the tapes can be listened to and the clothes worn tomorrow too, resources are also being expended today that yield satisfaction tomorrow. This is the essence of saving.

Definition: Saving is an activity in which resources are used in the current period and yield satisfaction in future periods.

The purchase of cassette tapes and the purchase of clothing are examples of activities that are simultaneously consumption and saving. So is the purchase of a car or other durable good.[1] Pure saving occurs when households use some of their current resources to increase their bank balances, buy stocks and bonds, or lend money to an individual or firm. Indeed, increasing their bank balances is, in reality, simply lending money to the bank. In cases of pure saving the resources saved increase satisfaction in the period in the future when they are consumed.

Consumption–saving is, therefore, a continuum with pure consumption at one extreme and pure saving at the other. As with other continua, we will simplify matters by investigating only the extremes: pure consumption and pure saving. With an understanding of household behavior at each of the poles of the continuum, we can better understand the behavior at any point along the continuum.

We have discussed saving as if it were always either zero or some positive amount. Nothing can be further from the truth. Households can also dissave and frequently do. Dissaving is the reverse of saving.

Definition: Dissaving involves the transfer of future resources to the present so as to increase current consumption.

Dissaving involves borrowing, then. When we borrow money to buy a house, a car, or an education, we are transferring resources we expect to have in the future for use in the present period. If debts outstanding are subtracted from assets (i.e., total savings), the result is *net assets* or *net worth*. We can say, then, that saving occurs when net worth increases and dissaving occurs when net worth declines. Paying off debts, then, is just as much saving as increasing one's bank balances.

The major question addressed in this chapter is how the household allocates its resources through time: what factors determine its total consumption, and what factors determine its total saving. One of the important determinants of consumption and saving is income, and therefore, much space is devoted to it in this chapter. The question of the relation of consumption to income, that is, the fraction of income that is saved, has very important monetary and fiscal policy implications and, in consequence, has engaged the interests of economists since the Great Depression of the 1930s. In this chapter we will discuss some of the enduring answers to the question in the context of a simple two-period model of household consumption and saving. We will also examine how household borrowing and lending behavior responds to changes in interest rates. Finally, we will examine how price changes through time (i.e., inflation and deflation) affect household consumption and saving behavior.

A consumption and saving model of the household

The factors from the past and the future that bear on a household's current consumption and saving decisions can be examined within a very simple model containing two periods: today and tomorrow. Interpret "today" as the current year and "tomorrow" as next year. Assume that the household will not exist "the day after tomorrow" and that it leaves no inheritances when it departs the scene. Assume, moreover, that the household knows for certain today what tomorrow will be like: that is, what its income tomorrow will be, what tomorrow's prices will be, and what its preferences will be tomorrow.

Such a circumstance is a gross caricature of the actual situation in which families must make their decisions. The restriction of the model to "today" and "tomorrow" is made so that we can represent the model on a two-dimensional diagram rather than with more complicated mathematics. The assumption that the household leaves no bequests is likewise to contain the model to two dimensions. And presuming that the household knows the future with certainty allows us to ignore the very much more complicated mathematics required to model uncertainty. Nonetheless, the model sheds much light on actual behavior, and its simplicity dispenses with much irrelevant detail.

The household is pictured as being poised at the beginning of year one and is faced with deciding how much to consume in years one and two, denoted by C_1 and C_2, respectively, such that it exhausts its total resources. Its total resources include its income in years one and two, denoted by Y_1 and Y_2, along with whatever net assets (assets minus debts), denoted by A_1, it brought into the current period from the past. A_1, therefore, will be negative if the household's total debts exceed its total assets. A_1 will be positive if its total assets exceed its total debts. The household will make its consumption and saving decisions so as to maximize its satisfaction; that is, so as to achieve the goals it has set out for itself, subject to the resources at its disposal.

As with the model in Chapters 2 and 3, the intertemporal household model contains three parts: the household's intertemporal budget constraint, the household's preferences, and the behavioral hypothesis that it makes decisions so as to maximizes satisfaction. We deal with each in turn.

The household's intertemporal budget constraint

At this point we need an accurate representation of the resources at the household's disposal at the beginning of year one when it makes its decisions. Think about it in the following way. The household has its net assets, A_1, plus its current income, Y_1. In addition, it has the maximum amount of money it can borrow using year two's income, Y_2, as collateral. Let the maximum sum it can borrow be denoted by B_1^m. B_1^m can be viewed as the household's credit line. Thus, total household resources at the beginning of year one, R_1, equal

$$R_1 = A_1 + Y_1 + B_1^m. \tag{4.1}$$

Can we be more precise about B_1^m? Anything the household borrows in year one must be paid back with interest in year two. Thus, supposing the rate of interest to be r, then in year two B_1^m must be paid back plus the interest on B_1^m, which is rB_1^m. What will this amount to? No lender will loan more than the household can pay back with its income in year two. Consequently, the principal and interest on the maximum loan will equal year two's income, Y_2:

$$B_1^m + rB_1^m = Y_2. \tag{4.2}$$

Factoring out B_1^m from the left-hand side and dividing through by $(1 + r)$ yields the size of the maximum loan:

$$B_1^m = Y_2/(1 + r). \tag{4.3}$$

Example: If the household's expected income in year two was $100 and the rate of interest was 10 percent, then the household could borrow a total of $100/1.10 = $90.91 in year one. In year two the $90.91 principle would be paid back along with $9.09 in interest in year two. $Y_2/(1 + r)$, then, is the value of year two's income in year one. Alternatively, $Y_2/(1 + r)$ is referred to as the *present value* of Y_2, valued at the beginning of year one (see mathematical note 1). The total resources of the household at the beginning of year one, then, sum to

$$R_1 = A_1 + Y_1 + Y_2/(1 + r). \tag{4.4}$$

Another way of looking at R_1 is to view it as representing the maximum expenditure on current consumption the household could make in year one if it spent its entire resources on current consumption and consumed nothing in year two. Thus,

$$p_c C_1^m = R_1 \tag{4.5}$$

where C_1^m represents the maximum quantity of goods and services the household could consume in year one, given the price of goods and services was p_c. Thus,[2]

$$C_1^m = R_1/p_c. \tag{4.6}$$

On a graph with consumption in year one ("today") on the horizontal axis and consumption in year two ("tomorrow") on the vertical axis, $(C_1^m, 0) = D$ plotted on the horizontal axis represents the maximum possible consumption in year one and the minimum consumption in year two given the household's resources, the market rate of interest at which money can be borrowed, and the price of consumption goods. Such a graph is pictured in Figure 4.1.

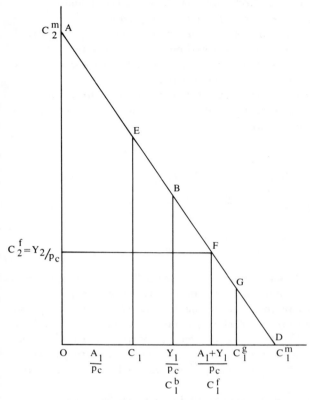

Figure 4.1 The household's budget line between consumption in year one and consumption in year two

Likewise, we can compute the maximum quantity of goods and services the household could consume in year two if it saved all of its year one income and net assets. Saving this amount would yield $A_1 + Y_1$ in year two *plus* the interest on this sum, $r(A_1 + Y_1)$. Adding to this sum income received in year two, Y_2, the maximum expenditure on goods and services consumable in year two would be

$$p_c C_2^m = (1 + r)(A_1 + Y_1) + Y_2 \tag{4.7}$$

where C_2^m is the maximum quantity of goods and services consumable in year two, or

$$C_2^m = [(1 + r)(A_1 + Y_1) + Y_2]/p_c. \tag{4.8}$$

Plotting $(0, C_2^m) = A$ on the vertical axis of Figure 4.1 represents the maximum quantity of goods and services purchasable in year two and the minimum quantity purchasable in year one. A straight line joining A and D represents the household's budget line. It represents all the combinations of C_1 and C_2 available to the household if it exhausts its total resources between the two years. This budget line is exactly analogous to the budget lines that were developed in Chapter 2 and used to analyze demand in Chapter 3.

The slope of the budget line in Figure 4.1 represents the rate at which the household is able to exchange consumption in year one for consumption in year two in the market. Algebraically, the

$$slope = \frac{rise}{run} = -\frac{[(1+r)(Y_1+A_1)+Y_2]/p_c}{\{(Y_1+A_1)+Y_2/(1+r)\}/p_c}$$
$$= -\frac{(1+r)(Y_1+A_1)+Y_2}{[(1+r)(Y_1+A_1)+Y_2]/(1+r)}$$
$$= -\frac{1+r}{1} = -(1+r).$$

Thus, a dollars' worth of consumption in year one can be exchanged for $(1+r)$ dollars' worth of consumption in year two. This is reasonable: giving up a dollar's worth of consumption in year one implies that \$1.00 is saved. By year two, the saved dollar is worth \$1.00 $(1+r)$ and thence can buy $(1+r)$ dollars' worth of consumption in year two. Conversely, borrowing a dollar from year two for use in year one yields $1/(1+r)$ dollars of purchasing power in year one since the dollar next year must pay off both the loan and the interest on the loan.

The intertemporal budget line in Figure 4.1 does more than illustrate possible consumption combinations in years one and two. It also illustrates regions of saving and borrowing. Saving is income minus consumption. If consumption in year one is C_1, saving is $S_1 = Y_1 - C_1$. Thus, at point B in Figure 4.1, $C_1^b = Y_1/p_c$ and $S_1 = 0$. Point E, lying to the left of point B, represents a situation in which consumption, C_1^e is less than at point B, and therefore, saving, S_1^e, must be positive. Point G, lying to the right of point B, represents a situation in which consumption, C_1^g, is greater than at point B, where it equals Y_1/p_c, and therefore, saving, S_1^g, must be negative. Negative saving, of course, is the equivalent of borrowing. Point B, therefore, represents a situation in which the household represented by this budget line would be neither a saver nor a borrower. Any point on the budget line to the left of B is the saving region, whereas any point to the right of B is the borrowing region.

Point F and the region between B and F in Figure 4.1 are also of interest. At F, $C_1^f = (Y_1+A_1)/p_c$ and $C_2^f = Y_2/p_c$. Thus, if the household were consuming at point F it would consume all of its year one resources in year one and all of its

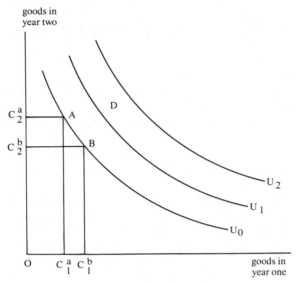

Figure 4.2 The household's time preference map

year two resources in year two. In this case the household would be consuming all of its net assets, A_1. By consuming its net assets the household is, in a sense, borrowing from itself. This occurs at any point between B and F. To the right of F, say at G, the household consumes more $(Y_1 + A_1)/p_c$ in year one and can only do so by borrowing in the credit market.

The household's time preference map

Just as the consumer has preferences among combinations of goods at any point in time (see Chapter 2), the consumer also has preferences among consumption in different years. Figure 4.2 illustrates a representative set of indifference curves between consumption in year one, C_1, and consumption in year two, C_2. Each of the indifference curves in Figure 4.2 is the locus of all points representing combinations of C_1 and C_2 among which the household is indifferent. The household, for instance, is indifferent between (C_1^a, C_2^a) and (C_1^b, C_2^b) on indifference curve U_0. It prefers combination D on U_1 to either A or B because D contains more consumption in both years.

The slope of each of these indifference curves represents the marginal rate of substitution of C_1 for C_2, $\text{MRS}_{1,2}$; that is, the rate at which the household is willing to substitute consumption in year one for consumption in year two and still be as satisfied as it was before. And, as with the marginal rate of substitution between goods at a single point in time, the marginal rate of substitution between consumption through time diminishes. Hence, the indifference curves in the household's time preference map are negatively sloped and convex to the origin.

Time preference and other motives for saving

The $MRS_{1,2}$ can be used to characterize a household's *time preference*. Household's are said to be *present oriented, future oriented*, or have *neutral time preference*. The essential characteristic of a present-oriented household is that given no other motive to transfer resources between periods, such a household prefers to consume more in the current period than in future periods. Consequently, such a household will borrow against future income so as to consume more today. A future-oriented household will save in similar circumstances, whereas a household with neutral time preference will neither borrow nor lend.

From what has been said earlier, it is clear that an understanding of time preference and its rigorous definition require a discussion of other motives for saving and the specification of conditions that remove all motives for saving except the relative preference for consumption now or in the future. Consequently, we must discuss other motives for saving.

Evening out the income stream. The first motive arises because the receipt of one's resources through time is uneven and will not match the desired time path of consumption. By saving or borrowing, one can rearrange one's resources in time so that they match the desired time path of consumption.

This is an important reason for saving. It is commonplace knowledge that an individual's income is low while that individual is young, rises after the completion of one's education, rises more with the pursuit of one's occupation, and subsequently falls in retirement. In the face of this life-cycle pattern of income, people commonly borrow against future income when young in order to finance educations, houses, and the like. In contrast, middle-aged people typically save in order to increase their resources during retirement. The earlier borrowing and the later saving are attempts to even out the receipt of one's income stream over the life cycle to make it coincide more closely with desired consumption patterns.

Consuming when goods are cheap. A second motive for saving and borrowing is to transfer resources into time periods when goods are relatively cheap and to transfer resources out of periods when goods are relatively expensive. High interest rates today mean that today's income can buy more goods tomorrow than they can today. Similarly, if prices are expected to be lower tomorrow than today, a dollar saved today can buy more goods tomorrow than if spent today. In contrast, low interest rates today or the expectation of higher prices tomorrow each create incentives to borrow from the high-priced future in order to consume more today when goods are cheaper. Rearranging one's income stream through time so that it coincides with the pattern of prices and interest rates through time is, then, the second motive.[3]

Time preference, per se. The third motive, time preference, is simply the desire to rearrange one's consumption pattern through time – unaffected by the expected pattern of prices, interest rates, and income through time. As such, time preference is reflected in the shapes of the indifference curves between consumption now and consumption then. Thus, the $MRS_{1,2}$ can reveal a consumer's time preference in circumstances in which the other two motives for saving and borrowing are removed.

Motives for saving other than time preference are removed when a consumer's resources are distributed evenly through time (i.e., $A_1 = 0$ and $Y_1 = Y_2$), when interest rates provide no incentive either to borrow or to lend (i.e., when $r = 0$), and when the pattern of prices in time provides no incentive either to borrow or to lend (i.e., when $p_c^1 = p_c^2 = p_c$).

Definition: A consumer with neutral time preference will neither borrow nor lend when $A_1 = 0$, $Y_1 = Y_2$, $r = 0$, and $p_c^1 = p_c^2 = p_c$.

Definition: A present-oriented consumer will borrow when $A_1 = 0$, $Y_1 = Y_2$, $r = 0$, and $p_c^1 = p_c^2 = p_c$.

Definition: A future-oriented consumer will save when $A_1 = 0$, $Y_1 = Y_2$, $r = 0$, and $p_c^1 = p_c^2 = p_c$.

Such preferences are illustrated in Figure 4.3. Budget line AB is drawn with a slope of -1; that is, if $r = 0$ and p_c is a constant, then the slope of $AB = -(1 + r)/1 = -1$. Given that the household's resources are equal in the two years, $Y_1 = Y_2 = Y$ and $A_1 = 0$, the point at which the household neither borrows nor saves is $(Y/p_c, Y/p_c)$; that is, point N. Budget line AB, then, sets up the conditions under which the motives other than time preference are set aside.

Three households, each with different time preferences and represented by U_f, U_n, and U_p, are shown. Each maximizes satisfaction at a different point when faced with the same circumstances, AB. Household N, possessing indifference curve U_n, maximizes satisfaction at point N, where it consumes its income in each year and neither borrows or saves. It has *neutral time preference*. Household P, with indifference curve U_p, maximizes satisfaction between N and B at P. It borrows, $C_1^p - (Y/p_c)$, and so consumes more than its income in the present. It is *present oriented*. Household F, represented by indifference curve, U_f, maximizes its satisfaction at point F between A and N. At point F its consumption in year one is C_1^f, less than its income. Consequently, it saves, $(Y/p_c) - C_1^f$, so that it can consume C_2^f in year two, an amount more than its income in year two. Household F, therefore, is *future oriented*.

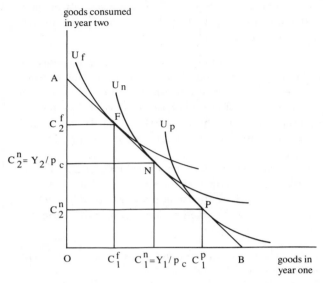

Figure 4.3 A present-oriented household, *P*, a future-oriented household, *F*, and a household with neutral time preference, *N*

If, therefore, the $MRS_{1,2}$ of a family at point N is -1, the family has neutral time preference. If the $MRS_{1,2}$ of a family at N is less than -1 (i.e., the indifference curve through point N has less slope than AB), the family is future oriented. If the family's $MRS_{1,2}$ at N is greater than -1 (i.e., the indifference curve through point N is steeper than AB), the family is present oriented.

Intertemporal satisfaction maximization

When faced with its current and expected future resources, the prices of consumption goods, and interest rates, the household will choose that combination of current consumption and net saving (positive, if saving exceeds borrowing; negative, if borrowing exceeds saving) that will maximize satisfaction (see mathematical note 2). This is illustrated in Figure 4.4.

The household represented by Figure 4.4 maximizes satisfaction at point E, where the budget line is tangent to the highest attainable indifference curve. At point E the family's marginal rate of time preference, as represented by the slope of the indifference curve, equals the rate at which goods in year one can be exchanged for goods in year two in the marketplace, as represented by the slope of the budget line. This family consumes C_1^e in year one saves $Y_1 - p_c C_1^e = S_1^e$. In year two it consumes C_2^e, spending an amount in excess of its income in year two

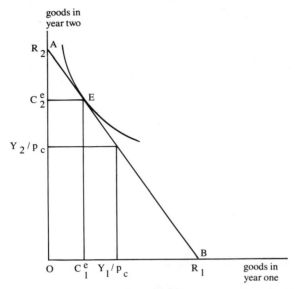

Figure 4.4 Maximization of intertemporal household satisfaction subject to the household's resource constraint

by the amount saved in year one, S^e_1, plus the interest on that saved, rS^e_1.

Figure 4.4 makes clear that the household's current consumption and saving depend on the household's present and future expected resources, R_1, the price of consumption goods, p_c, and the interest rate, r, in addition to its time preference; that is, whether it prefers current consumption to future consumption, or the reverse. We now turn to a discussion of the role played by the household's resources in determining its consumption and saving.

The resource–consumption–saving relation

Households with different total resources will devote different amounts to current consumption and to saving. A household's total resources, R_1, are composed of current income, Y_1, future expected income, Y_2, and net assets, A_1. If current consumption is a normal good, an increase in Y_1, Y_2, or A_1, holding interest rates and prices constant, will increase current consumption. This means that a household's current consumption can be expected to increase if its future expected income rises even though the family experiences no increase in its current income. Likewise, two families, each with the same current and future expected incomes, will have different current consumptions and savings if one has borrowed more in the past and enters the current period with smaller

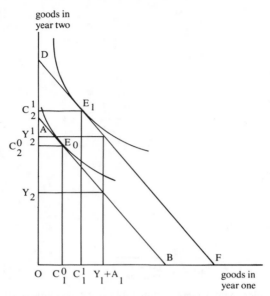

Figure 4.5 The effect of an increase in expected future income on current consumption and saving

net assets. The fewer total resources depresses the family's current consumption.

The effect of one such change in resources, an increase in future expected income, on current consumption and saving is illustrated in Figure 4.5. Initially the household faces budget line AB given its resources of A_1, Y_1, and Y_2, the interest rate, r, and the price level, p_c. Given these conditions, the family maximizes satisfaction at point E_0, involving current consumption of C_1^0 and saving of $S_1^0 = (Y_1 + A_1) - p_c C_1^0$.

Now suppose that the family gains information on the basis of which it can now expect Y_2^1 income in the future rather than Y_2. The increase in future expected income increases the household's total resources and, thus, expands its opportunities, shifting the budget line from AB to DF. Given that present and future consumption are both normal goods (which is, in fact, the case empirically), the family's current consumption and future consumption will both increase. The increase in current consumption to C_1^1 brought about by an increase in future expected income leads to a decline in current saving to $S_1^1 = (Y_1 + A_1) - p_c C_1^1$.

The logic of this decline in current saving is that the increase in current consumption necessarily results in a decline in current saving because the in-

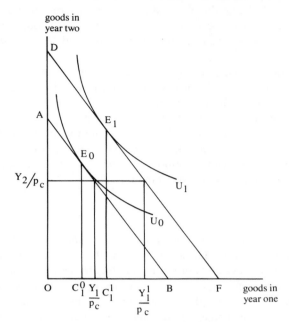

Figure 4.6 The income effect on current consumption and saving

crease in income will not actually occur until year two. Moreover, with the increase in future expected income the family need save less currently in order to provide for desired future consumption. This is exactly the behavior of a household that learns of a previously unexpected increase in future income via, for instance, a previously unforeseen future promotion or a previously unforeseen future inheritance. Current consumption rises and current saving falls.

A more likely change in a household's resources is a change in its current income. As a result of a rise in current income, its total resources increase, expanding consumption opportunities in both the present and the future periods. Current consumption and current saving will both rise. If the household was a net borrower prior to the increase in current income, the increase in saving will take the form of a decline in net borrowing. Figure 4.6 illustrates such a situation. When current income, Y_1, rises to Y_1^1, current consumption increases from C_1^0 to C_1^1 and saving increases to $Y_1^1 - p_c C_1^1$.

Economists have long had an interest in the relation between income and consumption because the relation has been the basis of policies combating depressions and unemployment. Some governmental policies seek to stimulate consumption by increasing peoples' income in the expectation that the increased consumption will stimulate an increase in employment. Such policies and the relationships underlying them are discussed in macroeconomics courses. Suffice it to say here that crucial to the effectiveness of such policies is the relationship between income and consumption, or the so-called *consumption function*.

The simple framework that has just been introduced is well suited for a discussion of the several conceptions of the consumption function that economists have developed. The relation between income and consumption is the familiar Engel curve that was introduced and discussed in Chapter 3. There, the Engel curve was used to examine the relation between income and the demand for particular goods like food, toys, or electricity. Here in Chapter 4, we use it to examine the relationship between consumption and income, where consumption is expenditures on all the goods the household buys.

The absolute income hypothesis

The first conception of the consumption function was the *absolute income consumption function* introduced by John Maynard Keynes in 1936. Keynes did not begin with the framework we have laid out in this chapter. Instead, he postulated that the "fundamental psychological law . . . is that men are disposed as a rule and on the average to increase their consumption as their income increases but not by as much as the increase in their income" (1936, p. 96). This hypothesis implies that there is a positive relationship between current income and current consumption and that the change in current consumption due to a change in current income, $\Delta C_1/\Delta Y_1$ in terms of the notation introduced in Chapter 3, is between 0 and 1; that is,

$$0 < \Delta C_1/\Delta Y_1 < 1.$$

Keynes called $\Delta C_1/\Delta Y_1$ the *marginal propensity to consume* (MPC), and subsequent authors have followed him.

Keynes's hypothesis, that the MPC is between 0 and 1, has been borne out by all subsequent empirical studies: the MPC has been found to be between .7 and .8 in most cross-section empirical studies. That is, if the current consumption expenditures of two groups of otherwise similar families are compared, one with current income $1,000 higher than the other, the higher income families will have current consumption expenditures about $700–$800 higher than the lower income families.

Keynes also hypothesized that high-income people save a higher fraction of their current income than low-income people. Again, this hypothesis is borne out by studies comparing the saving/income ratios of otherwise-similar rich and poor families.

The absolute income consumption function is illustrated by the Engel curve drawn in Figure 4.7. Current consumption, C_1, and current income, Y_1, are

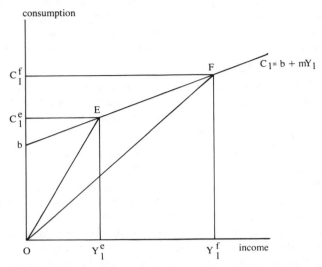

Figure 4.7 An example of a consumption function based on the absolute income hypothesis

plotted on the vertical and horizontal axes, respectively. The consumption function,

$$C_1 = b + mY_1,$$

is a positively sloped, straight line. The MPC is equal to m, the slope; that is, given an added dollar of current income, the household will increase its current consumption by m dollars, the increase being less than 1.

The second hypothesis, that the rich save a higher fraction of current income than the poor, is also illustrated by the consumption function in Figure 4.7. Take two points on the consumption function, one representing a low-income consumer, E, and the other representing a high-income consumer, F. Draw straight lines from E and F to the origin. The slopes of OE and OF, C_1^e/Y_1^e and C_1^f/Y_1^f, respectively, represent the consumption/income ratios at these points.[4] Note that OF has less slope than OE, indicating that the high-income family has a lower consumption/income ratio than the poor family. Since $S_1 = Y_1 - C_1$, the saving/income ratio must be higher for the rich family at F than for the poor family at E.

The consumption function in Figure 4.7, then, captures the two features of the absolute income hypothesis:

(1) $0 < \text{MPC} < 1$, and
(2) S_1/Y_1 rises as current income rises.

Any straight-line consumption function with $0 < m < 1$ and a positive intercept, b, is consistent with the absolute income hypothesis. Finally, recall from Chapter 3 that linear Engel curves with positive intercepts on the quantity axis exhibit income elasticities of demand that are less than 1. Thus, the absolute income hypothesis also implies that

> (3) the current income elasticity of current consumption, N_c, is less than 1: $N_c < 1$, where $N_c = (\Delta C_1/\Delta Y_1)(Y_1/C_1)$. Thus, Keynes expected that a 1 percent increase in current income would result in a less than 1 percent increase in current consumption.

Although consumption functions estimated on the basis of Keynes's absolute income hypothesis contribute importantly to the explanation of differences between families' consumption patterns at any point in time, they predict badly what happens to aggregate consumption when aggregate income changes through time. Studies of the saving/income ratio for the nation as a whole over a long stretch of time (from the 1870s to the 1940s), ignoring depressions and inflations, showed that saving as a fraction of income remained *constant* at about .1 (Goldsmith 1955; Kuznets 1942). Real family income, however, quadrupled over this period. Keynes's absolute income consumption function, in which people save a higher fraction of income as their income rises, would predict that the saving/income ratio for the nation would have risen in the face of this massive increase in income. Yet, it did not. Something is wrong with the hypothesis.

The permanent and life-cycle income hypotheses

Several alternative hypotheses have been put forward as replacements for the Keynesian absolute income consumption function. Two have become quite important: the *permanent income* and the *life-cycle income* consumption functions.[5] Both are special cases of the model of intertemporal satisfaction maximization already presented. We will treat them as if they are the same hypothesis but we will use the permanent income hypothesis terminology. Both differ from the Keynesian consumption function in that they measure income by total resources, R_1, rather than by current income, Y_1. Also, both take note of the long-run constancy of the saving/income ratio.

Implicit in the absolute income hypothesis is the view that the family bases its consumption and saving decisions solely on the size of its current income. However, the household as well as lending institutions expects a stream of earnings and other income to accrue to the household in future periods. Current consumption can be financed out of net assets and out of loans against future expected income as well as out of current income. Consequently, the relevant relationship is between total resources and consumption, not current income and consumption.

That people base their consumption and saving decisions on their views of their total resources and not just on their current income also accords well with one of the major motives for saving. Not only do people realistically expect a stream of income in future periods, they also realistically expect that stream to vary over their expected life. Young people expect low incomes because they have yet to complete their education or are just beginning their careers. They also expect their incomes to rise as they gain experience and responsibility. Too, they expect their incomes to level off and to fall upon retirement. Furthermore, people in occupations with unstable employment patterns also expect some unemployment and, consequently, some variability in their earnings over their work life. In contrast, employees in secure occupations expect little unemployment-related income variation.

Although people expect their incomes to vary over their lifetimes, they expect less variation in their consumption patterns over time: they must continue to be fed, clothed, and housed. Consequently, there is a need to shift resources from periods of high income to periods of low income in order to provide for consumption. The way this is done is by borrowing from the future in times of low income to provide for current consumption and by saving in times of high income to pay back past debts and to provide for future consumption. Not only are total resources important to the saving–consumption decision, therefore, but the expected pattern of income over time is also important.

Both the permanent income and the life-cycle income hypotheses emphasize this reason for saving and borrowing: to even out the variations in one's income stream over time so as to make it match a relatively constant demand for goods and services through time. Indeed, both hypothesize that in the absence of changes in prices, if interest rates are zero and family size is constant, households with the same total resources will demand the same quantities of goods and services each year and so demand a constant consumption stream through time. Households with different total resources will demand different consumption streams: those with few total resources will consume less and those with more total resources will consume more. But, regardless of the quantity of resources households posses, each will try to have a constant consumption stream over their life cycle.[6]

The total resources of the family can be measured in two ways: as a stock of wealth or as a flow of income. We are already familiar with measuring the household's total resources as a stock of wealth, for that is what R_1 is: the present value of the family's net assets, current income, and future expected income. In the context of our two-period model

$$R_1 = A_1 + Y_1 + [Y_2/(1 + r)]. \tag{4.9}$$

The permanent income consumption function, however, has been phrased in terms of a flow of income, called permanent income and denoted as Y_p, rather than as a stock of wealth.

Definition: Permanent income is defined as the constant (i.e., equal in each time period) annual income the present value of which equals the family's net wealth, R_1.

That is,

$$R_1 = Y_p + [Y_p/(1 + r)]. \tag{4.10}$$

Solving for Y_p yields

$$Y_p = R_1(1 + r)/(2 + r). \tag{4.11}$$

This definition of Y_p is more in the spirit of Modigliani's life-cycle income hypothesis than of Friedman's permanent income hypothesis. Friedman defined permanent income as $Y_p = rR_1$, that is, the constant annual income that the family's net worth would yield if invested at the market rate of interest in perpetuity. Such a definition implies a bequest by the family to its heirs (valued in the current period) of R_1. Our diagrams of intertemporal resource allocation are based on a zero bequest. The first definition of Y_p is consistent with a zero bequest and, thus, with Modigliani's hypothesis that consumers act so as to leave no bequest to their heirs.

Having defined permanent income, what is its relationship with current income, Y_1? The relationship is depicted in Figure 4.8, where both permanent and current income are plotted. In both panels net assets, A_1, are assumed to be 0 and $p_c = \$1.00$/unit for simplicity. Current income in year one, Y_1, is higher than permanent income in year one, Y_p, in panel A. Consequently, $Y_p < Y_1$. The reverse is the case in panel B.[7]

The difference between current income and permanent income is defined as *transitory income, Y_t:*

$$Y_t = Y_1 - Y_p. \tag{4.12}$$

Transitory income, then, is simply the excess or the deficiency of current income over permanent income. Transitory income is positive if current income is greater than permanent income (i.e., panel A). Transitory income is negative if current income falls below permanent income (i.e., panel B).

Having defined permanent and transitory income, of what use are they in explaining consumption and saving patterns? Consider a consumer faced with the budget lines in Figure 4.8. In Figure 4.9 we have added an indifference curve to each budget line. It is the same consumer in each panel and, thence, the same indifference curve. The only thing that differs between the two panels is the time pattern of income. Total resources, prices, and interest rates are the same in the two panels. Because total resources are the same, permanent income, Y_p, remains the same. The time pattern of income differs from panel A to

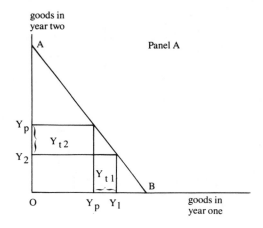

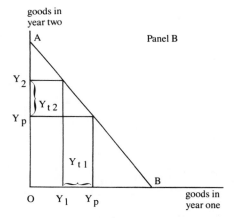

Figure 4.8 The relationship among current income, Y_1, permanent income, Y_p, and transitory income, Y_t

panel B: current income, Y_1, is higher in panel A than future income, and future income, Y_2, is higher than current income in panel B.

Now consider the consumer's consumption and saving behavior in the two circumstances. Despite the difference in the time pattern of income in the two panels, the consumer maximizes satisfaction at the same point on the budget line in each panel (at point E in panel A and E' in panel B) and, in consequence, has the same consumption, C_1. Why not? In each case he or she has the same total resources (i.e., the same permanent income) and faces the same prices and interest rate.

Although consumption is the same, saving is markedly different in the two

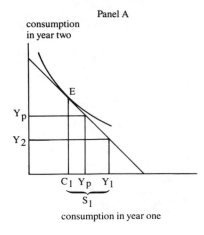

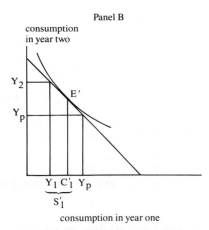

Figure 4.9 Permanent and transitory saving

panels. Faced with high current and low future income in panel A, the consumer saves $Y_1 - C_1 = S_1$. In contrast, when confronted with low current and high future income as in panel B, the consumer borrows $Y_1 - C'_1 = S'_1$. The consumer has positive saving in panel A but negative saving (i.e., he or she borrows) in panel B.

Now look more deeply into this behavior. In each case the consumer saves the same fraction of permanent income and in each case he or she saves all of transitory income! In panel A total saving amounts to $S_1 = (Y_1 - Y_p) + (Y_p - C_1) = Y_1 - C_1$. Note that all of transitory income, $Y_t = Y_1 - Y_p$, and some of permanent income, $Y_p - C_1$, is saved. In panel B, total saving amounts to $S'_1 = (Y_1 - Y_p) + (Y_p - C'_1) = Y_1 - C'_1$. Again, the same amount is saved from permanent income, $Y_p - C'_1$, and again, *all* of transitory income, $Y_t = Y_1 - Y_p$ is saved (i.e., borrowed in this case).

We can draw the following conclusions from this example. Regardless of the time pattern of income, when faced with the same total resources, prices, and interest rate, the consumer (1) consumes the same fraction of permanent income, (2) saves the same fraction of permanent income, and (3) saves all of transitory income: if transitory income is positive, the saving is positive; if transitory income is negative, the saving is negative (i.e., borrowed). (4) There are two components of saving: saving out of permanent income, which we can call permanent saving, and saving out of transitory income, which we can call transitory saving. Together, they equal current saving. Thus,

$$S_1 = S_p + S_t \qquad (4.13)$$

where S_1 = current saving, S_p = permanent saving, and S_t = transitory saving. In Figure 4.9, $S_p = Y_p - C_1$ and $S_t = Y_1 - Y_p = Y_t$.

Conclusions 1 through 4 constitute the permanent or life-cycle income hypothesis of consumption. Friedman's postulates are as follows.

1. In the absence of changes in prices and interest rates, consumers consume a constant fraction of their permanent income. If the constant fraction is k_p, then the permanent consumption[8] function is

$$C_1 = k_p Y_p. \qquad (4.14)$$

The fraction k_p is termed the *marginal propensity to consume out of permanent income*. It is the added consumption resulting from an added dollar of permanent income.

2. Given that consumption is a constant fraction of permanent income, permanent saving is also a constant fraction of permanent income; the permanent saving function is

$$S_p = Y_p - C_1 = Y_p - k_p Y_p = (1 - k_p) Y_p. \qquad (4.15)$$

The fraction $1 - k_p$ is termed the *marginal propensity to save out of permanent income;* that is, the added saving resulting from an added dollar of permanent income.

3. All transitory income is saved:

$$S_t = Y_t. \qquad (4.16)$$

Thus, the *marginal propensity to save out of transitory income* is hypothesized to be equal to 1.

Now return to the evidence that led economists to doubt the veracity of Keynes's absolute income hypothesis and to consider it in the light of Friedman's permanent income hypothesis. Recall that Kuznets (1942) found that the aggregate saving/income ratio, adjusted for the business cycle, remained constant from the 1870s to the 1940s. The depressions and expansions implicit in the business cycle, however, can be viewed as "transitory" phenomena when viewed in the long run. When the saving/income ratio was adjusted for the business cycle, the adjustments served to exclude transitory saving from the numerator of the ratio and transitory income from the denominator, leaving only the ratio of permanent saving to permanent income. This ratio measures the fraction $1 - k_p$. If, as the theory suggests, households really do base their consumption and saving decisions on their total resources (i.e., their permanent income) and not just on current income and if the fraction they save of permanent income is constant, then the saving/income ratio Kuznets constructed would be constant from the 1870s to the 1940s despite the fact that real income quadrupled. Kuznets' findings, therefore, are more consistent with the permanent than with the absolute income hypothesis.

We can follow the implications of the permanent income hypothesis farther. If the permanent saving/permanent income ratio remains constant as permanent income changes, then the permanent consumption/permanent income ratio must also be constant since $S_p = Y_p - C_p$. Furthermore, if the permanent consumption/permanent income ratio remains constant as permanent income increases, then the *permanent income elasticity of demand for consumption must be unitary:*

$$N_p = (\Delta C_p / \Delta Y_p)(Y_p / C_p) = 1; \tag{4.17}$$

that is, the demand for consumption must be unitary elastic with respect to permanent income (see mathematical note 3). But, since Y_p is simply a measure of total resources, the intertemporal income–consumption line must be a straight line emanating from the origin.

These relationships are pictured in Figure 4.10. Given market interest rates and the price level, the family's initial resources imply budget line AB. Here $p_c = 1$ and $A_1 = 0$ for simplicity. The family maximizes satisfaction at E_0 consuming C_1^0 and saving $S_1^0 = Y_1^0 - C_1^0$.

In the context of the permanent income hypothesis,

$$C_1^0 = C_p^0$$

because C_1^0 is the consumption planned in year one on the basis of the family's total resources as reflected by its permanent income in year one, Y_p^0. The

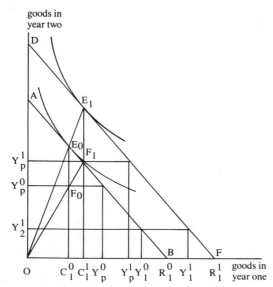

Figure 4.10 The permanent income hypothesis

difference between Y_1^0 and Y_p^0 is the difference between current and permanent income and is, therefore, transitory income in year one, Y_t^0; that is,

$$Y_t^0 = Y_1^0 - Y_p^0.$$

Because all transitory income is saved to even out consumption,

$$S_t^0 = Y_t^0.$$

The difference between Y_p^0 and C_1^0 is permanent saving, S_p^0, that is,

$$S_p^0 = Y_p^0 - C_1^0.$$

Total saving,

$$S_1^0 = Y_1^0 - C_1^0,$$

then, is the sum of permanent saving and transitory saving.

Following an increase in resources, say by an increase in Y_1^0 to Y_1^1, the family's budget line shifts to DF, leading to a new equilibrium at E_1. Permanent consumption increases to C_1^1 and current saving to

$$S_1^1 = Y_1^1 - C_1^1.$$

The increase in current income increases permanent income to Y_p^1. At the new equilibrium, permanent saving increases to

$$Y_p^1 - C_1^1 = S_p^1;$$

transitory income increases to

$$Y_1^1 - Y_p^1 = Y_t^1;$$

transitory saving increases to

$$S_t^1 = Y_t^1;$$

and current saving at the new equilibrium equals

$$S_1^1 = S_p^1 + S_t^1.$$

The income–consumption line through E_0 and E_1 is a straight line through the origin, as hypothesized by the theory. Points F_0 and F_1 are the points (C_1^0, Y_p^0) and (C_1^1, Y_p^1), respectively. Thus, the line joining them and extended to the axes is the permanent income Engel curve and is termed the *permanent consumption function*. It, too, is a straight line through the origin, showing that permanent consumption is unitary elastic with respect to permanent income as well as with respect to total resources, R_1. Given that it is unitary elastic with respect to Y_p, then the permanent consumption/permanent income ratio is constant, a fact consistent with the hypothesis. This, then, is the permanent income hypothesis.

Once the distinction between total resources (whether measured as total resources, R_1, or as permanent income, Y_p) and current income, Y_1, is made clear, the difference between the Keynesian absolute income and the permanent income hypotheses becomes clear. The absolute income hypothesis is phrased in terms of current income, whereas the permanent income, or life-cycle income, hypothesis is phrased in terms of total resources. The "income" to which each hypothesis refers is different. Also, the permanent income hypothesis argues that $C_p/Y_p = \Delta C_p/\Delta Y_p$.

The difference the different income concept makes in the income elasticity of consumption can be made clear. Denote the permanent income elasticity of consumption as N_p and define it (see Figure 4.10) as

$$N_p = [(C_1^1 - C_1^0)/C_1^0]/[(Y_p^1 - Y_p^0)/Y_p^0] = 1. \tag{4.18}$$

It is set equal to 1 according to the permanent income hypothesis. Since

$$Y_p = R_1(1 + r)/(2 + r)$$

and

$$R_1 = Y_1 + [Y_2/(1 + r)].$$

then, given an increase in Y_1 from Y_1^0 to Y_1^1, it is the case that

$$N_p = \frac{C_1^1 - C_1^0}{C_1^0} \bigg/ \frac{Y_1^1 - Y_1^0}{Y_1^0 + [Y_2^0/(1+r)]} = 1. \tag{4.19}$$

(see mathematical note 4). Likewise, denote the current income elasticity of consumption as N_c and define it as

$$N_c = \frac{C_1^1 - C_1^0}{C_1^0} \bigg/ \frac{Y_1^1 - Y_1^0}{Y_1^0}. \tag{4.20}$$

The difference between N_p and N_c is just their denominators. In the former case the denominator is

$$\frac{Y_1^1 - Y_1^0}{Y_1^0 + [Y_2^0/(1+r)]},$$

and in the latter the denominator is

$$\frac{Y_1^1 - Y_1^0}{Y_1^0}.$$

Because the latter excludes $Y_2^0/(1+r)$, it must be the larger. Consequently, if $N_p = 1$, then $N_c < 1$ and $\Delta C_1/\Delta Y_1 < C_1/Y_1$, which is in accordance with Keynes's hypothesis that the currently rich save a higher proportion of current income than the currently poor.

The economic (as opposed to the mathematical) reason why the currently rich save a higher fraction of their current income than the currently poor is, according to the permanent income hypothesis, as follows. On average the currently rich are made up of the temporarily rich and the permanently rich. The temporarily rich will tend to save the excess of their current income over their "usual," or permanent, income, increasing the fraction of current income saved above the S_p/Y_p ratio. Likewise, the currently poor are made up of the temporarily poor and the permanently poor. The temporarily poor will tend to save the difference between current and permanent income. However, because Y_t is negative, S_t will also be negative, pushing the current saving/current income ratio below S_p/Y_p.[9]

Friedman hypothesized that families consume a constant proportion of their permanent incomes (i.e., their total resources) and none of their transitory income. They save *all* of their transitory income, according to Friedman, in order to even out their consumption path through time. Subsequent empirical work has shown that families do tend to save a constant proportion of their permanent incomes. But Friedman was wrong about families' behavior with respect to transitory income. Although the marginal propensity to consume out of transitory income (MPC$_t = \Delta C/\Delta Y_t$) is less than the marginal propensity to consume out of permanent income (MPC$_p = \Delta C/\Delta Y_p$), it is not 0 (Mayer 1972).

The permanent and life-cycle income hypotheses, thus, postulate that families look *within* themselves to their own resources, both current and those they expect to have in the future. Then, they base their consumption and saving decisions on these resources along with market prices and market rates of interest. The basic difference between the two has to do with the pattern of households' net wealth through time. Friedman's permanent income hypothesis predicts that people will consume the annual return to their net wealth and leave their total resources to their heirs. Modigliani's life-cycle income hypothesis argues that people will attempt not to leave anything to their heirs and so they will consume their net wealth before dying. Reality lies somewhere between these two hypotheses. Both are very "economic" hypotheses in that they argue that people pay no attention to the consumption behavior of other people.

The relative income hypothesis

In contrast, the relative income hypothesis is quite "sociological." Duesenberry, the creator of the hypothesis, posited that people base their consumption and saving decisions not only on their resources (present and expected in the future) but also on the consumption behavior of their peers; that is, of the social class to which they belong.[10]

Specifically, a family gains great satisfaction from being able to consume more than other families it considers its peers, and it loses satisfaction if it is unable to consume as much as its peers. The issue is not how many resources the family possesses and what fraction of the resources will be consumed in the current period. Instead, the issue is how the family's total resources stand *relative to others* in its social class and whether the family consumes in accordance with the canons and standards of its social class. Hence, the name of the hypothesis.

According to this hypothesis families will resist changes in their consumption levels even in the face of changes in their income levels. Given a decline in income, a family will attempt to maintain its consumption at its previous level, equal to or greater than the consumption level of its peers. In order to maintain its consumption level in the face of a decline in income, the family must save a lower fraction of its current income. If the decline in income is large or of long duration, maintaining its previous consumption level may involve going deeply into debt. Only if the income decline is of very long duration will the family readjust its consumption standard downward to a level more in line with other families with similar incomes; that is, with families in the next lower social class.

According to the relative income hypothesis the reverse also occurs. If a family's income rises, it will continue to maintain its previous level of consumption, imitating the consumption standards of those it considers its peers. Conse-

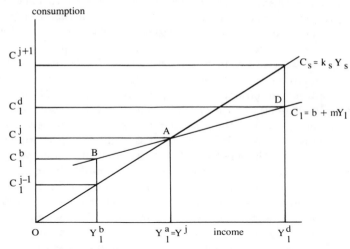

Figure 4.11 The relative income hypothesis

quently, it will save a higher fraction of its income. Only if the increase in income is of long duration will the family adjust its consumption upward to a level more in line with other families who have similar incomes; that is, who are in the next higher social class.

Families consume in accordance with the canons and standards of the social class to which they belong. Changes in income in either direction will not change their consumption behavior much so long as the changes are small, of short duration, and do not move them into another social class. Saving – positive or negative – takes up the slack caused in the short run by variations in family income. Once income changes are long term and sufficiently large to move the family into another social class, the family will adjust its consumption behavior and so adjust its saving behavior, too.

The relative income hypothesis is illustrated in Figure 4.11. Figure 4.11 contains two consumption functions, $C_s = k_s Y_s$ and $C_1 = b + m Y_1$, the latter being the Keynesian absolute income consumption function arrived at by plotting the current consumption–current income points of families.

The $C_s = k_s Y_s$ function arises in the following way. Divide families into social classes from the lowest to the highest. Compute the average income of each social class, Y_s. Likewise, compute the average consumption for each social class, C_s. The consumption function drawn from plotting the average consumption–average income points for each social class is $C_s = k_s Y_s$, where k_s is the MPC as one goes from one social class to the next higher class.

Now take three families, A, B, and D, who all consider themselves to be in the jth social class. Family A's current income, Y_1^a, is equal to the class average, Y^j. Family B's current income, Y_1^b, is currently somewhat below the class average, and family D's current income, Y_1^d, is somewhat above. Family A's income is sufficient to consume according to the standards of class j, and consequently, its consumption equals the class average, C_1^j. Family B currently has an income somewhat insufficient to consume according to class j's standards. However, so long as family B identifies with class j, it will attempt to equal those standards, falling a trifle short, however. If its income remains at Y_1^b, it will reevaluate its situation, begin to identify with the $j-1^{th}$ class, and lower its consumption from C_1^b to the $j-1^{th}$ class's standard, C_1^{j-1}. As it does so, its consumption/income ratio will fall to $C_s/Y_s = k_s$, and its saving/income ratio will rise to $1 - k_s$.

In contrast, family D has an income somewhat higher than the class average. Because it identifies with class j, it will maintain its consumption close to C_1^j at C_1^d. If its income remains at Y_1^d, however, D will begin to identify with the next higher social class, $j+1$, and adjust its consumption upward to the new standard, C_1^{j+1}. As it does so, its consumption/income ratio will rise to k_s, and its saving/income ratio will fall to $1 - k_s$.

Compared with the permanent and life-cycle income hypotheses, the relative income hypothesis is quite sociological in that people look *beyond* their own resources to the social classes to which they belong for directions as to their consumption and saving behavior. In David Reisman's (1950) terminology, the permanent income hypothesis postulates *inner-directed* behavior whereas the relative income hypothesis postulates *other-directed* behavior. Which of these two hypotheses – the permanent or the relative income hypothesis – is correct? Both have elements of truth. A study of the consumption behavior of Israeli kibbutzim showed that both permanent and relative income explained a part of their consumption behavior.[11]

From a different perspective, however, the relative income hypothesis may be interpreted as part and parcel of the permanent and life-cycle income hypotheses. How so? Despite the fact that the permanent and life-cycle income hypotheses postulate that families know their future expected incomes, in reality they do not, at least not with any accuracy or precision. How, then, is a family or an individual to estimate what resources will be available in the future? One way is to observe otherwise-similar families who are somewhat farther along in the life cycle and to base expectations for the future on these observations. Observing one's peers for guidance is the same as observing members of one's own social class for guidance. Therefore, patterning one's behavior after others in the same social class may simply be an efficient way to gather and act upon information about the future, and thus such behavior may be included in the permanent and life-cycle income hypotheses.

The interest rate–consumption–saving relation

To this point in the chapter we have held interest rates and prices constant while we have discussed how the household adjusts its consumption and saving behavior in the face of changes in income. It is now time to discuss how household consumption and saving change as interest rates change, holding resources and prices constant. Out of this discussion will come a better understanding of how changes in interest rates affect the borrowing and lending behavior of families.

Suppose that the market rate of interest rises from, say, r_0 to r_1. The increase in the interest rate has two effects that are like the effects of any price change: (1) future consumption becomes cheaper relative to present consumption (this is essentially a change in relative prices) and (2) the consumption alternatives open to the family are changed. As with price changes, the former is called a substitution effect and the latter is termed an income effect. We deal with the substitution effect first.

The substitution effect of the change in the interest rate

When the rate of interest rises (resources and market prices held constant), saving (i.e., future consumption) becomes cheaper relative to present consumption. Holding satisfaction constant, there is an incentive for the consumer to increase saving at the expense of current consumption; that is, to substitute future consumption for present consumption (hence, the term *substitution* effect). If the consumer was a net borrower prior to the rise in the interest rate, borrowing (i.e., using future income to pay for current consumption) becomes more expensive, and consequently, less is borrowed, holding satisfaction constant. The substitution effect of a rise in the interest rate, therefore, increases saving (or decreases borrowing) at the expense of current consumption.

The income effect of the change in the interest rate

When the interest rate rises, the consumer's real income is also altered. Whether real income rises or falls depends upon whether the consumer was a net borrower or a net saver prior to the rise in the interest rate. If the family was a net saver, then a rise in the interest rate means that the same dollars currently saved will yield more in the future. Thus, the family can consume more, both currently and in the future. The real income of net savers is increased by a rise in the rate of interest, therefore. The reverse is true for the net borrower. At a higher rate of interest current loans cost more than before. Consequently, the consumption options open to the net borrower decline with an increase in the interest rate. The real income of net borrowers, therefore, declines in the face

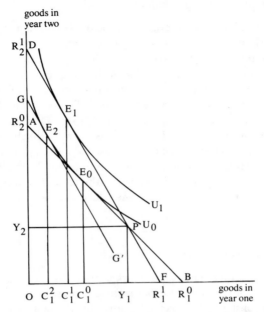

Figure 4.12 The effect of an increase in the interest rate on the consumption and saving behavior of a net saver

of a rise in the rate of interest.[12] Providing current consumption is a normal good (and we know it to be from the discussion in the preceding section), the real income effect of a rise in the interest rate will expand the current consumption of net savers and lower the current consumption of net borrowers (see mathematical note 5).

These effects are illustrated in Figure 4.12. Given resources Y_1 and Y_2, the market rate of interest at r_0, and the price level at p_c, the consumer faces budget line AB. Satisfaction is maximized at E_0, where the family purchases C_1^0 of current consumption and saves $Y_1 - C_1^0 = S_1^0$. The rise in the interest rate from r_0 to r_1 rotates the budget line around point P, the point at which the consumer neither borrows nor lends.[13] Since the slope of the budget line is $-(1 + r)$, the increase in r from r_0 to r_1 will increase the slope, rotating the budget line clockwise around P. The budget line when $r = r_1$ is DF. Given the new budget line, the consumer reestablishes equilibrium at E_1, where current consumption, C_1^1, is less than before and saving, $Y_1 - C_1^1 = S_1^1$, is more than before. The total interest rate effect on consumption is, therefore, $C_1^1 - C_1^0$.

The substitution and income effects of the interest rate rise are separated by drawing a straight line, GG', parallel to the new budget line, DF, and tangent to the old indifference curve, U_0, at E_2. The substitution effect of the interest rate rise is $C_1^0 - C_1^2$; that is, future consumption is substituted for current consumption by an increase in saving as future consumption becomes cheaper relative to current consumption.

The real income effect of the rise in the interest rate is $C_1^1 - C_1^2$. In response to the expansion of consumption alternatives (measured by distance GD) brought about by the rise in the interest rate, holding relative prices constant at the new level, $-(1 + r_1)p_c$ (as measured by the slopes of GG' and DF), the consumer increased current consumption and saving (i.e., future consumption) from C_1^2 to C_1^1.

Although not illustrated, the effect of a rise in the interest rate on a net borrower is also clear from Figure 4.12. The net borrower would have maximized satisfaction at a point between P and B on the original budget line AB. The rise in the interest rate would force such a family to the PF segment of the new budget line, DF, making that family less satisfied than before. While the substitution effect induces that family to decrease borrowing by decreasing current consumption, the decline in real income leads to a further decline in current consumption, provided current consumption is a normal good.

The empirical evidence on the interest rate effect on saving and consumption is restricted to evidence on the substitution effect. In a study of U.S. data from 1897 to 1949 and from 1929 to 1958 Wright (1969) found the compensated interest rate elasticity of saving to be very inelastic: 0.18 to 0.27. That is, consumers responded to a 10 percent increase in the interest rate by increasing their saving by 1.8 to 2.7 percent, holding satisfaction constant. More recently, Hall (1988) found the compensated interest rate elasticity of saving to be positive but close to 0. Both earlier and later data are consistent with the idea that the substitution effect of changes in interest rates, while consistent with economic theory, is quite small.

Changes in the prices of consumption goods through time

Prices have not entered the discussion up to this point because they were held constant through time; that is, it has been assumed that $p_{c1} = p_{c2} = p_c$. But what if inflation occurs? What are the effects of inflation on current consumption and saving likely to be? More correctly, what are the effects of *changes* in inflationary expectations; for instance, what if the family expects greater inflation than in the past?

Suppose initially the consumer expects prices to rise at a rate of $g_0 100$ percent per year, where $g_0 > 0$. Consequently, if the price level is currently p_c, then it will be $(1 + g_0)p_c$ next year. Then suppose that the consumer changes his or her price expectations so that next year prices are expected to be $(1 + g_1)p_c$ where $g_1 100$ percent is the new expected rate of inflation. What effect will this change in price expectations have on the family's consumption and saving behavior?

In the model presented thus far in this chapter prices of goods and services in the two periods have been assumed to be the same and equal to p_c. The slope of the household budget line was

$$-C_2^m/C_1^m = -(R_2/p_c)/(R_1/p_c) = -R_2/R_1 = -(1 + r)$$

where C_2^m = maximum consumption in year two if the household consumed nothing in year one, C_1^m = maximum consumption in year one if the household consumed nothing in year two, and R_2 and R_1 represent total resources evaluated in years two and one.

Now, suppose that the family expects prices in year two to be $p_{c2} = (1 + g)p_c$, where p_c is the price in year one and $g100$ percent is the inflation rate. As a result of this change in inflationary expectations, the slope of the budget line becomes

$$\text{slope} = -C_2^{m'}/C_1^m = -[R_2/(1 + g)p_c]/(R_1/p_c) = -(R_2/R_1)[1/(1 + g)]$$
$$= -(1 + r)/(1 + g)$$

where $C_2^{m'}$ = maximum consumption in year two given the new price expectations and zero consumption in year one.

So long as $g > 0$ (i.e., prices are expected to rise next year),

$$(1 + r)/(1 + g) < 1 + r,$$

and the larger the expected rate of inflation, g, the gentler the slope of the budget line; that is, the greater is g, the more expensive is future consumption relative to current consumption.

A change in consumer expectations about the rate of inflation therefore changes the intertemporal budget line facing the consumer. In consequence, not only are the consumption–saving options open to the consumer altered but the price of present consumption relative to the future is altered too. In short, changing expectations about inflation have both substitution and income effects.

As the expected inflation rate increases (the expected rate of inflation rises from 0 in our example to g, where $g > 0$), present consumption becomes cheaper than future consumption. The rise in the price of future consumption relative to present consumption creates an incentive for the consumer to substitute present consumption for future consumption by saving less, holding satisfaction constant. This is the substitution effect of expected increases in the inflation rate.

There is another, more common, way to formulate the argument underlying the substitution effect. When prices rise, loans become cheaper. They become cheaper because the loan is taken out today when "a dollar buys a lot" and paid off tomorrow when (given that prices are expected to rise) "a dollar will buy less." There is, in consequence, an incentive to borrow "dear" money today and pay the loan off with "cheap" money tomorrow. The loan increases consumption and reduces saving.

The income effect of increases in the expected rate of inflation concerns both the net saver and the net borrower alike. If future consumption is expected to become more expensive because of inflation, the net saver finds the real return on current savings smaller, reducing his real income. His savings will buy less in the future than they did before, and real income has declined. In consequence, his current consumption will fall so long as consumption is a normal good. For the net saver the income effect of rising inflationary expectations, therefore, tends to counteract the substitution effect.

The income effect on the net borrower is similar. Being a net borrower means that future consumption is reduced by the necessity of debt repayments. Rising prices mean that future consumption will be reduced even more because goods and services will be more expensive in the future than at present. Rising price expectations, therefore, reduce the net borrower's alternatives and, thus, real income in the same way they reduce those of the net saver and with the same results: a decline in current consumption so long as consumption is a normal good.

The net effect of rising inflationary expectations, then, depends on the relative sizes of the substitution effect and the income effect. If the substitution effect is the greater, saving falls and consumption increases. If the income effect is the larger of the two, rising price expectations will result in a decline in consumption and a rise in saving.

The effects of expecting price increases are illustrated in Figure 4.13. In Figure 4.13, AB is the initial household budget line prior to the increase in inflationary expectations, where point A represents $R_2/p_c = C_2^0$ and point B represents $R_1/p_c = C_1^0$. The consumer whose indifference curves are pictured maximizes satisfaction at E_0 consuming C_1^0 and saving $S_1^0 = Y_1 - p_c C_1^0$.

Expecting the rate of inflation to increase from 0 to g moves the budget line to $A'B$, where A' represents the new maximum possible consumption in year two, $R_2/(1 + g)p_c$. Maximum possible consumption in year two has fallen because the consumer expects prices to rise by $g100$ percent between years one and two. Maximum possible consumption in year one has not changed, because prices in year one have not changed. As a result of the expected increase in inflation, the pictured consumer reestablishes equilibrium at E_1, where he consumes C_1^1, more than before, and saves $S_1^1 = Y_1 - p_c C_1^1$, less than before. $C_1^1 - C_1^0$ is the total effect on consumption and $S_1^1 - S_1^0 = p_c C_1^0 - p_c C_1^1$ is the total effect on saving of the expected increase in inflation.

In order to reveal the income and substitution effects embedded in these total effects, draw line FF' parallel to the new budget line, $A'B$, and tangent to the old indifference curve, U_1. The point of tangency occurs at E_2. The substitution effect (that is, the effect of the expected increase in inflation on consumption,

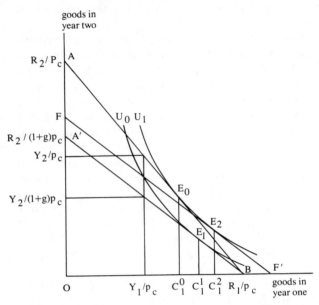

Figure 4.13 The effects of expectations of increasing inflation

holding satisfaction constant) is $C_1^2 - C_1^0$. This represents a substitution of current consumption for future consumption because future consumption is expected to become more expensive. Saving falls to $S_1^2 = Y_1 - p_c C_1^2$ as current consumption rises due to the substitution effect.

The reduction in real income resulting from the rise in inflationary expectations is represented by FA' on the vertical axis. As real income falls, the consumer reduces consumption from C_1^2 to C_1^1. In consequence, the consumer increases saving to $S_1^1 = Y_1 - p_c C_1^1$.

Given that current consumption is a normal good, the income effect of an expected rise in inflation tends to offset the substitution effect. For the consumer pictured in Figure 4.13 the offset is not complete and the total effect is to increase consumption somewhat. Clearly, the more income elastic is current consumption, the more likely the income effect will more than offset the substitution effect, leading to a reduction, rather than an increase, in current consumption.

Expectations about inflation are hard to measure, and therefore, empirical evidence is somewhat difficult to obtain. Nonetheless, a number of studies have measured the effects of changing rates of inflation on consumption and saving. The conclusions of Weber's study (1975) of consumption expenditures in the United States from 1930 through 1970 were that changes in the rate of inflation had no effect on personal consumption expenditures and, thus, none on saving. Over this long stretch of time, therefore, the income and substitution effects of changing rates of inflation about canceled each other out. However, studies focusing on the period between World War II and the early 1970s indicated that increases in the rate of inflation resulted in increasing rates of saving. During this period, then, the income effect more than offset the substitution effect of rising future prices, leading to a net decline in consumption and an increase in saving. A part of this increase in saving was found to be linked to the increased uncertainty that rising rates of inflation bring (Wachtel 1977).

In their study, which included data from the late 1970s, Campbell and Lovati (1979) point out that whereas purchases of consumer durables are largely acts of saving, they are not counted as saving in the National Income Accounts data, the data source commonly used in saving studies. Campbell and Lovati show that rising rates of inflation depressed purchases of consumer durables at the same time saving rates increased. In the 1970s, then, it appears that consumers reacted to rising rates of inflation by making their total saving more liquid by reducing their saving in the form of consumer durables and increasing their saving in the form of bank accounts, stocks, bonds, and the like. Thus, recent changes in the rate of inflation have had greater effects on the manner in which families have saved than on how much they have saved.

Summary

This chapter has made a beginning in explaining the consumption and saving behavior of the household. The household is pictured as allocating its present and future expected resources among time periods over its expected life so as to maximize its satisfaction. According to both the permanent and the life-cycle income hypotheses, the household engages in borrowing and lending activities to even out its income stream over its life cycle to better match its desired consumption plan over the life cycle. If the permanent income hypothesis were strictly correct, consumers could be expected to consume only the annual return on their resources, leaving their total resources to their heirs as bequests. If the life-cycle income hypothesis were strictly correct, consumers could be expected to live off their assets in their declining years and die leaving no bequests. As usual, reality is poised somewhere between these simple but extreme hypotheses. Nonetheless, these simple hypotheses capture much reality.

Besides income, both interest rates and price expectations are important determinants of household consumption and saving behavior. The former affect net savers and borrowers differently, whereas the latter affect the two in the same way. Much less is known empirically about interest rate and price expectation effects than about income effects.

This completes our introduction to the theory of the household as it relates to the demand and consumption activities of the household. Throughout Chapters 1 and 4 it has been presumed that the household has had no choice over the amount of income it receives, no choice over the number and spacing of children, and no choice over its form; that is, whether it is single, married, or divorced. And no recognition has been given to the household's role as a producer of goods and services. We will begin to rectify these deficiencies in the next chapter, which deals with the work activities of the household.

CHAPTER FIVE

Work and leisure: how the household spends its time

Introduction

During the twentieth century American males in nonagricultural employment have reduced the average annual weekly hours they work from 60 hr./wk. to about 40. This change took place by 1945 and took the form of a reduced workweek, longer annual vacations, and more holidays (Owen 1971). From the turn of the century these same Americans reduced the fraction of their lives they spent working in the labor market from 0.23 in 1900 to 0.15 in 1960 (Owen 1971). Although some of this is the result of lengthened life expectancy, also important is the increased amount of time spent in school and in retirement. The work patterns of American females have undergone similar revolutionary changes. The labor force participation rate of married females was approximately 4.5 percent in 1900 (Lebergott 1968). By 1985 it had risen to 48 percent for those with no children, 68 percent for those with children aged 6–17, and 54 percent for those with children under 6 yr. of age (Bloom 1986).

How Americans spend their nonmarket time has seen similar transformations in the twentieth century. This is much better documented for women than for men. The average married woman's workday in the home in 1900 has been reported to be about 12 hr./day, too high to be believed on a 7-day-per-week basis but nevertheless, indicating a very long workday. By 1929 it had been measured accurately at 7.6 hr. It had fallen to about 6 hr. by 1967 (Bryant 1986). By 1975 the average amount of time spent by married women in household work activities was, perhaps, 5.0 hr./day (Hill 1985, Table 7.3). This contrasts with the average of 2.0 hr. of household work married men performed per day in 1975 (Hill 1985, Table 7.3). Although the time spent in household tasks by married men has been much more constant over the century, the amount of time men spend in leisure activities has increased as their market work time has fallen.

The patterns of time use of single men and women are very different from those of married people. In 1975 single females spent about 3.4 hr./day in household work and 3.2 hr. in market work. Single males, however, spent 4.7 hr. in market work per day and 1.7 hr./day in household work (Hill 1985,

Table 7.3). We know very little about the time use patterns of unmarried people in the past.

These are just a few of the radical changes in the patterns of work and leisure that Americans have experienced in the eight decades of the twentieth century. What caused these changes? Did employers by themselves reduce the amount of work they have offered household members or have the households themselves exercised choice over how much they work, when, and where? This chapter argues that households do have considerable choice over the way time is spent, develops a small economic model by which the household's time use choices can be understood, and discusses the major economic determinants of households' time use choices.

In the preceding chapters we have analyzed the household's demand, consumption, and saving activities. The analysis in Chapter 3 began with whatever income the household possessed and then asked how it allocated that income across various expenditure categories given market prices. Chapter 4 was concerned with the pattern of consumption over the family's expected life. The analysis began with a particular pattern of income receipts across the household's expected life. Then it asked how the household would, so to speak, rearrange its resources, via borrowing and lending, to create the family's desired pattern of consumption through time.

To this point, therefore, it has been presumed that the household has no control over how much income it receives or over when it receives it. But we know that this is incorrect in major ways. People do choose whether to look for work and which job offer to accept. Since earnings from employment are the most important source of a household's income, the household does, therefore, exert control over how much income it has and the timing of its receipt over the life cycle.

The decisions by which the household orders the size and timing of its income turn out to be about how family members spend their time: how much time will be spent in income-earning activities, how much in household production activities, and how much in recreation, or "leisure," activities. As with the discussion on demand in Chapter 3, the discussion in this chapter will be restricted to one period. That is, the questions asked will be how the household allocates its time *within* any time period. The final section of the chapter, however, does consider the allocation of time over the life cycle.

Just as the household's work and leisure decisions were ignored in earlier chapters so we could focus on its demand, consumption, and saving decisions, we will deemphasize these decisions in this chapter so as to focus on the family's time use decisions. Doing this does not deny that the decisions as to the allocation of income and the allocation of time do not interact. It merely simplifies things in the hope of making the time allocation decision process clearer. As in earlier chapters we begin by building a small model of the household within which the discussion can be cast. Despite the gross simplifications that are made in the model, it contains major insights about how families actually do allocate their available time.

A work–leisure model of the household

We will begin the discussion by supposing that we are observing a single-person family over a period of time, say a week, a month, or a year. We could equally begin with a family in which only one family member has the opportunity of being employed in the labor market. The model will focus on the allocation decisions with respect to this person's time. As in earlier chapters our model of the household must have three components: a description of the family's preferences, a description of the household's resources and how they restrict the alternatives open to the family, and a behavioral relation describing the rule by which decisions are made. Let us describe the household's preferences first.

The utility function

Suppose that during any time period under analysis, say a week, the household derives satisfaction from three composite goods: goods and services purchased in the market, called "market goods" and denoted by C; goods and services produced and consumed by the household, called "home goods" and denoted by G; and the leisure time of the individual in the single-person family or the individual who has the opportunity of being employed in the multiperson family. The quantity of this person's leisure time will be denoted by L.

We can express the consumer's preferences with respect to these three goods algebraically with the following general utility function:

$$U = u(C, G, L). \tag{5.1}$$

These preferences could be represented geometrically on a three-dimensional graph with quantities of C, G, and L measured along the three axes. Thus, each point in the three-dimensional space would represent a particular combination of market goods, home goods, and leisure. Instead of using indifference curves to represent all the combinations of goods among which the consumer is indifferent, one would have to use *indifference dishes*. A good drafter could draw such diagrams, but they would be hard to understand. Because graphs are supposed to aid rather than hinder understanding, we must find some way to utilize two-dimensional graphs.

One useful simplification is to assume that the consumer regards market and home goods, C and G, as *perfect substitutes*. That is, the consumer derives as much satisfaction from a bakeshop cake as from a homemade cake, from a flute solo played by Jean-Pierre Rampal as played by himself or herself. Although this

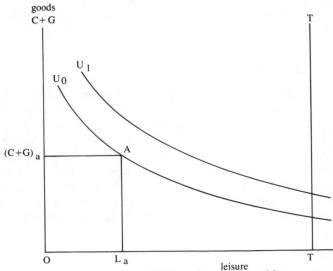

Figure 5.1 The household's preference map with respect to goods and time

assumption is patently false, it will be made anyway because its falsity has little effect on the conclusions that can be drawn from the model. So long as we keep the assumption firmly in mind, we can adjust our conclusions by relaxing the assumption that C and G are perfect substitutes and considering the changes in the conclusions that result.

Assuming that home and market goods are perfect substitutes allows us to write the consumer's utility function as

$$U = u(C + G, L). \tag{5.2}$$

Thus, the three-dimensional diagram of the household's preferences collapses back into two dimensions with this assumption: one dimension representing goods, $C + G$; and one representing leisure, L. And the indifference dishes collapse into the more familiar and understandable indifference curves.

Figure 5.1 is an illustration of the consumer's preference map with respect to goods, $C + G$, and leisure time, L. U_0 and U_1 are two of the many indifference curves in the map, each point in the map on an indifference curve. Point A, for instance, represents the combination of L_a hours per week of leisure and $(C + G)_a$ quantity of goods that yields the consumer U_0 amount of satisfaction, where

$$U_0 = u(C + G, L) \tag{5.3}$$

is the equation for the indifference curve U_0.

The time constraint

Figure 5.1 also contains a straight, vertical line, *TT*. Although the consumer may prefer to have more leisure per week than there are hours in the week, it is physically impossible. *TT*, therefore, is drawn at $7 \times 24 = 168$ hr. and represents one aspect of the time constraint. Any point on *TT* or to the left of it represents a physically possible combination of goods and leisure. Points to the right of *TT* represent physically impossible combinations simply because there cannot be more than 168 hr. in any week.

The other aspect of the time constraint requires further specification of the way households use time. Suppose the various uses to which the individual in the single-person family (or the individual in the multiperson family whose time is the focus of study) devotes her time are classified into three categories: market work, household work, and leisure. *Market work* includes all the time the individual spends per week working for pay. It is denoted by *M*. *Household work* includes all the time the individual spends per week in household production activities like cooking; laundry; house, car, lawn and garden maintenance; child care and the care of sick persons; and planning, shopping, and other family managerial activities. Household work time will be denoted by *H*. We have already introduced the concept of *leisure, L*. We define it formally as the time *not* spent in market work or household work. Finally, we can denote the total time available (168 hr. in the case of a week) as *T*.

The time constraint, then, simply makes the point that the sum of all the possible uses of time must equal the total time available:

$$T = M + H + L. \tag{5.4}$$

Note that the model of the household states that satisfaction is derived from the consumption of goods, $C + G$, and from leisure, *L*. No satisfaction arises directly from spending time either in market work or in household work. This, again, is a simplification of reality. Most employed people do get some satisfaction as well as income from their jobs. And most of us do get some satisfaction from some aspects of household work. We may hate to cook but like to garden, for instance.

Our simple model of the household neglects these sources of satisfaction for two reasons. First, job (whether market or household work) satisfaction appears to have more to do with the *type* of job we have than it does with the time we spend on the job. Since our model is being built expressly to lead to a greater understanding of how much time we spend in market work, in household work, and in leisure pursuits, we can safely neglect these sources of utility. Second, experience has proved that models that include job satisfaction do not explain much more about work and leisure behavior than those that exclude job satisfaction from consideration. Consequently, we ignore it for simplicity, knowing that our model will not be far wrong.[1]

The household production function

Not only is the household physically bound by the time constraint, it is bound by the technology of household production. Household goods and services are produced by combining household members' labor in specific ways with other inputs (i.e., purchased goods and services that are used, in turn, as inputs into household processes) to produce cooked and served meals; cleaned and pressed clothes; clean and maintained houses, gardens, lawns, cars and other durables, and furniture; and clean, fed, healthy, and developing children. The household production function specifies the technological constraints involved in these productive processes.

The household production function, as it appears in this simple model, emphasizes the relationship between the time spent by the individual in household work activities and the quantity of household goods produced. And it is conditioned by the quantity of goods and service inputs with which the individual's household work time is combined. Let the quantity of goods and service inputs that the family combines with the individual's labor to produce household goods be represented by X; then the household production function can be expressed algebraically as

$$G = g(H; X). \tag{5.5}$$

Equation (5.5) can be interpreted as follows: Given that the household has quantity of X of other inputs on hand, if H hours of household labor are used in household production per week, G quantity of household goods will be produced. The semicolon dividing H from X in the equation indicates that the household can alter the amount of time the individual spends in household work, H, but cannot alter the quantity of inputs with which the labor is combined. Thus, the focus is on the household's time use decision and not on its decisions about the quantity of inputs to demand.

The easiest way to think about the fixed quantity of X is to link it with the array of appliances, furniture, and housing characteristics that tend to be fixed for any household in the short run. This array of appliances and the like partially determine the technical relationship between the time spent in household work and the quantity of household goods and services that results. A much smaller quantity of clothes can be washed, dried, and pressed per hour, for instance, if the individual is working with a scrub board, a laundry tub, a bar of brown soap, a clothesline in the backyard, and sad irons[2] than if one performs the same functions with a modern complement of automatic clothes washer, detergents, dryer, and steam iron. Similarly, a microwave oven as opposed to a self-cleaning electric stove will alter household labor productivity.

A representative household production function is illustrated in Figure 5.2. The horizontal axis of Figure 5.2 represents hours per week. Measuring from

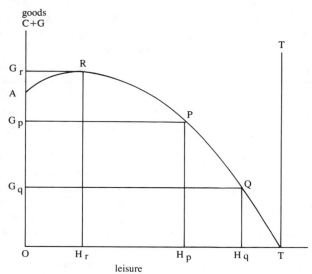

Figure 5.2 The household production function: $G = g(H; X)$

left to right along the horizontal axis beginning at 0 are measured hours per week of leisure, L. The vertical line TT again represents the idea that no more than 168 hours per week are available for any activity. Measuring from right to left along the horizontal axis beginning at T are hours per week spent in household work, H. The vertical axis represents increasing quantities of household goods produced by the household per week, G.

The line TA represents the household production function. Thus, if TH_q hours of the individual's time are devoted per week to household work, then G_q quantity of household goods and services is produced per week. If more time is spent, say TH_p hours per week, then more households goods and services, G_p, are produced.

Note that the slope of TA is positive (reading the graph from right to left), being quite steep for few hours spent and shallower as more time is spent in household production per week. Past point R, the household production function becomes negatively sloped. The slope of the household production function represents the marginal product of labor in household production, which we will denote by g_h (see mathematical note 1).

Definition: The marginal product of labor in household production is the change in the quantity of household output due to a small change in the quantity of labor used.

The fact that the household production function is drawn as a line concave to the hours axis represents the principle of *diminishing marginal productivity*. The principle says that when one input in a production process is increased, holding all other inputs constant, the marginal product of that input falls; that is, as more of the input is used, holding other input use constant, the input's productivity falls. The productivity of the input may even turn negative, as is pictured in Figure 5.2. In the region to the left of point R, output actually falls as more than TH_r hours per week of the individual's time are devoted to household production. Thus, the more time that is spent in household production, the less productive yet another hour will be: g_h, therefore, falls as H increases and beyond point R in Figure 5.2 becomes negative.

The principle of diminishing marginal productivity is based on two common phenomena: tiredness and congestion. An individual can work continuously for so many hours and, consequently, become so tired that further labor destroys more than is produced. Students who study all night prior to an examination frequently experience this. During the first hour or two of studying, the student learns much. But as each hour wears on without a break, less additional material is learned until, past some point, forgetting takes place.

The classic folk injunction that "too many cooks spoil the broth" conjures up a scene in which many cooks fight for space at the stove and in the process ruin or spill the soup. It exemplifies the problem of congestion. Increasing congestion also occurs when an individual spends more and more time with a given amount of other inputs. Added minutes spent ironing and folding clothes can increase quantity and quality of the ironing. Many more minutes spent ironing the same clothes, however, leads either to no more cleaned and pressed laundry or even to scorched and burned clothes. Too much time was spent with the same iron and the same clothes. Congestion reduces productivity and can even destroy output.

Equilibrium in a Robinson Crusoe household

For a Robinson Crusoe (i.e., an individual with absolutely no access to paid employment or other source of income and no access to consumer markets; thus, he or she is someone who must home-produce everything consumed), the line TA in Figure 5.2 represents the budget line. This is so because purchased goods, C, and market work, M, do not exist, and whatever time is spent in household production, say TH_q, leaves OH_q as leisure. Furthermore, the TH_q household work produces G_q quantity of household goods, which Crusoe consumes. Implicit, then, is the notion that for a Crusoe there are simply two uses of time, H and L, and they must sum to the total time available, T. Therefore,

$$T = H + L. \tag{5.6}$$

By substituting the relation $H = T - L$ from equation (5.6) into the household production function, one obtains

$$G = g(T - L; X). \tag{5.7}$$

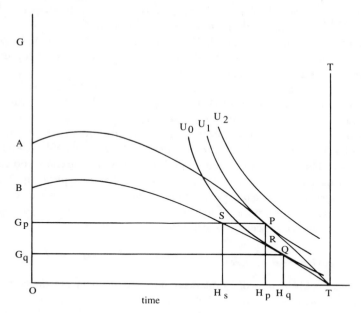

Figure 5.3 A Robinson Crusoe household

Equation (5.7) can be regarded as the budget line for such a household. Equation (5.7) is essentially the equation for AT in Figure 5.2.

One could, then, superimpose Robinson Crusoe's preference map on the diagram, assume that he allocates his time between household production and leisure so as to maximize satisfaction, and have a simple model of such households. Figure 5.3 illustrates such a case. Given his preferences for goods and leisure represented by indifference curves U_0, and U_1, Crusoe maximizes satisfaction by spending TH_p hours each week producing G_p goods, which he consumes, and OH_p hours each week in leisure pursuits.

Suppose, now, he injures himself – say he hurts his leg while bodysurfing in the waters off his island one day. As a result he must spend more time per week in order to produce a given quantity of goods. Thus, his household production function would shift down to, say, BT. Whereas before the injury TH_p hours per week are sufficient to produce G_p quantity of goods, after the injury it takes him TH_s per week to produce the same quantity. Thus, his labor productivity falls as a result of his injury.[3] After the injury he would maximize satisfaction at point Q, where he spends TH_q hours per week producing G_q goods, which he consumes, and OH_q hours of leisure. As a result of his injury he spends less time working and more time in leisure pursuits and consumes fewer goods than before. If his production function had been differently shaped or his preferences between goods and leisure different (as represented by the shapes of the indifference curves), the result might have been different.

Although Figure 5.3 has been explained in terms of a fictional Robinson Crusoe household, it still has much relevance in today's world for it captures important elements of the reality faced by peasant families in Third World countries. Household models only a little more complicated than Figure 5.3 are used by development economists to better understand the behavior of peasants and to evaluate policies that would improve their lot.[4]

The typical American family, however, faces opportunities in the labor market as well as opportunities for home production. American families also are confronted with a myriad of consumer goods that they can purchase and consume if they have the money. In consequence, a model of the typical American family must incorporate the possibility of employment in the labor market and the purchase and consumption of market goods from the family's labor and nonlabor income. We proceed to specify these other relations.

The market work budget constraint

The family's weekly income of Y dollars is composed of earnings from employment, E, and nonlabor income, V. Thus,

$$Y = E + V. \tag{5.8}$$

Nonlabor income includes such things as rent from real property, dividends from stocks, interest on bonds and savings accounts, and gifts received; that is, income that does not result from employment and is not affected by the amount one works. Benefits from most welfare programs like Aid to Families with Dependent Children Program, the Supplemental Security Income Program, and the Food Stamp Program are affected by the amount one works and, therefore, are not included in nonlabor income.

The family's expenditures on market goods are pC, where p is the price index for market goods. Since expenditures exhaust income,

$$pC = Y = E + V. \tag{5.9}$$

Recognize that earnings depend on how much time is spent per week in market work. If the individual can command a wage rate per hour of $\$w$/hr., then weekly earnings must be

$$E = wM. \tag{5.10}$$

And, therefore, by substituting equation (5.10) into (5.9) the budget constraint can be expressed as

$$pC = wM + V. \tag{5.11}$$

Equilibrium in a household with no household production

We can make use of this simple market work budget line to construct a model of a household that is the *reverse* of Robinson Crusoe's. Whereas the Robinson

Crusoe household could work only in household production and consumed only household-produced goods and services, its opposite can perform only market work, has no household production, and consumes only market goods. This implies that time can be spent only in market work, M, and leisure, L, and that they must sum to the total time available; that is,

$$T = M + L. \tag{5.12}$$

Substituting equation (5.12) into the equation for the budget line, equation (5.11), yields

$$pC = w(T - L) + V$$

or, after multiplying through and shifting wL to the left-hand side,

$$pC + wL = wT + V. \tag{5.13}$$

The expression on the right-hand side of equation (5.13) represents the total income the household could have if the individual worked every minute of every day in the labor market at the wage rate w. In consequence, $wT + V$ has been called *full income*. It represents the resources available to the household. The expression on the left-hand side of equation (5.13) shows how full income is spent; pC on purchased goods and services and wL on leisure.

The budget line, equation (5.13) is graphed in Figure 5.4. As before, quantities of goods (market goods in this case) are measured up the vertical axis and time is measured along the horizontal axis. Leisure hours are measured from left to right beginning at O, and market work is measured from right to left beginning at T. Point B represents the combination of market goods (V/p) and leisure (OT hours) that the individual could have if he did no work and had only the market goods purchasable with his nonlabor income, V. In contrast, point A represents the quantity of market goods purchasable, $(wT + V)/p$, if the individual had no leisure and, therefore, worked TO hours. Points on line AB represent other possible combinations of market goods and leisure and, therefore, work. Point D, for instance, represents a situation in which the individual works TM_d hours per week and with the income so generated purchases and consumes $C_d - V/p$ quantity of market goods and services over and above what was purchased with nonlabor income, V, and spends OM_d hours per week in leisure.

The slope of the budget line has the same interpretation as the slope of any budget line. It represents the market rate of exchange between goods and leisure. This is seen by computing the slope:

$$\text{slope of } AB = -[(wT + V)/p - V/p]/T = -[(wT)/p]/T = -w/p.$$

w/p is the quantity of market goods and services that must be given up in order to gain an added hour of leisure. w/p is, therefore, the *real price of leisure*.

If the preference map of such a household is superimposed on the budget line in Figure 5.4, one can observe the household's equilibrium quantities of market

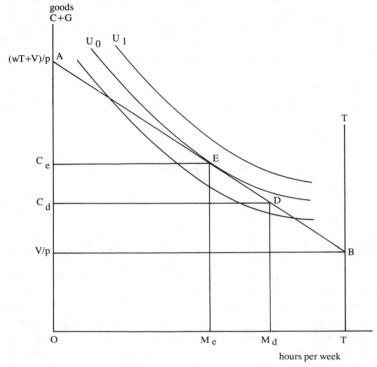

Figure 5.4 The household that does no household work

goods, leisure, and market work. This occurs at point E, where the household's budget line is tangent to the highest attainable indifference curve, U_0. At point E the individual has OM_e hours per week of leisure and spends TM_e hours per week in the labor market earning wM_e earned income. Total income, $wM_e + V$, is then spent on C_e market goods and services.

Such a model of the household is quite useful if one wishes to focus *only* on market work. The distinction between time spent in leisure and time spent in household production is lost in such applications.[5] Figure 5.4 or variants of it are often used by labor economists in analyzing the household's supply of labor to the labor market.

However, our focus is on household behavior in and out of the household and not just on its supply of labor to the labor market. The typical American household (indeed, the typical household in most countries in the world) faces a more complicated set of circumstances, in which some household work is done, some market work is done, and some time is spent in leisure activities. In order to understand how the household allocates its time among market work, household work, and leisure a more complicated budget line must be built. It must include aspects of both the market work budget line, equation (5.13), and the household work budget line, equation (5.7). We proceed to build the total budget line.

The total household budget line

Definition: The total budget line is the locus of points representing the maximum quantity of goods (either market or household) obtainable from each number of hours worked at either market or household work and nonlabor income.

To derive this line a behavioral rule must be introduced. The behavioral rule derives from the assumption that more is better so long as more is free. The rule is that the household allocates time to market and to household work so as to maximize the quantity of goods derivable from each hour worked.

An example will help. Suppose the household production function is

$$G = 40H - 0.5H^2;$$

the price of market goods, p, is \$1.00/unit; and the wage rate the individual can command in the labor market is \$10.00/hr.

Now, compare the quantity of goods the individual can produce with one hour spent in household production with the quantity of goods that the individual can purchase with the earnings from one hour of market work. If $H = 1$, then $G_1 = 40(1) - 0.5(1)^2 = 39.5$ units. If $M = 1$, then earnings are \$10.00 and $C_1 = w/p = 10/1 = 10$ units of market goods can be purchased. The first hour spent in household work yields more goods than the first hour in market work. In consequence, if the individual were to spend one hour working, she or he would spend it in household production and not working in the labor market.

The calculations for succeeding hours worked in household production are contained in Table 5.1. The leftmost column shows the hours worked in household production per week, H. The middle column displays the quantity of household goods, G, produced per week given the hours worked in the first column. The rightmost column displays the marginal product of labor in household production, g_h, given the hours worked in the first column; that is, the added household output produced given an added hour of labor. Thus, if 4 hr. are worked in household production per week, 152 units of household goods, G, are produced and the marginal product of the fourth hour is 36.5 units; working the fourth hour in the household yields $152 - 115.5 = 36.5$ additional units of household goods.

The thirtieth hour worked in the household per week yields $750 - 739.5 =$

Table 5.1. *Total hours worked, total product, and marginal product in household production*

Hours worked (H)	Total product (G)	Marginal product (g_h)
0	0	0
1	39.5	39.5
2	78.0	38.5
3	115.5	37.5
4	152.0	36.5
⋮	⋮	⋮
29	739.5	11.5
30	750	10.5
31	759.5	9.5
⋮	⋮	⋮

Note: Figures based on household production function $G = 40H - 0.5H^2$.

10.5 added units of household goods. If the thirtieth hour were spent in market work instead, the earnings from it would buy $w/p = 10$ units of goods. Clearly, if 30 hr. are to be spent working per week, they are better spent in household work than in market work. However, the thirty-first hour worked will yield more goods if spent in market work than in household work because the marginal product of the thirty-first hour in household work is only 9.5, whereas it is 10 in market work. If the individual were to work 31 hr./wk., therefore, he or she would produce the maximum quantity of goods by spending 30 hr. in household work and 1 hr. in market work. If this were done, then 750 units of household goods would be produced and 10 units of market goods would be purchased for a total of 760 units. If the entire 31 hr. had been spent in household production, 759.5 units would have been produced. If the 31 hr. had been spent in market work, only 310 units of goods would have been purchased. Because any hours worked beyond 30 per week yield more goods if spent in market work than in household work, the individual possessing this production function and who can command $10/hr. in the labor market will spend no more than 30 hr./wk. in household work.

Notice that the individual ceases to do more household work when the marginal product of labor in household work, g_h, equals the real wage rate, w/p:

$$g_h = w/p. \tag{5.14}$$

This condition, then, determines the point at which an individual ceases to do

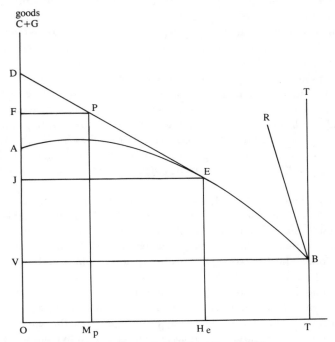

Figure 5.5 The total household budget line, *DEBT*

more household work and begins to do market work. For fewer hours worked, $g_h > w/p$, and the time is more productively spent in household work. For more hours worked, $g_h < w/p$, and the extra time is more productively spent in market work.

These relationships are illustrated in Figure 5.5. Point B represents the combination of goods and leisure available to the household if no work whatsoever is done and it has V dollars of nonlabor income per week to spend on market goods. Since we are assuming that $p = \$1.00/\text{unit}$, then point B represents V market goods and $T = 168$ hr. of leisure per week.

Line AB is the household production function; any point on it represents a quantity of hours per week spent in household work, say, H_e, and the output of household goods produced with that labor, say VJ (OV quantity of goods are market purchased with the household's nonlabor income so that H_e hours of household work yield VJ units of G-goods). The slope of AB at any point represents the marginal product of labor in household work, g_h.

Line DE is the market work portion of the total household budget line. The slope of DE is w/p; that is, the real wage rate. Since no market work is contemplated until enough household work is done to drive the marginal product of labor in the household down to the real wage rate ($g_h = w/p$), DE is not drawn from the T axis but rather begins at point E on AB, where DE is tangent to AB. At the point of tangency, E, the slopes of AB and DE are equal; that is, $g_h = w/p$ at E.

Any point on DE, say point P, represents the total quantity of goods (market purchased and household produced) available to the household if it works TH_e hours per week in the household and H_eM_p hours per week in the market and uses its nonlabor income, V, to purchase goods also. In particular, at P the household purchases OV goods with its nonlabor income, produces VJ household goods by spending TH_e in household work, and purchases JF market goods with the earnings from H_eM_p hours of market work.

Line $DEBT$, then, is the total household budget line. It is made up of three parts. The TB part represents the quantity of market goods purchasable with the household's unearned income, V. The EB part is derived from the household production function and represents the region in which household work is efficiently done. The DE part represents the region in which both household work and market work are done.

The household budget line, $DEBT$, implies that market work will never be done unless some household work is done. Put differently, so long as the marginal product of labor in household production is higher than the real wage rate commanded by the individual in the labor market, the individual will do no market work. The reason is simple but needs repeating: no market work will be done so long as more goods can be produced in an added hour worked at home than in the labor market.

Figure 5.5 is representative of all but a very few American families in that most adult members of most families do some household work (even if it is simply showering, dressing, and cleaning their teeth each morning) and some family members also engage in market work. Only those individuals whose real wage rates are higher than the productivity of their first hour in household work will do no household work. In such a case the market work portion of the budget line would be steeper than even the steepest part of the household production function. This is represented by the line RB in Figure 5.5, which is steeper than AB at zero hours. While such may be the case for the highest paid entertainers, it is unrealistic for most families.

To summarize: The household's total budget line is made up of pieces of the household production function and the market work budget line. The household will produce and/or purchase goods so as to maximize the total quantity of goods it can consume for the hours it spends working. Because the first few hours of work are most productively spent in household production, the household will be employed in the labor market only if its real wage rate, w/p, is at

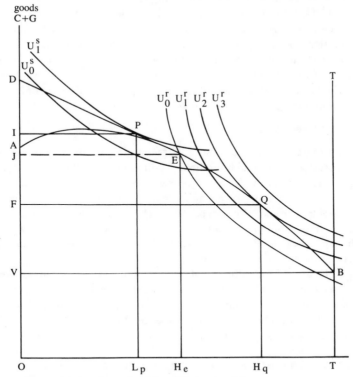

Figure 5.6 Two households' equilibrium positions

least equal to its marginal productivity in home production, g_h. Geometrically, this occurs when the slope of the household production function equals the slope of the market work budget line; that is, where *DE* is tangent to *AB* in Figure 5.5.

Equilibrium in the household work–market work–leisure model

With the total household budget line and the household's preferences we can now introduce satisfaction-maximizing behavior and use the model to discover the household's equilibrium allocations of time to household work, market work, and leisure activities. We illustrate this in Figure 5.6.

Figure 5.6 illustrates the preference maps of two households that happen to face the same total household budget line, *DEBT*. The S family's preferences are represented by indifference curves U_0^s and U_1^s and the R family's preferences are represented by indifference curves $U_0^r - U_3^r$. The preferences of these two families are between goods (whether market purchased or home produced) and leisure in accordance with the assumptions that C and G are perfect substitutes and that market work, M, and household work, H, yield satisfaction only through the goods produced or purchased by the labor. Assume for the sake of discussion that both the S and the R families are single individuals.

Individual R maximizes satisfaction at point Q, where the total household budget line, $DEBT$, touches his highest attainable indifference curve, U_{ξ}^{s}. At Q, R's marginal rate of substitution of leisure for goods equals his productivity in home production, g_h. Thus, for R at Q

$$\mathrm{MRS}_{lc} = u_l/u_g|_Q = g_h|_Q,$$

where u_l = marginal utility of leisure, u_g = marginal utility of goods, and g_h = marginal product of labor in household production.[6] At Q the rate at which R is willing to exchange leisure for goods is exactly equal to the rate at which he can exchange leisure for goods by engaging in household production. R consumes OH_q hours of leisure and OF goods per week. He also spends TH_q hours per week engaged in household production activities in which he produces VF units of household goods. In addition, he purchases OV quantity of goods in the market with his weekly nonlabor income of V.

In equilibrium R is unemployed. He is unemployed because in equilibrium his marginal product of labor in household work exceeds the real wage rate he can command in the labor market, w/p; that is, $g_h|_Q > w/p$. The real wage rate he commands in the labor market is represented by the slope of DE. The slope of EB at Q is $g_h|_Q$ and is greater than at E, where it equals the slope of DE (i.e., w/p).

R is not unemployed because he cannot find work. Work is available to him at a real wage rate of w/p. Rather, R is unemployed because at a wage rate of w/p per hour his time is worth more to him at home in household production or in leisure. R could be a retired individual, in which case V represents his weekly pension. R might also be sufficiently independently wealthy so that his nonlabor income and his household production provide him with enough material goods and services that he is happiest not working. R could also be a student whose time is worth more studying than if spent in the labor market. Or R has a great enough relative preference for leisure that he would rather make do with fewer goods and services than give up more of his leisure and do any more household work or any market work.

That R prefers to do no market work is evident from Figure 5.6. The slope of R's indifference curve, U_{δ}^{s}, through point E (the point at which it would be efficient for him to cease further household work and work the first hour in the labor market instead) is greater than the slope of DE (i.e., w/p). That it has greater slope than w/p indicates that the price he is willing to pay for added leisure at E is greater than he must pay. Consequently, he "buys" more than OH_e hours of leisure by sacrificing FJ units of goods and working TH_q hours rather than TH_e hours in household production per week. The real wage rate would have to be at least equal to the slope of his indifference curve at point Q to induce him to enter the labor market at all. The slope of U_2^R at Q, therefore, is R's *reservation wage rate* – the wage rate at which R would be indifferent between working in the labor market or not.

Now consider individual S. She maximizes satisfaction at point P, where she consumes OI total goods (market purchased and home produced) and OL_p hours of leisure per week. S spends TL_p hours per week working: TH_e of them in household production and H_eL_p in market work. The OI goods she consumes each week are made up of OV goods purchased with her weekly nonlabor income, VJ home-produced goods and services, and JI goods and services purchased with her earnings from employment.

For individual S at point P

$$u_l/u_g|_P = w/p = g_h|_E;$$

that is, S's marginal rate of substitution of leisure for goods at point P (i.e., the slope of U_3^S at P) equals the real wage rate (i.e., the slope of DE), which also equals her marginal productivity in household production (i.e., the slope of BE at E) (see mathematical note 3). Thus, the rate at which S is willing to exchange leisure for goods (u_l/u_g) is equal to the rates at which she is able to exchange leisure for goods (w/p via the labor and purchased goods markets and g_h via household production).

Figure 5.6 is a remarkable diagram. It indicates the equilibrium allocation of time among market work, household work, and leisure for the person being analyzed. It also shows how the equilibrium total consumption of goods arises: from goods purchased with unearned income, from goods purchased with earned income, and from goods produced within the household.

Before we begin to use the model in Figure 5.6 to analyze the time use decisions in families, we need to point out that it is capable of being interpreted in a wider context than it has been thus far in the discussion. To this point it has been interpreted as a model of a single individual's time allocation or of the employed individual in a one-earner family. It can also represent the time allocation of either spouse in families in which both may be employed. In the latter interpretation of the model, nonlabor income is made to include the earnings of the spouse whose time allocation is not being analyzed.

We can interpret Figure 5.6 as a picture of the time allocation of either spouse in a family, therefore. Suppose, for example, we interpret Figure 5.6 as a model of the time allocation of the married woman in the typical family. The horizontal axis, then, refers to her time and the vertical axis refers to total goods, purchased and home produced. The husband's earnings (his labor income) are included in nonlabor income because the married woman does not earn it. When interpreted in this way, however, we will still consider a change in nonlabor income as a change only in that part of family income that is unearned by both spouses; the earned income of the spouse included in V will remain constant (see mathematical note 4). With these assumptions, we can now begin to use the model to analyze the time use decisions of family members.

Income effects on the work behavior of the household

Family income has two sources: labor and nonlabor income. Since labor income is the product of the wage rate, w, and the hours employed in the labor market, M, a change in earned income can arise because either w or M changes. But w is the price of leisure and any change in w can be expected to affect the household's equilibrium in a fashion similar to the way changes in the price of any other consumption good affect it. However, if a change in M is the source of the change in earned income, then the work behavior of the household has changed and we are interested in explaining why it changed. Consequently, when we talk about the effects of income changes on the work behavior of family members, we must not be referring to changes in earned income. Instead, we must be referring to changes in nonlabor income, V.

An increase in nonlabor income, V, increases the resources available to the household and, thus, increases the available combinations of goods (purchased and produced) and leisure that are available. Such a change cannot be expected to change the wage rates family members command in the labor market, the price at which goods can be purchased in the goods market, or the basic parameters of the production function by which goods and services are produced in the home. An increase in nonlabor income, therefore, simply increases the resources available to the family but does not change the market rates of exchange between goods and leisure or conditions of household production. An increase in nonlabor income, therefore, shifts the household's total budget line up in a parallel fashion. Consequently, the family's demand for goods and for the leisure of each family member will increase so long as they are normal goods.

The increase in the demand for leisure time will, of course, mean that the amount of time spent working by each family member will fall. For individuals who are unemployed, the reduction in work time must be a reduction in household work time. For individuals who are employed, how is the reduction in work time taken? Do such individuals reduce their market work time, their household work time, or both? So long as the increase in unearned income has no effect on the household production function, then all the reduction in work time will be in market work time, and household work time will be unaffected. This is so because the increase in nonlabor income does not affect the trade-off between market and household work.

Figure 5.7 illustrates these points. The total household budget line, *DEBT*,

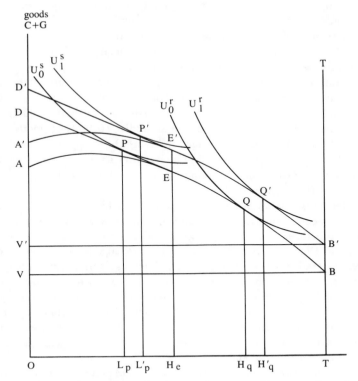

Figure 5.7 The effects of an increase in unearned income on household work behavior

represents the initial alternatives open to the household. The households facing this total household budget line (i.e., our friends, the R and S families) have V nonlabor income per week (the units in which goods are measured being such that $p = \$1.00/\text{unit}$) and the family member whose time use is pictured can command a wage rate of $\$w/\text{hr}$. in the labor market (the slope of DE). Indifference curves U_0^s and U_1^s represent the preferences of household R, and U_0^s and U_1^s represent those of household S.

Initially, family S is in equilibrium at point P, and family R maximizes satisfaction at point Q. At P, the individual in family S spends TH_e hours per week in household work, H_eL_p hours employed in the labor market, and OL_p hours in leisure activities. The individual under study in family R is unemployed, spending TH_q hours per week in household work and OH_q hours in leisure pursuits.

Now presume that each household receives an added VV' dollars of unearned income per week. Recall, this additional income does not emanate from the labor earnings of any family member. It is additional nonlabor income, perhaps from an increase in the return to some of the family's assets.

The increase in nonlabor income shifts the new total household budget line to $D'E'B'T$, a shift that is simply a vertical and parallel translation of $DEBT$. It is vertical and parallel because the increase in nonlabor income has no effect on the wage rate at which R and S can find employment; employers will not alter what they are willing to pay R and S simply because R and S are now wealthier. Nor has the increase in nonlabor income any effect on the household production function; if R and S could produce an added 10 units of goods in the twenty-first hour of household production before the receipt of the nonlabor income, then they can do no more and no less after its receipt. Consequently, the additional nonlabor income simply adds to the households' purchases of market goods (from OV to OV').

Consider household S. With the receipt of VV' added nonlabor income, S reaches a new equilibrium at P', at which TH_e hours are spent in household work (the same as before), $H_eL'_p$ hours per week are spent in market work (less than before), and OL'_p hours are spent per week in leisure activities (more than before). Clearly, leisure is a normal good and, just as clearly, so are goods. The increase in nonlabor income has been used partly to buy more market goods and partly to "buy" more leisure. The added leisure is obtained by reducing the number of hours per week of market work. The amount of time devoted to household work is unchanged by such an increase. This is so because the number of hours of household work for which $g_h = w/p$ remains unchanged by the increment in nonlabor income.

The household work of an employed person would be affected by an increase in nonlabor income only if market- and home-produced goods are not perfect substitutes (see mathematical note 5 for the case in which C-goods and G-goods are not perfect substitutes) or if the increase was large enough to induce the individual to cease market work altogether. The latter frequently happens when the increase in nonlabor income is huge; for example, when someone wins \$2 million in a lottery. Here, the desired increase in leisure is more than the total number of hours worked in the market per week. Consequently, the individual quits market work and also reduces somewhat his or her weekly household work.

Now turn to household R. Household R is unemployed before and after the increment in nonlabor income. After its receipt R spends TH'_q hours per week working at household tasks (less than before) and OH'_q hours per week in leisure activities (more than before). Leisure is a normal good for R as well as for S but because R is unemployed, the only way R can consume more leisure is to reduce the amount of household work she performs.

Do we have any evidence to support the hypotheses about the effects of nonlabor income? Yes. Consider first the effects of changes in nonlabor income on the market work behavior of individuals. There is wide agreement based on cross-section data that both males and females, married and single, devote less time to market work as nonlabor income rises.[7] Pencavel (1986, p. 70) hazards the opinion that the nonlabor income elasticity of men's market work is about −0.23. The studies of female labor supply summarized by Killingsworth and Heckman (1986, Table 2.26) contain estimates of the nonlabor income elasticity for women in the same neighborhood.

Several scholars have studied labor supply in the aggregate over the period 1929–67. Their findings are similar. Kiefer (1977) combines the market work of males and females and estimates the income elasticity of hours worked to be −0.08. That is, a 10 percent increase in nonlabor income results in a decline in total (male plus female) labor supplied to the labor market of about 0.8 percent. Owen (1971) studied the aggregate annual hours of market work of nonagricultural males from 1929 to the 1960s and found the income elasticity of hours worked to be between −0.37 and −0.57. Owen maintains that part of the reason the workweek for American males has fallen from around 60 hr./wk. at the turn of the century to about 40 hr./wk. after World War II has been the increase in American affluence.[8]

Turn now to the question of the effect of nonlabor income on the time spent on household work. Cross-section studies of the household work time of American married males and females are entirely consistent with Figure 5.7. As nonwage income rises, the household work times of employed married men and women are unaffected but that of unemployed married women falls.[9] Gronau's results (1977) are the most evocative. He finds that an increase in nonlabor income of $1,000/yr. leads to a decline of 44 hr. in the annual time spent in household work by white unemployed married women. No such decline is observed for white employed married women (1977, Table 3). Kooreman and Kapteyn (1987, pp. 242–3) find the household work time of employed married men, employed married women, and unemployed married women in 1975 to be unresponsive to changes in nonlabor income.

One must conclude, therefore, that the hypotheses contained in Figure 5.7 are founded in empirical fact. For both men and women leisure is a normal, income-inelastic good. The household work of unemployed married females falls by a small amount as nonwage income rises, where that of employed men and women does not.

Wage rate effects on time use

As has been pointed out before, the wage rate an individual can command in the labor market is also the price of leisure; that is, the amount of money that has to be sacrificed in order for the household to consume an added hour of leisure.

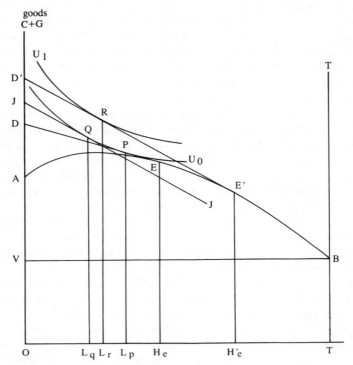

Figure 5.8 The own-wage-rate effect on time use

When wage rates change, therefore, the price of leisure changes and one can expect the family to respond by changing its demand for leisure.

The wage rate, however, is also an integral part of the individual's productivity in gaining purchased goods; that is, w/p represents the quantity of market goods that can be gained by doing an hour of market work and using the earnings to purchase goods. Therefore, a change in the wage rate also changes the individual's "market productivity" relative to household productivity (i.e., g_h) and, thus, affects the trade-off between market and household work. The altered trade-off, in turn, affects the distribution of work time between market and household production.

Figure 5.8 disentangles these effects of an own-wage-rate change; that is, a change in the wage rate of the individual whose time allocation is under study. *DEBT*, as usual, is the total household budget line facing the household prior to the wage rate change. The initial wage rate facing the individual is w and, therefore, the slope of *DE* is w/p. The household maximizes satisfaction at point P, where the individual spends OL_p hours per week in leisure activities, H_eL_p

hours in the labor market, and TH_e hours in household work activities.

Now consider the change in the individual's behavior in response to an increase in his or her wage rate from w to w'. First, the relationship between the individual's market productivity, w/p, and household productivity, g_h, changes. With an increase in w, the quantity of goods the individual can purchase with the first hour of time spent in market work, w/p, becomes greater than the quantity of goods he or she can produce with the last hour spent in household work at point E; that is, $g_h|_E < w'/p$. Consequently, the household finds that it can have more goods with the same hours devoted to work if the amount of time the individual spends in household work is reduced and the amount of time spent in market work increases. Thus, the rise in the real wage rate induces the individual to substitute market work for household work, holding the total amount of work time constant.

This substitution of market work for household work is illustrated by the shift in the total household budget line from $DEBT$ to $D'E'BT$, the decline in household work time from TH_e to TH'_e, and the increase in market work by $H_eH'_e$. Prior to the rise in the wage rate point E is the point of tangency between the household production function AB and the market work budget line, DE. At E, $w/p = g_h|_E$. When w rises to w', $w'/p > g_h|_E$ and the individual substitutes market for household work, finding a new equilibrium at point E', where $w'/p = g_h|_{E'}$. $D'E'$, then, has slope w'/p.

We can call this substitution of market work for household work as the own wage rate changes a *production substitution effect*. In the production substitution effect the individual does not change the total amount of time he or she spends working. Rather, one way of gaining access to goods is substituted for another way. In Figure 5.8, the production substitution effect is the substitution of $H_eH'_e$ hours of market work for $H_eH'_e$ hours of household work. Total hours of work, TL_p, remain constant.

The production substitution effect is, however, not the only substitution effect caused by a wage rate change. As the real wage rate rises from w/p to w'/p, the individual's leisure becomes more expensive relative to goods. Holding satisfaction constant, the household is induced by this relative price change to substitute the now-cheaper goods for the now relatively more expensive leisure. This is done by increasing the time the individual spends working and by using the extra earnings to increase the family's consumption of goods. This can be called the *consumption substitution effect* because the substitution occurs in consumption, not production.

The consumption substitution effect is illustrated geometrically in the same way as the substitution effect was illustrated in Chapter 3: by drawing a straight line parallel to the new budget line (i.e., $D'E'$) and tangent to the original indifference curve (U_0). JJ is such a line and is tangent to U_0 at Q. Hypothetically, JD' is the amount of real income that must be taken away from the household to make it as satisfied at the new wage rate as it was at the old wage rate. The consumption substitution effect of the wage rate increase, then, is the decline in the quantity of leisure consumed from OL_p to OL_q, holding satisfaction constant.

The *total substitution effect* of the own-wage-rate increase on market work, then, is the sum of the production substitution and the consumption substitution effects. As the wage rate rises, the production substitution effect induces the individual to substitute market work for a like amount of household work, holding total hours of work constant. The consumption substitution effect induces the individual to work more in order to earn the income required to buy the added goods that the household substitutes for its now more expensive leisure, holding satisfaction constant.

Thus far, we have neglected the fact that a rise in the individual's wage rate increases the household's real income. With the increase in real income come increases in the household's demands for goods and leisure, so long as both are normal goods. This is the *income effect* of the rise in wage rate. It is illustrated by the parallel shift from JJ to $D'E'$ in Figure 5.8 and the consequent increase in the demand for the individual's leisure from OL_q to OL_r, as the household equilibrium moves from Q to R. The income effect of the wage rate increase, therefore, serves to increase the demand for leisure and decrease the individual's supply of labor. But the decrease in the supply of labor comes totally out of market work; time spent in household work does not decline due to the income effect.

The *total own-wage-rate effect on market work* is the sum of the production and consumption substitution effects and the income effect. In Figure 5.8 the total own-wage-rate effect on market work is

$$L_r H'_e - L_p H_e = H_e H'_e + L_p L_q + L_q L_r.$$

Whereas the two substitution effects of a wage rate increase market work, the income effect reduces market work. The total own-wage-rate effect, therefore, is negative or positive depending on the ability of the income effect to offset the two substitution effects. Thus, the supply curve of labor to the labor market can be conventionally positive (the higher the wage rate, the more labor is supplied to the labor market) or "backward bending" and negative (the higher the wage rate, the less labor is supplied to the labor market).

The *total own-wage-rate effect on household work* is made up solely of the production substitution effect: as the wage rate rises, the time spent in household work declines as more and more labor is shifted from household to market production. In Figure 5.8, this is represented by $H_e H'_e$.

The *total own-wage-rate effect on leisure* is composed of the consumption substitution effect and the income effect. As the price of leisure rises relative to goods, the household substitutes goods for leisure. As the rise in the wage rate increases real income, more leisure is demanded. Since the two effects oppose each other, the total effect on leisure depends on which is the stronger. In terms of Figure 5.8,

$$L_r L_p = L_p L_q + L_q L_r.$$

What evidence do we have that these hypothesized effects occur in the real world? We have more evidence with respect to market work than with respect to household work or leisure. There is wide agreement that the supply of labor by American males is "backward bending"; that is, as male wage rates rise, the amount of time American males spend in market work declines. In a time-series study of the hours worked by American nonagricultural males between 1929 and 1961, Owen (1971) found the wage rate elasticity to be about -0.20. Burkhauser and Turner (1978) extended Owen's period of analysis and estimated the wage rate elasticity to be between -0.15 and -0.33. Because both of these studies utilized aggregate time-series data, they are subject to the criticisms with respect to aggregation discussed in note 8. Owen attributes most of the fall in the weekly hours worked by American males from 60 hr./wk. in 1900 to 40 hr./wk. in the 1940s to the rising wage rate over the period.

Evidence from cross-section studies of market work behavior abounds and is summarized by Pencavel (1986) for men and by Killingsworth and Heckman (1986) for women. Again, most of the evidence indicates that the total own-wage-rate effect on males' labor supply is negative and quite inelastic – in the neighborhood of -0.12 (Pencavel 1986, p. 69).

The compensated wage rate elasticity of labor supply is the sum of the consumption substitution and production substitution effects expressed in elasticity terms. As illustrated in Figure 5.8, both are expected to be positive, and so the total substitution effect is also expected to be positive. From estimates of the uncompensated wage rate elasticity (i.e., the sum of the production and consumption substitution effects and the income effect) and the nonlabor income elasticity, Pencavel (1986) deduces that the compensated wage rate elasticity (the sum of the production and consumption substitution effects on labor supply) for men is in the neighborhood of 0.11. Holding satisfaction constant, therefore, the average male can be expected to increase his labor supply by 1.1 percent in response to a 10 percent increase in his wage rate. In quite a different study, which took into account the future consumption of leisure in much the same way as consumption and saving were discussed in Chapter 4, Smith (1977) derived direct estimates of the compensated wage rate elasticity of labor supply for American men by education and by race. Smith estimates the compensated wage rate elasticity of market work for both black and white males to be 0.33. For college-educated white males, Smith estimates the compensated own-wage-rate elasticity to be 0.26, compared with 0.44 for white males with only elementary school education. The signs of these elasticities are consistent with the hypotheses in Figure 5.8: the total substitution effect is positive; holding satisfaction constant, American males increase their labor supply in the face of a rise in wage rates. The extent of their response depends on their demographic characteristics.

In contrast with males, the evidence for married females indicates that American married women have a positively sloped supply curve of labor to the market. Killingsworth and Heckman (1986) summarized thirty-three cross-section studies. With few exceptions females' uncompensated and compensated wage rate elasticities are positive and their nonlabor income elasticities are negative: as female wage rates rise, the production and substitution effects more than offset the income effects so that females increase the time they spend employed in the labor market. Again, the sizes of these effects depend on the characteristics of the women studied. For instance, Cogan (1980) estimates that the uncompensated wage rate elasticity for white married women aged thirty to forty-four is 0.65 and the compensated wage rate elasticity is 0.68. Estimates for black married women have been calculated by Dooley (1982). He estimates that the uncompensated wage rate elasticity for black married women aged thirty to thirty-four is 0.67 and the compensated wage rate elasticity is 1.01. Interestingly, his estimates of the wage rate elasticities for older black married women become negative.

Much less is known about the effects of wage rate changes on the household work of individuals. Gronau (1977) has performed one of the few studies on total housework. For employed American married women he found that the annual hours of household work declined by 500 hr. (about 1.4 hr./day) for each 1 percent increase in the wage rate. This is an estimate of the production substitution effect in Figure 5.8. These results are consistent with those of Gramm (1974), who studied Chicago high school teachers, and those of Cochrane and Logan (1975), who studied college graduates in South Carolina. Gramm found, for instance, that the amounts of time married women spent cooking and cleaning each declined as women's wage rates rose. Time spent doing laundry, however, did not decline. It is clear, therefore, that married women respond to wage rates as Figure 5.8 suggests.

Even less is known about the time married men spend doing household work. What little research has been done suggests that married men's household work time is very unresponsive to changes in their wage rates (or to anything else, for that matter!). Stafford and Duncan (1985) estimate the compensated wage rate effect on husband's household work time (i.e., the production substitution effect expressed in elasticity form) to be about -0.17. Although this result is consistent with the hypothesis laid out in Figure 5.8., the statistical confidence of the result is low and not much weight can be placed on it.

Since economists have typically defined *leisure* as the time not spent in market work, they have combined the time spent in household work and the time spent in leisure pursuits. In consequence, much less is known about leisure as we are defining it. Gronau, in his study of American married women's time use (1977), found that employed married women devoted less time to leisure activities as their wage rates rose. Cochrane and Logan (1975) found that married South Carolinian women who were college graduates also reduced the amount of time they devoted to leisure activities as their wage rates rose. Using the 1975 national time use sample (see Juster et al. 1978), Kooreman and Kapteyn (1987) studied three categories of leisure: (1) organizational activities and sports; (2) entertainment and social activities; and (3) reading, watching TV, and listening to the radio. They find that married females spend more time in entertainment and social activities and less in both of the other two leisure time activities as their wage rates rise. Married men's behavior with respect to these three leisure time activities is similar. The only other study of men's leisure time was done by Lange (1979). His sample consisted of farm operators in Iowa in the 1970s, and his results indicate that farmers also reduce the time they spend in leisure activities as their labor productivity in work activities rises.

The theory is not restricted to developed country households. The theory has also been used with great success to explain the behavior of peasant households in less developed countries. One such study is that of Evenson (1978), which analyzed the time allocations of husbands and wives in rural Philippine households. Increases in the wage rates of women in farm households led to increases in the time they spent in market work and decreases in the time they spent in both farm and household work. Nonfarm Philippine women increased their market work and decreased their home time as their wage rates increased. Increases in men's wage rates led nonfarm husbands to increase their market work, and it led farm husbands to increase their market work and decrease the time they spent in farm work.

Specialization of function and the division of labor

The results of the above research indicate that the effect of female wage rate changes on the household work of married women is larger than the effect of male wage rate changes on the household work of married men. How does one account for this difference? Why is the household work time of married women more responsive to wage rate changes than men's? One explanation is grounded in the specialization of function and division of labor between spouses that occur in two-spouse households. Therefore, we will now outline the economics of the specialization of function and division of labor in the household.

To the extent that the husband and wife are substitutes in household work – either can do it – there are powerful economic incentives for a division of labor between spouses. The reason is that the household can have more goods and services (i.e., the sum of market-purchased and home-produced goods in terms of our simple model) for any given amount of time spent working if each spouse specializes in market work or household work in accordance with their comparative advantage.

Define the wife's comparative advantage for market work over household work as w_f/g_f, where w_f is the wage rate she commands in the labor market and g_f is the marginal productivity of her time in household work. Likewise, define the husband's comparative advantage for market work over household work as w_m/g_m, where w_m is the wage rate he commands in the labor market and g_m is the marginal productivity of his time in household work.

If $w_f/g_f < w_m/g_m$, then the household will have more total goods and services for any given time they spend working if the wife specializes in household work and the husband specializes in market work. If, however, $w_f/g_f > w_m/g_m$, then total goods and services are greater if he specializes in household work and she specializes in market work. (See mathematical note 4, equation [31].)

How so? To make things simple suppose that both husband and wife are equally productive in household work ($g_f = g_m$) but that the wife commands a higher wage rate than the husband ($w_f > w_m$). Suppose that initially both spouses are employed and also do some household work. Now suppose that she works an hour longer at her job and he works an hour less in his. Further, suppose that he works an hour more in the household and she an hour less. Both work the same amount of time as before: she, an hour more in market work and an hour less in household work; he, the reverse.

Because their household productivities are equal, their output of home-produced goods remains the same: the household production lost because she worked an hour less is exactly made up by the added household output produced by his additional hour. Because her wage rate is higher than his, their output of market-purchased goods and services has increased. The household loses w_m/p units of market goods and services because he spends an hour less working in the labor market.[10] It gains w_f/p units of market goods and services because she spends an hour more at her job. Since $w_f > w_m$, the household gains more purchased goods and services than it loses and, thus, benefits from this relative specialization of function.

So long as their household productivities, g_f and g_m, are equal and so long as $w_f > w_m$, the incentive exists for her to substitute market work for household work while he substitutes household work for market work. This will continue until she ceases all household work and he ceases all market work. Complete specialization of function by both spouses occurs. Only if the couple has a great demand for goods and services will the husband increase his total work time and reenter the labor market. His wife, however, will continue to do no household work.[11]

Current reality, of course, is the reverse of the simple example given above. While there is active debate as to whether female and male time are substitutes in household work,[12] women's wage rates are less than men's. It is equally clear that currently married women are more specialized in household work than married men even though over one-half of all married women also work at paid jobs.

The presence of such specialization implies that the household work of those specialized in market work will be less responsive to wage rate changes than the household work of those specialized in household work. An increase in the wage rate of males will have a consumption substitution effect and an income effect on the times married men spend in leisure and in market work. But there will be little if any production substitution effect of the wage rate increase on their household work for the simple reason that they do little or no household work anyway. Only if their wage rates were less than their wives' would one expect much change. In contrast, an increase in female wage rates can be expected to affect the time married women spend in household work because they either specialize in household work or divide their work time between the labor market and the home. An increased wage rate will induce some of those married women who are totally specialized in household work into the labor market, substituting market for household work. The same wage rate increase will induce those married women working both in the market and in the home to shift more of their time away from household work and toward market work. Thus, the current and historical specialization of function and division of labor between married men and women partially explains the greater response by women than men to changes in their own wage rates.

In sum, although the sizes of the effects vary from study to study, the market work, household work, and leisure time of both men and women do, in general, respond to changes in their wage rates in the fashion hypothesized by our model as modified by specialization of function and division of labor.

Cross-wage-rate effects

Cross-wage-rate effects refer to the effect of changes in the wage rate of one spouse on the time use of the other spouse. As such they are similar to cross-price effects. Indeed, since wage rates are the prices of leisure, the analogy is exact.

Consider an increase in the wage rate of the husband. This constitutes an increase in the price of his leisure. The consumption substitution effect of the increase will lead the family to substitute goods for his leisure given that his leisure has become more expensive. The income effect of the increase in his wage rate will increase the family's demand for his leisure, it being a normal good.

Now trace the impacts of his wage rate increase through to his wife's time use. Since neither her home productivity nor her market productivity is affected by the increase in his wage rate, the trade-off between her household production and her market work remains unchanged. Consequently, the amount of time she devotes to household work will not change if she was employed prior to the increase in his wage rate. The amount of time she spends in market work, however, will be affected. If the spouses' leisure times are *complements* and, therefore, tend to be consumed together by the family, her leisure will fall as his falls due to the consumption substitution effect of his wage rate increase. If, however, the spouses' leisure times are *substitutes* for each other, then the family will substitute her leisure for his leisure as the consumption substitution effect reduces his leisure time. Furthermore, regardless of the status of their leisure times as substitutes for or complements of each other, the income effect of the rise in his wage rate will increase the demand for her leisure. The net effects on her leisure and market work, therefore, depend on whether her leisure is a substitute for or complement of her husband's leisure and on the strength of the income effect.

If the wife was unemployed prior to the increase in his wage rate, the substitution and income effects bear directly on the division of her time between household work and leisure. The cross-substitution effect (between his and her leisure) will increase (decrease) her leisure time and decrease (increase) her household work time if her leisure is a substitute for (complement of) her husband's. The income effect will increase the demand for her leisure time and, in consequence, lower the time she spends in household work.

Although the cross-wage-rate effect has been explained in terms of the effect of the husband's wage rate on the wife's time use, the effects are symmetric; that is, the effect of the wife's wage rate on the husband's time use can be expected to be the same. Indeed, the results are completely general. In principle, the effect of any family member's wage rate on the time use of any other family member can be expected to have the very same components.

We, again, turn to the work of Gronau, Cochrane and Logan, and Kooreman and Kapteyn, as well as others, for evidence of the cross-wage-rate effects. Gronau (1977) found that the employed married female's market work time falls, her leisure time rises, and her household work time remains unchanged when her husband's wage rate increases. Among unemployed married women, an increase in the husband's wage rate increases their leisure and reduces the time spent in household work. On the basis of this evidence, then, her leisure is a gross substitute of his. Cochrane and Logan (1975) also found employed wives' household work time unresponsive to the husband's wage rate while their leisure rose with the husband's wage rate.

Kooreman and Kapteyn's (1977) results are more complicated because they disaggregated household work into three categories of "household activities" (cooking, cleaning, laundry, etc.; child care; and shopping). Leisure is also broken down into the three categories (organizational activities and sports;

entertainment and social activities; and reading, TV, and radio), and the time spent in personal care is classified separately. As the husband's wage rate rises, the time the wife spends in market work falls, indicating that *in total* the wife's time is a substitute for the husband's in household work and leisure activities. The distribution of the increased time she spends in household work and leisure activities is interesting. As his wage rate rises, she spends more time in all three of the household work activities. And although she spends more time in reading, TV, and radio and in entertainment and social activities, she spends less time in organizational activities and sports as his wage rate rises.[13]

In contrast, Kooreman and Kapteyn (1987) found husbands' time use to be much less responsive to changes in wives' wage rates than wives' time use is to changes in husbands'. Although husbands do slightly reduce the amount of time they spend in market work in response to increases in their wives' wage rates, the increased nonmarket time is spread evenly across the several categories of household work and leisure. The overall reduction in husbands' market work time in response to changes in wives' wage rates is consistent with the results of other studies of the labor market behavior of males. Gerner and Zick (1983), for instance, in a study of husbands in two-parent, two-child families find that husbands do, in fact, reduce the time they spend in market work in response to increases in their wives' wage rates, but the reduction is quite small.

The smaller response of male time use to changes in female wage rates is consistent with the observed specialization of function and division of labor by spouses. Given that male wage rates are higher than females' and given that most husbands are specialized in market work and most wives in household work, changes in female wage rates should have little effect on the time use of married men except through the income effect and through any complementarities that may exist between husbands' and wives' leisure times. There will be little if any cross-substitution between husbands' and wives' household work time.

Family size, family composition, and time use

When we think of changes in family size and composition we typically think of changes brought about by the arrival of children, what happens to the family as they grow and mature, and what happens when they leave to form a new household. Consequently, we will deal with the effects of family size and composition by considering the effects children have upon parents' time use.

The relationships between children and parental time use are complicated. Not only does the presence of children of different ages affect parental time use differently, but the relationship is quite different in the short run from that in the long run. In the short run it is clear that the causation runs from children to time use. In the long run it is equally clear that neither parental time use nor children are the cause or effect of the other. Rather, they are both planned responses to an underlying set of forces.

Over the long run parental time use, especially that of the mother, and the number and timing of children are consequences of long-run planning the family executes on the basis of family goals in the light of resources and the alternatives family resources and resource prices allow. This long-run view will be dealt with extensively in the chapter on fertility. Here, we shall consider the short-run effects of the presence and development of children on parental time use.

The arrival of a child has three effects on parents. It increases the home productivity, g_h, of each spouse, because it induces each to increase the time spent in household work, at the expense of market work. It also leads, as we have seen in past chapters, to an increase in the demand for market goods and services (more food, clothes, furniture, housing, etc.), inducing increases in the market work of each spouse to earn the income to buy them. Finally, the increase in home productivity possesses an income effect that increases the demands for parental leisure.

Because time is limited, each spouse cannot simultaneously increase market work, household work, and leisure time. However, all of these forces can partially be responded to through parental division of labor. Due to a complex of social and economic forces, parents have practiced rather extreme division of labor. Men specialized in market work and women specialized in household work. Although there may be less sex typing of household tasks today than in the past, most household activities, especially those dealing with the care and development of children, were and are performed by women (see Hill 1985). Consequently, the addition of a child to a family typically induces the father to increase his market work and the mother to increase her household work at the expense of market work.

But why does the arrival of a child increase household productivity. The increase in household productivity arises out of increased opportunities for *joint production* and out of *economies of size* that the family can exploit given the larger family size. Joint production occurs when more than one good or service is produced with the same inputs, as when clothes are washed, a meal is cooked, and a child cared for all at the same time. The opportunities for joint production with the addition of a child occur because much child care allows other tasks to be carried out simultaneously.

Size economies are instances in which the average cost of a good or service falls as its output rises. The new infant increases the demand for all home-produced goods and services (meals, laundry, cleaning, shopping, etc., as well as child care). Given the increased demands, the family can enlarge its production of these goods and services and so exploit a number of cost-reducing (and, therefore, home productivity increasing) economies.

A number of these economies are obvious. Home appliances are "lumpy" in that each has a minimum capacity that is larger than that demanded by many childless couples. Instead, their services are rented or done without entirely. Laundry equipment is an example. Many childless couples find it much more economic to have their washing done at a hand laundry or to do it themselves at a nearby laundromat. The arrival of a child, however, increases the demand for laundry services sufficiently to warrant the purchase of laundry equipment. Owning a freezer is, likewise, uneconomic for small families but increasingly economic as family size rises. Food preparation is another example. Increasing family size reduces food loss and spoilage. Also, the increase in food preparation time is proportionately less than the increase in family size. In each of these cases, household productivity, g_h, rises.

We know that the demand for goods and services also rises as family size increases for the simple reason that there are more members to be housed, clothed, transported, and fed. And we know that the demands for certain goods and services change with changes in family composition: the demand for health care is greater, for instance, in families with elderly and very young family members than in families made up of teenagers and middle-aged adults. How do these same forces affect the time use patterns of men and women?

The arrival of a child constitutes both an increase in family size and a change in family composition. Neither unearned income nor the wage rates commanded by the parents are changed. As argued earlier, the household productivity, g_h, of the mother and, perhaps, also the father increases because of economies of size and joint production.

The arrival of a baby also creates a demand for child care, a service that is quite expensive when purchased and considerably cheaper when produced in the home. Given the large commitment to child care that one child entails, added children do not increase the commitment in proportion to the increase in family size. Thus, efficiency in the home production of child care is high and becomes higher as more children are added.

What about preferences? Do changes in family size alter the family's preferences for goods and services relative to leisure? Certainly more goods and services, purchased or home-produced, are demanded simply because there are more members to feed, clothe, house, transport, etc. But does the demand for leisure rise also (we refer here to parental leisure and not the leisure of other family members)? Parents' preferences for their own leisure probably do increase with the arrival of children because of the satisfaction obtained from playing with children. The arrival of a child, however, probably increases the demand for goods and services, purchased and homemade, relative to parental leisure, as any new parent lacking sleep can attest.

The increased demand for goods relative to leisure, of course, induces family members to work longer hours in the market or at household tasks, or both, in

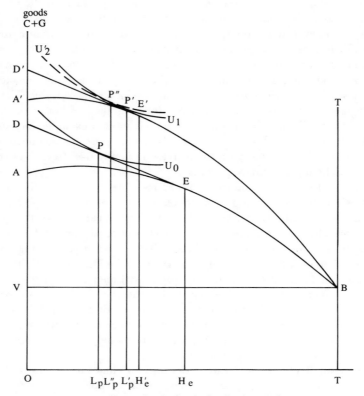

Figure 5.9 The effects of a change in family size on time use

order to supply them. Given the sexual division of labor within the family, however, the pressure to work longer hours induces the father to do more market work while it induces the mother to do more household work. Indeed, the rise in the mother's household productivity, g_h, tilts the trade-off between market and household work toward the latter and typically induces her to increase household work at the expense of market work. And the increased demand for purchased goods induces fathers to spend more time in paid employment earning the money to buy them.

The forces affecting the time use of the mother are illustrated in Figure 5.9. Prior to the arrival of a child the total household budget line is *DEBT*, with the household maximizing satisfaction at point P. The wife, consequently, spends TH_e hours per week in household work, H_eL_p hours per week in market work, and OL_p hours in leisure activities.

The arrival of a child raises the mother's household productivity throughout the range of hours worked. Consequently, the household production function rotates clockwise from AB to $A'B$ so that its slope at any given hour of work is steeper than it was before. Given her increased household productivity and the fact that her market productivity, w/p, remains unchanged, the mother will increase the amount of time she spends in household production until she drives her marginal productivity down equal to her real wage rate once again. This occurs at E' rather than E. Thus, the family's total household budget line shifts from $DEBT$ to $D'E'BT$. $D'E'$ is parallel to DE because the child does not affect the woman's market productivity, w/p. Because her household productivity increased relative to her market productivity, the mother substitutes household work for market work by the amount $H_e H'_e$ in response to the advent of the child. Thus, one of the effects of an added child is essentially a *production substitution effect* – from market work to household work as household production becomes the cheaper way to acquire goods and services.

The increase in her household productivity also acts to increase the household's total resources and, thus, increases the household's demand for the woman's leisure as well as for goods through an *income effect*. This increase is shown by the move from P to P', the new equilibrium combination of total goods and leisure. Not only will the extent of the mother's market work be reduced by the production substitution effect of her increased home productivity, it will also be reduced by the income effect.

To the extent that the advent of the child also increases the household's preference for goods relative to leisure, the indifference curves become less steep at P' (i.e., the family becomes more willing to give up some leisure for added goods and services with the added child). With the new indifference curve (represented by the dashed-line curve, U'_2), the mother willingly gives up $L'_p L''_p$ leisure in order to earn the money required to afford the extra goods demanded as a result of the added child. The new equilibrium is, then, P''.

Unless the child-induced decline in the relative preference for leisure is quite large, the net effect of a new child on the mother's time use will be a reduction in the amount of time she spends in leisure and market work and a large increase in the time she spends in household work. Indeed, the increase in the mother's household productivity is frequently large enough to induce her to cease market work entirely, at least temporarily.

So much for an increase in family size via childbirth. What about the effects of changes in family composition as children grow and mature? One can classify activities as "goods-intensive" or "time-intensive" according to the ratio of goods to time used in the activity: the higher the ratio of goods to time, the more goods-intensive. Child rearing begins as a time-intensive activity and becomes more goods-intensive as children gain physical, emotional, and intellectual independence from their parents as they grow older. Economic independence is not typically gained until the schooling process is complete and the child has formed an independent household.

A crucial point in the drift toward the goods-intensive period of the child-rearing process occurs when school begins. Once in school (or in purchased child care) the time burden of children becomes much less. One would expect, then, that the time spent in household work by mothers would decline as the age of the youngest child increases and that the time spent in market work or leisure or both would increase; that is, the reverse process to that depicted by Figure 5.9 should occur as the child grows up. Also, in order to meet the increased demands for purchased goods and services, as the child grows up one would expect the father's market work to remain high or to grow until the child leaves home. Of course, the entry or reentry of the mother into the labor force also importantly meets the increased demands for purchased goods and services.

Gronau's work, again, offers empirical evidence with respect to the effects of children on the time use of married women. The household work of unemployed married women increased by 328 hr./yr. and their leisure fell by a like amount with the addition of a preschool child. Employed married women increased their household work by 276 hr. annually and reduced their market work by 190 hr. and their leisure by 89 hr. with the addition of a preschool child (Gronau 1977). These are the effects of an increase in family size by one infant.

The evidence of the effects of changes in family composition when children grow up is as clear. When the child becomes school-aged, Gronau (1977) found that the household work time of unemployed married women fell by 125 hr. annually. If employed, the married woman's household work time declined by about 100 hr., her market work time increased by a like amount, and her leisure time was unaffected as the child reached school age.

The work of Gerner and Zick (1983) on two-parent, two-child families holds family size constant and allows the effects of children's ages to be isolated. They found that the likelihood that the mother would be employed rose as the age of the younger child rose. Likewise, the hours of market work performed by the mother, if she was employed, also rose by about 1 hr./wk. for each year of the child. Gerner and Zick also found that the wider the spacing between the two children, the less likely it would be that the mother would be employed and the fewer hours per week she worked if she was employed. Clearly, the age distribution of the children is as important as the number of children and whether they are school-aged or not.

It is a commonplace to observe that married men have higher labor force participation rates and work more hours per year than single men. Likewise, married men with children work longer hours per year than others. Owen (1971) found that the market work of American males rose in the 1950s as the cost of educating a family rose in terms of both the cost per child and the cost per family as family size rose. In their study of American males' market work behavior from 1929 to 1971, Burkhauser and Turner (1978) found that average weekly hours worked per year by males increased by 0.3 percent for each increase in family size by one person. Sanik (1983) has conducted one of the few studies of the household work of married men. Working with a sample of husbands in two-parent, two-child families in New York, she finds that the age of the younger child has no effect on the father's household work time at all, whereas the age of the older child does: as that child becomes older, the father spends less time engaged in care of family members and more time in household management activities. The increase in the one almost exactly offsets the fall in the other, leaving total household work time constant.

Income taxes and welfare payments

There is probably no subject more infused with political rhetoric than the long-standing debate over the impact that income taxes and welfare payments have on the incentive to work. Political conservatives take it as a matter of faith that the high marginal income tax rates faced by affluent people induce them to work less and, thus, rob society of their productivity. Likewise, political conservatives fervently believe that the welfare payments received by the poor blunt their incentive to work and impede their progress to economic independence. Political liberals have argued equally passionately that income taxes do not penalize ambition and welfare payments do not reward laziness and sloth.

Our model of the time use activities of the household is ideally suited to analyzing the effects of both income taxes and welfare payments on the way individuals spend their time. Here we will analyze simple versions of both an income tax and a welfare program to show how the model can be used to shed light on such controversies.

An analysis of an income tax

The federal income tax, even as simplified in the 1986 Tax Reform Act, is much too complex to analyze completely. Instead, a simple proportional income tax similar in spirit to the Social Security tax will be investigated.

Suppose that a simple proportional income tax of $t \cdot 100$ percent (where $0 < t < 1$) is levied on all earned income. The total tax paid by an individual, Tx, is, therefore,

$$Tx = tE = twM, \tag{5.15a}$$

and after-tax income, AY, is

$$AY = E + V - Tx = wM - twM + V = (1 - t)wM + V. \tag{5.15b}$$

The time constraint $M = T - H - L$ can be substituted into (5.15) and expenditures on purchased goods, pC, can be equated with after-tax income to yield the market work portion of the household's budget constraint:

$$pC + (1 - t)wL + (1 - t)wH = (1 - t)wT + V. \tag{5.16}$$

What equation (5.16) makes clear is that the proportional income tax alters the price of time. In the absence of any income tax, the price of time is the wage rate, w, for employed individuals. In the presence of the income tax, however, the price of time is $(1 - t)w$. Since t is a fraction like 0.10 or 0.20, the price of time is lower in the presence of the income tax than in its absence. That being said, we can analyze the imposition of an income tax in exactly the same way as a drop in the wage rate would be analyzed.

The income tax lowers the real wage rate and, therefore, the individual's market productivity from w/p to $(1 - t)w/p$. This reduction induces the individual to substitute household work for market work as market productivity falls below household productivity, g_h. In consequence, through the vehicle of the production substitution effect, the income tax relocates some of the individual's work time from the labor market to the home. Since market work is readily observable and recorded in national statistics whereas household work is not, political conservatives mistakenly believe that work effort has been reduced when, in fact, it simply has been relocated from the office and factory to the home.

The incentives for substitution are not completely encompassed by the production substitution effect, however. The reduction in the price of time due to the income tax rate also lowers the price of leisure relative to goods, inducing a consumption substitution effect. As leisure is made cheaper than goods as a result of the imposition of the income tax, individuals are induced to increase their consumption of leisure and reduce their consumption of purchased goods, holding satisfaction constant. Here, via the consumption substitution effect of the income tax rate, is the reduction in work focused on by political conservatives and ignored by political liberals.

But the effects of the income tax have not yet been exhausted. The reduction in the after-tax wage rate also lowers the individual's real income and induces an income effect too. Since we know that leisure is a normal good, we know that the income effect of the imposition of the income tax is to lower the individual's consumption of leisure, thereby increasing his or her work effort. This effect is ignored by political conservatives and liberals alike.

In reality, of course, the beliefs of both conservatives and liberals are about the total effect of the income tax. Most are unaware of the complexities of substitution and income effects. What is clear, however, is that individuals' responses to income taxes will depend upon their marital status and their gender if the own-wage-rate elasticities discussed earlier in the chapter are applicable to cases in which wage rates are changed by taxes. If so, and most economists believe they are applicable, then we would expect (1) people's work effort to be quite inelastic with respect to changes in income tax rates, (2) men to increase their work effort in the face of increases in income tax rates given their backward-bending labor supply curve, and (3) married women to decrease their work effort. What is clear is that political rhetoric from the Left and from the Right both overstate reality: labor supply responses to income taxes are smaller than conservative ideology states and larger than liberal ideology maintains.

Welfare programs

Programs like Aid to Families with Dependent Children, Supplemental Security Income, and New York State's Home Relief are all examples of welfare programs to provide cash income to families and individuals temporarily destitute and to those with no possibility of supporting themselves completely. These programs are like income tax programs in their complexity. We, therefore, will analyze a simple program that has facets common to all such programs.

Suppose that a simple program is begun that pays D dollars per month to a family if the family has no other source of income.[14] In welfare program language, D is referred to as the "guarantee." To the extent the family does have earnings, however, the monthly welfare payment is reduced by b times \$1.00 for each dollar of monthly earnings. b is typically called the "benefit reduction rate" and is a fraction between 0 and 1. The monthly welfare payment goes to zero and the individual becomes ineligible for the program when earnings reach B dollars per month. B is usually called "break-even income."

The monthly welfare payment formula, then, can be written as

$$N = D - bE \qquad \text{for} \qquad E < B, \tag{5.17a}$$

$$N = 0 \qquad \text{for} \qquad E \geq B \tag{5.17b}$$

where N is the monthly welfare payment to the family and E is monthly family earnings.

Total monthly family income, Y, is the sum of the family's earnings and the monthly welfare payment:

$$Y = E + N = D + (1 - b)wM \qquad \text{for} \qquad E < B, \tag{5.18a}$$

$$Y = E \qquad \text{for} \qquad E \geq B. \tag{5.18b}$$

Given the welfare payment formula (5.18), we can come to a better understanding of break-even income, B. Since $N = 0$ when $E = B$, we can set N equal to 0 and E equal to B in (18a) and solve for B:

$$B = D/b; \tag{5.19}$$

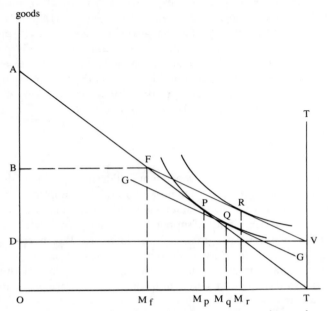

Figure 5.10 The effects of welfare payments on market work

that is, break-even income is the ratio of the guarantee to the benefit reduction rate.

A simple diagram exposes the features of the welfare program and increases understanding of its effects. In Figure 5.10 the focus is entirely on market work, M, measured from right to left on the horizontal axis so that leisure and household work are summed and not considered separately. Also for simplicity, the units of purchased goods are defined so that $p = \$1.00/$unit and we can measure dollars of income on the vertical axis.

Line AT represents the household's budget line in the absence of any welfare program. The slope of AT equals the individual's real wage rate, w. Given there is no program, this individual will maximize satisfaction at point P on AT, work TM_p hours per month, and spend OM_p hours in home activities (leisure and household work).

In the presence of the program the family's budget line is AFV. The distance TV equals the guarantee of D dollars. Thus, the individual would receive a monthly welfare payment of D dollars per month and consume OT leisure if he or she were unemployed. The slope of FV equals $(1 - b)w$, the net wage rate after taking into account the benefit reduction rate. FV meets AT at M_f monthly hours of work, which, at a wage rate of w, earns the break-even income, B. Given the welfare program, this individual maximizes satisfaction at R, working TM hours per month in the labor market and OM_r hours in home activities.

The welfare program has two distinct effects, then. The guarantee, D, operates like an increase in unearned income, shifting the whole budget line upward. The benefit reduction rate serves to reduce the price of time from w to $(1 - b)w$ and, thus, flattens the budget line to the right of point F.

Focus first on the effect of the benefit reduction rate. The benefit reduction rate of the welfare program serves to lower the price of time for eligible families from w to $(1 - b)w$. In this, the benefit reduction rate behaves exactly like an income tax and, in consequence, economists have, at times, angered politicians by calling b a tax rate.[15] So, as the price of the recipient's home time is lowered by the benefit reduction rate, the recipient is induced to substitute home time for market work time, holding satisfaction constant. This is shown in Figure 5.10 as the move from point P to point Q.

Additionally, since the real wage rate is reduced, the recipient's real income falls as a result of the benefit reduction rate and the individual is induced to consume less home time and to work more. The benefit reduction rate will increase or decrease recipients' work effort, therefore, depending on whether the income effect offsets the substitution effect; that is, whether the wage rate elasticity of labor supply is positive or negative. Consequently, we can expect women (by far the majority of the recipients of the Aid to Families with Dependent Children Program) to reduce the time they spend in the labor market as a result of the benefit reduction rate and men to increase their work effort. As with income taxes, however, we can expect the effects to be small given the inelastic own-wage-rate elasticities of men and women.

The effect of the guarantee, D, has not been discussed. For recipients D is simply the same as an increase in nonlabor income. We can expect that the larger the guarantee level built into a welfare program, the less market work recipients will do because of its income effect.

Finally, since the welfare program increases rather than decreases recipients' total income, Y, the income effect due to the guarantee must be larger than the income effect due to the benefit reduction rate. This is shown in the move from Q to R, which contains the two income effects: the increase in work effort due to the decline in income brought about by the benefit reduction rate, and the decline in work effort due to the increase in real income brought about by the guarantee. Consequently, the total effect of the welfare program (the income and substitution effects of the benefit reduction rate and the income effect of the guarantee) will be to reduce the time spent by recipients in market work.

As with their ideological positions on income taxes, the positions of both conservatives and liberals overstate the work disincentive effects of welfare programs. Welfare programs do, indeed, induce recipients to work less than they would in the absence of such programs, to the dismay of doctrinaire

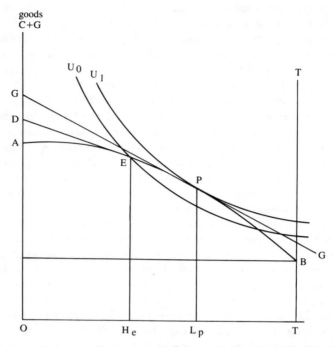

Figure 5.11 Voluntary unemployment and the reservation wage rate

liberals, but the effect is far less than doctrinaire conservatives would like to believe (Danziger, Haveman & Plotnick 1981).

Unemployment, the reservation wage, and the value of time

Voluntary unemployment and the reservation wage

The only kind of unemployment that has been recognized up to this point is *voluntary unemployment.* A person is voluntarily unemployed when the wage rate the person is offered is lower than the person's *reservation wage.* A person's reservation wage rate is that wage rate at which the individual is indifferent between being employed and not. Another way of saying this is that a person is voluntarily unemployed when his or her leisure and household production activities are worth more to the individual than the goods that could be purchased if he or she were employed.

These concepts are illustrated in Figure 5.11. As usual *DEBT* is the individual's total household budget line. The person is in equilibrium at point *P*, at which he spends TL_p hours per week in household work and OL_p hours in leisure activities. Clearly, he would be less satisfied if he did any work at the wage rate employers offer (i.e., the slope of DE): U_0, the indifference curve through point E, where market work would begin if he did any, is well below U_1. The individual is, therefore, voluntarily unemployed. Work is available to him at a wage rate of w/p (the slope of DE), but the wage rate is not sufficiently high to draw him into the labor force.

At point P the individual's marginal rate of substitution of leisure for goods (the slope of U_1 at P) is equal to his household productivity (the slope of $DEBT$ at P). And both are much higher than the wage rate he can command in the labor market (the slope of DE). That is,

$$u_l/u_g|_P = g_h|_P > w/p.$$

In order to emphasize this difference in Figure 5.11, line GG has been drawn through point P and tangent to both $DEBT$ at P and U_1 at P so that the slope of GG can be compared with that of DE: GG is steeper than DE.

What is also clear from Figure 5.11 is that the wage rate the individual is offered in the labor market must be greater than the slope of GG if the individual is to be induced into any market work. Indeed, a real wage rate equal to the slope of GG is the wage rate at which the individual would be indifferent between working an added hour in the household, having an additional hour of leisure, and working the first hour in the labor market. The slope of GG, therefore, is the reservation wage rate.

The value of time and the reservation wage

As a practical matter, empirical measures of the value of time are some of the most sought after numbers in all of economics. The values of the time of unemployed people are especially sought.

Economists are quite interested in the value of the work done in the household. If the goods and services produced in the household could be valued, they could be added to the nation's gross national product and we would have a much better idea of the true wealth and productivity of the nation. Since much of the value of home-produced goods and services is contributed by household work time, an accurate measure of the value of time spent in the household would greatly improve our national economics accounts.

Measures of the value of time are also of great importance in political and legal arenas. The benefits in accident, product liability, and divorce cases all hinge on estimates of the value of time. If, for instance, a housewife or househusband is permanently disabled and no longer can perform household tasks, insurance benefits will depend on the lost value of the individual's time in household work. Likewise, divorce settlements may depend on the relative contributions of the two spouses and their contributions depend on their respective values of time and on how much each worked – in the home and in the labor market. In the political arena it is argued that the Social Security benefits of married women who have never been employed should be linked to the value of their household production. Again, this hinges on the value of the individual's time.

What, then, is the value of an individual's time? The answer is the individual's *opportunity cost of time.*

Definition: The opportunity cost of time is the value of what was forgone in order for the individual to spend his or her time in the manner he or she did.

For the employed person, the opportunity cost of time is his or her wage rate. Recall that in equilibrium

$$u_l/u_g = g_h = w/p$$

for the employed person; that is, the marginal rate of substitution of leisure for goods equals the individual's productivity in household work and also the individual's real wage rate. The employed person, therefore, gives up consuming w/p quantity of goods for each hour spent in leisure activities or in household work. The individual must judge that this sacrifice is worth it, else he or she would alter behavior to reduce the sacrifice. The real wage rate, then, must equal the opportunity cost of time and, thus, be the value of the individual's time either in household work or in leisure activities.

The wage rate the unemployed individual can command in the labor market is lower than the value of his or her time. Recall that for unemployed individuals in equilibrium,

$$u_l/u_g = g_h > w/p,$$

as is shown in Figure 5.11. If this were not true, then the individual would increase satisfaction by spending some time in market work. To use the wage rate unemployed individuals command in the labor market as the measure of the value of their time, then, is to underestimate it.

For the unemployed individual the opportunity cost of the time spent in household work is the value of the forgone leisure the individual could have had. Likewise, the opportunity cost of the time the individual spends in leisure pursuits is the value of the forgone goods and services that could have been produced and consumed had the individual chosen to spend the time in household work instead. What is this value per hour? It is the reservation wage rate. This is clearly seen in Figure 5.11, where the slope of GG (i.e., the real reservation wage rate, w^r/p, where w^r is the reservation wage rate) equals the marginal rate of substitution of leisure for goods (i.e., $u_l/u_g|_P$) and also equals the marginal product of labor in household work (i.e., $g_h|_P$).

Table 5.2. *Estimates of the value of time of married women*

Age of younger child	Employed married woman ($/hr)	Unemployed married woman ($/hr)
12–17	4.69	4.11
6–11	4.37	4.30
2–5	4.29	3.88
1	4.62	3.94
< 1	3.96	3.65
Overall	4.45	3.95

Source: Zick & Bryant 1983. The estimates are for women in two-parent, two-child families living in Syracuse, N.Y., in 1978.

The techniques by which reservation wage rates are estimated have become firmly established in the past decade. One study has estimated the reservation wage rates for employed and unemployed married women in two-parent, two-child families in 1978. The estimates, by age of younger child, are presented in Table 5.2. That the value of time of unemployed married women is lower than that of employed married women ($3.95 vs. $4.45) is consistent with the notion that it is generally those married women who can command higher real wage rates who choose to enter the labor market. That the value of time for housewives rises with the age of the younger child may be due to the fact that women with older children have been married longer, are thereby more experienced in household work, and, therefore, more productive.

Involuntary unemployment

To argue that all unemployment is voluntary is to misrepresent reality; involuntary unemployment does exist. *Involuntary unemployment* occurs when a person is willing to work more hours than they are allowed to work at the wage rate offered by employers. What is the behavior of the family in the face of involuntary unemployment?

Not being able to work as many hours as would be preferred at the offered wage rate implies that the individual would prefer to reduce the amount of time spent in leisure and household work in order to do more market work. Put another way, the individual has more leisure and does more household work that he or she would prefer. The individual's marginal rate of substitution of leisure for goods, u_l/u_g, and the individual's household productivity, g_h, must, therefore, be lower than the individual's real wage rate, w/p. Economic conditions in the labor market, not in the household, prevent the person from shift-

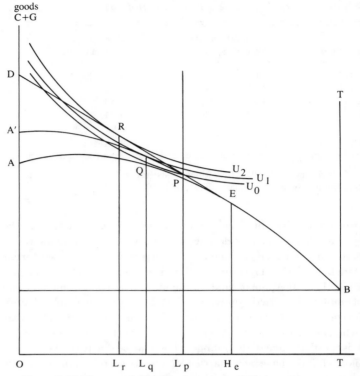

Figure 5.12 Time use during involuntary unemployment

ing hours from the household to the labor market and so equate the value of her time in household activities (leisure and household work) with her real wage rate. Nothing prevents the individual, however, from allocating her time within the household so as to be as satisfied as possible given the unemployment situation. Thus, she will arrange her household activities so as to equate the value of time in leisure activities with the value of time in household work. Consequently, for the involuntarily unemployed person it will be the case that

$$u_l/u_g = g_h < w/p.$$

This is illustrated in Figure 5.12. The total household budget line facing the individual is $DEBT$. In the absence of any constraints on hours worked, the pictured individual would maximize satisfaction at point R on U_2, at which she would spend TH_e hours per week doing household work, H_eL_r hours per week in market work, and OL_r hours per week in leisure activities.

What she prefers cannot be realized, however. Given conditions in the labor market, she can work only $H_e L_p$ hours in the labor market; more hours are not available. At point P the slope of U_0 is less than the slope of DE; that is,

$$u_l/u_g|_P < w/p = g_h|_P.$$

Clearly, she would give up additional leisure (a maximum of $L_p L_r$ hours) if she could work more hours per week. Although she cannot work more hours in the labor market, she can do more household work and will, since her marginal rate of substitution of leisure for goods ($u_l/u_g|_P$) is less than the marginal product of her time in household work ($g_h|_E$). She will continue to exchange leisure for household work until her marginal rate of substitution of leisure for goods equals her household productivity; that is, until

$$u_l/u_g = g_h < w/p.$$

Geometrically, this occurs at point Q. How is point Q determined? Since involuntary unemployment induces the individual to do more household work than she would prefer had she a choice, she must do more household work than TH_e. How much more depends on the relationship between the marginal productivity of her time in household work (i.e., the slope of the household production function) and her relative preference for leisure (i.e., the slopes of her indifference curves).

To find out how much more household work (and how much less leisure) she will do, one must take the AE portion of the household production function and shift it up to point P, where it becomes $A'P$. Any additional household work performed, then, is measured along $A'P$ beginning at P. The individual will maximize satisfaction, given the restrictions in the labor market, at point Q, where she is more satisfied than at point P ($U_1 > U_0$) but less satisfied than at point R ($U_1 < U_2$). At Q she will work $H_e L_p$ hours per week in the labor market, work $TH_e + L_p L_q$ hours per week in household production, and have OL_q hours of leisure.

Is such behavior reasonable? Certainly. Faced with involuntary unemployment, people do not simply lie around the house "doing nothing" with the excess time ($L_p L_r$) at their disposal. Instead, they will spend some of it ($L_p L_q$) in various productive activities: gardening, painting and fixing up, lawn and car maintenance, etc. The rest ($L_q L_r$) will be spent in added leisure activities.

Time allocation over the life cycle

To this point in the chapter we have discussed time allocation in a single period in the same sense that Chapters 2 and 3 discussed the demands for goods and services in a single period. But as Chapter 4 made clear, people make decisions about their consumption of goods and services today in the light of what they expect in the future. If this is true with respect to the consumption of goods and

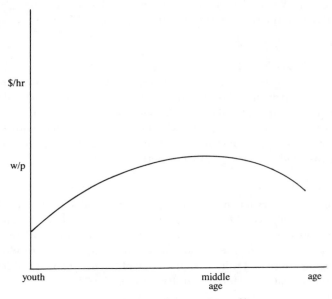

Figure 5.13 Typical age–real wage rate profile

services, then it should be the case with respect to time allocation as well, since leisure and home-produced goods are "goods" too.

What, then, might be said about the demands for home time ($H + L$) and consumption (in the sense used in Chapter 4) over the life cycle? Do people demand more home time and less consumption during some periods in their lives and less home time and more consumption in other periods in accordance with their expectations as to how expensive home time will be in the future relative to goods? The answer is yes; it appears to be the case. The question, of course, is why.

It is a common expectation of people that the wage rates they command will increase as they grow older. They also expect that their earning power will flatten out or fall as they reach and pass middle age and approach retirement. These expectations are with respect to their "real" wage rates, w/p, not simply their money wage rates, w. In fact, such expectations are realistic, for this is exactly how real wage rates move as individuals grow older. Figure 5.13 illustrates the typical relationship between age and the real wage or earning power; the curve rises to middle age and falls after middle age. The more education an individual possesses, the more rapid is the rise and the less rapid is the fall.

Faced with such expectations, how would a satisfaction-maximizing individual plan his or her pattern of consumption and home time over the life cycle? At each age such an individual would seek to equate his or her marginal rate of substitution of home time for consumption with the market rate of exchange of home time for consumption at that age (see Chapter 2); that is,

$$(u_l/u_c)_a = (w/p)_a \qquad (5.20)$$

where $(u_l/u_c)_a$ is the individual's marginal rate of substitution of home time for consumption at age a, $(w/p)_a$ is his or her wage rate or earning power at age a, u_l is his or her marginal utility of home time at age a, and u_c is his or her marginal utility of consumption at age a.

As the individual's age increases, earning power, w/p, rises, making home time more expensive relative to consumption. In response, the individual will substitute consumption for home time and, in so doing, reduce u_c and increase u_l to equate his or her marginal rate of substitution with his or her real wage rate. As a result the individual's demand for consumption will rise and the demand for home time will fall (i.e., hours of paid employment will increase).

The process of substituting consumption for home time and thereby increasing annual hours worked as w/p rises with age will continue until middle age, when the individual's real wage flattens out and begins to fall. At that point, the process of substitution will reverse: the individual will begin to work less and take more home time per year and his or her consumption will begin to fall (i.e., saving will begin to rise). On either side of middle age the individual will substitute the good becoming cheaper for the good becoming more expensive. From youth through middle age, home time gets more expensive relative to consumption, whereas after middle age home time becomes less expensive relative to consumption.

In other words, the satisfaction-maximizing individual will emphasize household activities (household work and leisure activities) when time is relatively cheap and emphasize the consumption of purchased goods when time is expensive. Such an individual's youth is devoted to education, which is preeminently a time-intensive activity. The prime of such a person's life is devoted to paid employment and goods-intensive activities. Old age is spent in time-intensive, household activities.

The evidence for this intertemporal substitution of leisure for consumption is accumulating. The first study addressing the question of leisure over the life cycle was conducted by Ghez and Becker (1975) and based on 1960 census data. Figure 5.14 is taken from their study and shows five-year moving averages of hourly earnings and hours worked per year by age for employed white males. Clearly evident is the rise in hours worked per year with age as age and the real wage rate both increase and the ultimate fall in hours worked as wage rates flatten out and ultimately fall.

Ghez and Becker (1975) estimate that the wage rate elasticity of annual home time across the life cycle for white males is −0.12: that is, a 10 percent increase

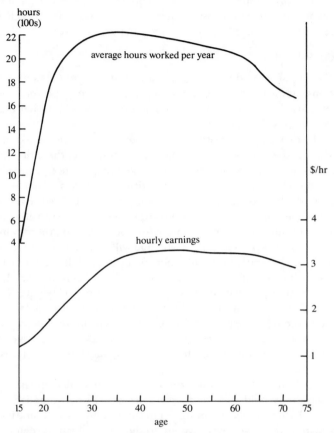

Figure 5.14 5-yr. moving averages of hourly earnings and average hours worked per year for employed white males in the United States in 1960 (*source:* Reprinted, by permission, from Ghez & Becker 1975, Figure 3.1, p. 85)

(decrease) in the real wage rate induces a 1.2 percent fall (rise) in annual home time. Thus, as white males' real wage rates rise as they grow older, they reduce the amount of home time they consume annually. Conversely, as real wage rates fall when they are in middle to late middle age, they begin to increase the time they spend in household production and leisure time activities. Over their life cycle it does appear that white men work when their wage rates are high and spend their time in other activities when their time is cheap. The analogous wage rate elasticity for black males is − 0.05. The same tendency is present but the responsiveness to wage rate changes is much less. The reasons for this decreased responsiveness are not clear.

Summary

In contrast to the preceding chapters, which focused upon the demand for goods and services and assumed that household income was fixed, this chapter has demonstrated that the household does have some control over its income by deciding when, where, and how much to work. Depending on individuals' market and household productivities and their preferences for consumption and leisure, individuals allocate their available time among market work, household work, and leisure pursuits. Consequently, as their market and household productivities change $(w/p$ and $g_h)$, they trade off household work and market work and change the time they spend in leisure activities.

Throughout this chapter we have assumed that wage rates are set by employers and that employees have no control over them. Likewise, we have assumed household productivities are totally determined by the state of technology and not affected by individuals' behavior other than the amount of time devoted to household production. Neither assumption is very realistic, however, because we can and do have great influence over what we are paid for our market work and over how productive we are in household work activities. Chapter 6 discusses these issues.

CHAPTER SIX

Human capital: investing in oneself and one's family

Fully 24 percent of the U.S. population, 60.1 million people, were enrolled in school in 1986. Of those in school, 4 percent were in nursery schools, 52 percent were enrolled in kindergarten or elementary schools, 23 percent were enrolled in high schools, and 21 percent were enrolled in institutions of higher education (U.S. Bureau of the Census 1989, Table 205, p. 127). These numbers exclude the millions of people who took private lessons in everything from sewing to music, from religion to skiing and hang gliding. The United States devoted 6.7 percent of its gross national product, $169.6 billion, to schools and schooling in 1980. Of this sum, $142.6 billion was spent on school operating expenses (including fees, tuition, and interest on debts), and $9.6 billion was spent on capital outlays (U.S. Bureau of the Census 1982, Table 213, p. 135). These figures ignore the billions of dollars of potential income students chose not to earn by virtue of their being in schools and colleges. The facts show that Americans spend great amounts of time and money investing in themselves.

What goes on under one's very nose is frequently noticed and dealt with long after things more remote. So it is with human capital. Although people (and even economists) have been investing in themselves and their children for as long as there have been people (or economists), economists have paid serious attention to the fact only in the past thirty years. Although economists have striven to understand households' saving behavior, they neglected until lately the process by which people invest in themselves, one of the most important ways of saving.

We do not yet have a full grasp of the magnitude of the nation's capital stock held in human form. Nor are the implications of saving by investing in oneself or one's family fully understood. It is clear, however, that the concept of human capital has been and is central to the understanding of the economic organization of the household. Consequently, this chapter is devoted to an introduction of the concept and to some of the ways that it has shed light on family behavior.

Most introductory treatments of human capital focus on the demand for education and the roles that schooling and experience play in influencing the

168

labor market behavior of individuals. Because of the focus of this text on the household and the recognition that its behavior in the labor market is only one of its many activities, some of the non-labor-market implications of human capital will also be addressed.

Human capital as saving

In Chapter 4 we dealt with a two-period model (today and tomorrow) in which the household balances the demands for consumption today against the demands for future consumption. Depending on the household's time preference (i.e., the marginal rate of substitution of today's consumption for tomorrow's), the market rate of interest, and expected changes in prices (i.e., the expected rate of inflation or deflation), the household puts aside a fraction of its current income for use in the future. The equilibrium condition expressing this decision is that the household equates the rate at which it is willing to exchange present for future consumption with the rate at which it can do so in the marketplace. This is expressed concisely by the equilibrium condition

$$u_1/u_2 = (1 + r)/(1 + g) \tag{6.1}$$

where u_t ($t = 1, 2$) denotes the marginal utility of consumption in period t, and therefore, u_1/u_2 represents the household's marginal rate of substitution of present consumption for future consumption; r is the rate of interest, g is the expected rate of inflation (deflation), and therefore, $(1 + r)/(1 + g)$ is the market rate of exchange of present consumption for future consumption. You will recall that u_1/u_2 is the slope of the highest indifference curve attainable by the family with the resources it has available, and $(1 + r)/(1 + g)$ is the slope of the household's intertemporal budget line (see Figure 4.4, Chapter 4).

The process just summarized determines the total amount that the household plans to save but it leaves unanswered the question of how. What form will the saving take? Will the household augment its savings account, buy added stocks and bonds, buy a house or improve one it owns, pay off some of its debts, or invest in family members?

Investing in family members – that is, investing in human capital – can take many different forms. The most recognized way to invest in human capital is through *formal schooling*. Additional education usually means additional study for a degree or for a high school diploma, but there are, in fact, a bewildering array of ways to augment one's formal schooling and a bewildering array of purposes for which formal schooling is relevant. These range from added schooling to complete requirements for a degree to a two-week class in word processing, knitting, painting, or ways of saying no.

One can also invest in human capital through *on-the-job training and experience* either in one's market job or in a household activity. Here, one takes time

out from one's job or from a household activity (or does it more slowly, deliber-
ately, and reflectively) in order to learn how to do it better. In so doing, one may
have to accept a somewhat lower current income or accept lower current output
from the household activity in order to increase one's productivity in the long
run. In the case of market work, the difference between the income earned
while receiving on-the-job training and what would have been received if one
had not engaged in the training is the amount saved or invested in human
capital via experience. In the case of a household activity, the forgone output
from the household activity constitutes the investment in human capital in the
form of experience.

Another way of investing in human capital is by spending time and money in
maintaining and augmenting one's *health.* Just as one invests in a car or a house
by repairing it and making improvements on it, one invests in health by maintaining and augmenting one's physical and mental health. Thus, aerobics
classes, jogging, physician visits, annual dental checkups, and good nutrition are
all means to invest in our health. The results are fewer days of sickness per year,
longer life expectancy, and higher productivity on the job and in household
activities.

Formal education, experience, and health are only the three most obvious
types of human capital investments. Another is *migration* from one city, state, or
country to another in search of a better job or a different life-style. The issue,
here, is that one forsakes the opportunities in one location in order to exploit
those in another. The millions of people – our parents, grandparents, and
great-grandparents – who left home and families in other countries to carve out
new lives in North America all were making large investments in human capital
by migrating. So too were the millions of people who have migrated from farms
to cities in search of better lives and livelihoods during the twentieth century.

But there are more subtle ways of investing in human capital. Having children and raising them in particular ways may, in part, be ways by which a couple
can provide for economic security in old age. This motive is very minor or
absent in developed countries, which have other ways of providing economic
security for elderly people, but it cannot be dismissed if one is to understand
fertility behavior in less developed countries. Fertility behavior – the demand
for children – is discussed more fully in Chapter 7. Marriage has been described by a wag as one of the few gambles fainthearted people take. It is also
one of the few ways by which very poor people can invest: one gives up the
advantages of remaining single for the future benefits of being married.
Marriage and divorce are analyzed in this fashion in Chapter 8.

Having surveyed the types of investments in human capital, we can return to
the question of the form in which the household will save: will it save in the form
of physical capital (a new car, a house), financial capital (bank accounts, stocks
and bonds, or lowering of debts), or human capital? As usual, this decision is

most easily understood through simplification. We simplify by assuming that the household can save only in the form of financial or human capital and the motive for saving is to maximize total wealth.[1] We will begin our discussion of human capital by examining it in the context of the labor market, and we will first consider only one type of human capital: formal schooling.

Human capital and the labor market

A major reason individuals invest in human capital through formal schooling is to augment their income in the future and so to increase their total wealth. Suppose, initially, that additional schooling increases an individual's productivity in the labor market, and employers, recognizing this, pay higher wage rates to individuals with more formal schooling. Consider an individual concerned only with the monetary payoff to formal schooling. Such an individual will invest in added schooling only if the payoff to added schooling is higher than or, at the margin, is equal to the payoff in alternative investments. In the simple case being analyzed, the only alternative to formal schooling is financial investments (stocks, bonds, savings accounts, etc.) at the going market rate of interest, r. The individual, will, then, compare the "rate of return" from added schooling with the market rate of interest, r, and invest in the opportunity with the higher rate of return. If formal schooling initially has the higher rate of return, the individual will maximize his or her wealth by continuing to invest in schooling until the rate of return on schooling has been driven down to the market rate of interest.

The rate of return on education

What is the rate of return on schooling? *Formally, it is the interest rate that equates the cost of the investment with the present value of the stream of future benefits from the investment.* We can define the rate of return to the investment (the so-called internal rate of return) more precisely through an example.

Suppose that Bob is contemplating a final year of high school at age eighteen and expects to retire at sixty-five. Let Bob's annual earnings in year t without the added year of school be E_t and his annual earnings in year t with the added year of schooling be E_t', where $E_t' > E_t$.

The cost of the added year of school for Bob has two components: the earnings Bob forgoes while he is in school for the final year rather than working at a paid job, E_0; and the out-of-pocket costs of the final year of school (such as tuition, fees, and books), C. Denote the cost of the added year of school by MC, standing for marginal cost. Then,

$$MC = E_0 + C \qquad (6.2)$$

where $t = 0$ is Bob's eighteenth year.

The benefit to Bob from the added year of school is the difference between:
(1) the future stream of annual earnings Bob expects given he has the added
year of schooling and (2) the future stream of annual earnings Bob expects if he
does not have the added year of schooling. The stream of differences is

Year	1	t	n
Bob's age	19	$18 + t$	65
Difference	$(E_1' - E_1), \ldots,$	$(E_t' - E_t), \ldots,$	$(E_n' - E_n)$

where n = the expected number of years until retirement.

Now find the interest rate, i, that equates the present value of the expected
stream of benefits from the added year of schooling with the cost of the added
year of school:

$$\sum_{t=1}^{n} (E_t' - E_t)/(1 + i)^t = MC = E_o + C. \tag{6.3}$$

Then i is the *rate of return* on the investment in the added year of school. If i is
greater than the market rate of interest on financial investments, r, Bob will
increase his net wealth by getting the added year of formal schooling. If $i = r$,
Bob will be indifferent between investing in financial capital or human capital.

Here, then, is the answer to the question concerning which form saving will
take: it will take the form of the investment with the higher rate of return. In
equilibrium, when the household is maximizing its total wealth, the rates of
return on competing types of investment – financial, physical, and human –
will all be equal.[2]

One can calculate the rate of return for each possible year of schooling Bob
may take beginning with kindergarten. There are three prominent reasons why
the rate of return to schooling, i, will decline with each added year of school.
One raises the marginal costs, and two lower the marginal benefits of added
schooling.

First, each additional year of schooling increases the opportunity cost of any
succeeding years of schooling, E_0 in the marginal cost formula, because the
wage rates employers are prepared to pay employees rise with education. Suppose, for instance, that people with grade 11 are paid \$7.00/hr. and high school
graduates earn \$8.00/hr. On the basis of a 2,000-hr. year, these translate into
annual earnings of \$14,000 and \$16,000, respectively. Consequently, the individual who completes grade 12 forgoes \$14,000 whereas the individual who
completes the first year of college forgoes \$16,000 for the added year of school.
Clearly, then, the marginal cost of schooling rises with additional schooling as
E_0, rises, and this will depress the rate of return, i.[3]

Second, each additional year of schooling reduces the remaining years during
which an individual works, shortening the expected stream of benefits of added

schooling and reducing the marginal benefit. This can easily be seen in equation (6.3). With added years of schooling, the sum,

$$\sum_{t=1}^{n} (E'_t - E_t)/(1 + i)^t,$$

becomes smaller because the remaining working life becomes shorter. The smaller the marginal benefit, of course, the lower the interest rate must be that equates the present value of the benefits with the marginal cost.

Third, the principle of diminishing marginal productivity also operates to reduce the marginal benefits. Recall that the principle of diminishing marginal productivity states that, holding other inputs in a production process constant, the marginal product of a particular input will fall as more of the input is used. The particular application of this principle here is that additional years of education are applied to a single individual who is in a real sense fixed. Consequently, an individual's productivity per hour in the labor market will rise with additional education but at a declining rate. If, as in the previous example, the twelfth year of schooling raises Bob's annual labor productivity from $14,000 to $16,000 (an increase of $2,000), the thirteenth year may increase it by only $1,500, to $17,500. Thus, the more schooling an individual already has, the lower the marginal benefit of an additional year. Therefore, this, too, means that as the number of years of schooling rises, the rate of return to additional education falls.

The demand curve for formal education

The fact that the rate of return to schooling falls as the number of years of schooling rises allows one to plot an individual's demand for formal schooling as in Figure 6.1. The number of years of schooling demanded by the individual is plotted along the horizontal axis, and the rate of return to schooling, i, as well as the market rate of interest on financial investments, r, are plotted on the vertical axis.

Line DD shows the rate of return yielded for each year of schooling obtained by the individual. For instance, the rate of return to S_a years of schooling is i_a. Line DD slopes downward to the right, indicating that the rate of return to education falls as the number of years of schooling rises.

Also in Figure 6.1 is a horizontal line, rr. It represents the market rate of return on financial investments. Line rr is horizontal because the market rate of return on financial investments does not depend on how many years of schooling are being "purchased." The wealth-maximizing individual will invest in formal schooling until the rate of return to education is driven down to the rate of return on alternative investments. Consequently, the wealth-maximiz-

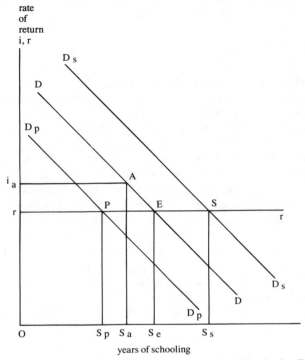

Figure 6.1 An individual's demand curve for formal schooling

ing individual possessing *DD* in Figure 6.1 will "demand" S_e years of schooling when the rate of return on financial investments is r. He would demand more education only if the market rate of interest were lower. Line *DD*, then, is the individual's demand curve for formal education.

DD is the demand curve for formal schooling for the wealth-maximizing individual, the individual who goes to school only for the increase in future income more education promises. There are, however, few such people. Most people either like or dislike school. What are their demand curves for education like?

Consider an individual who likes school (a student[4]) and, therefore, derives satisfaction as well as future income from schooling. Such an individual will attend school until the marginal benefit of added schooling equals the marginal cost. But, compared with the wealth-maximizing individual, the marginal cost of the added education to the "student" is less, and therefore, his or her rate of return for any given number of school years will be higher. That is,

$$MB = \sum_{t=1}^{n} (E'_t - E_t)/(1 + i)^t = E_o + C - V_s = MC \qquad (6.4)$$

where MB = marginal benefit and V_s = the dollar value of the added satisfaction the student obtains from an added year of school. As V_s becomes larger, MC falls, and i must be greater in order to equate MB with MC. Consequently, the demand curve for a student will lie above that for a wealth maximizer. The demand curve for such a person is represented in Figure 6.1 by $D_s D_s$. Faced with the same array of alternative financial investments and, hence, the same r, the student will invest in more schooling (S_s rather than S_e) than the wealth maximizer.[5]

In contrast, the individual who dislikes school (a pupil[6]) derives added wealth from an additional year of school but faces an added cost in terms of the added displeasure with school. Denoting the dollar value of the added dissatisfaction experienced by a pupil as V_d, the rate of return to education calculation becomes

$$MB = \sum_{t=1}^{n} (E'_t - E_t)/(1 + i)^t = E_o + C + V_d = MC. \qquad (6.5)$$

V_d inflates the marginal cost of schooling, implying that i here must be lower than i for the wealth maximizer in order to equate the marginal benefits with the marginal costs. For any given number of years of schooling, therefore, the rate of return to education for a pupil will be lower than that for a wealth maximizer. Consequently, the demand curve for schooling will be lower than that for the wealth maximizer; see $D_p D_p$ in Figure 6.1. Faced with the same market rate of interest, r, the pupil will demand fewer years of school, S_p, than either the wealth maximizer or the student.

Experience as a form of human capital

If formal schooling were the only way by which human capital was augmented, then the earnings of full-time employees would not rise with age after adjusting for prices. Yet one of the most common expectations people possess, and one of the best documented facts about earnings, is that they rise with age to late middle age or beyond and then flatten out or decline to retirement. Why?

According to neoclassical economic theory employers pay employees a real wage rate equal to their marginal productivity to the employer; that is,

$$w/p = MP \qquad (6.6)$$

where MP is the marginal product of the employee's labor in the employer's production process.[7] Now, education will raise the employee's marginal product in market employment, resulting in higher real wages. This explains why more highly educated people earn more than the less well educated. But once formal education has been completed, why would a forty-year-old high school graduate earn more than a twenty-year-old high school graduate? A good answer is "experience." Either through on-the-job training or learning-by-doing, the individual's marginal productivity, MP, continues to grow, and as it grows, real wage rates and, hence, earnings continue to rise.

There are two kinds of experience, *general* and *specific*. General experience raises the MP of an individual in all firms, whereas specific experience increases the individual's MP only in the firm where the experience is gained. Examples of general experience are work habits, personnel skills, problem-solving skills, and general skills of the trade or occupation that increase an individual's productivity for any employer. Examples of specific experience are knowledge of one company's administrative and accounting decision structures and personnel policies and experience with equipment that is used only by one particular firm.[8]

Employers have no incentive to pay the costs of general experience gained by employees, because they can leave after gaining the experience, taking the investment in human capital with them. Not reaping the benefits of general experience, employers visit the costs of general experience on their employees in the form of lower wage rates during the periods general experience is gained.

Because the investment in specific experience raises employees' labor productivity only in the firm in which the specific experience is gained, other employers will not pay them higher wages because of it. Consequently, even though a company's employees' MP is higher by virtue of the specific experience, the company has no incentive to pay them more for their specific experience. Employers reap the gains, therefore, from the investments in specific experience gained by their employees. On their part, employees will not accept lower wages while they are gaining specific experience, because they will reap no benefits from it in the future. And if employers did try to pay them less during the period in which they gain specific experience, the employees could respond by finding work elsewhere at a higher wage rate.[9]

In general, however, the individual reaps the benefits and pays the cost of any general experience gained on the job. How much experience will the individual choose to gain? The answer is the same as for formal schooling: more experience on the job will be gained until the marginal benefits of added experience are driven down to the level of the marginal costs of the added experience. Put differently, the individual will gain more experience until the rate of return on added experience is driven down to the rate of return on alternative investments.

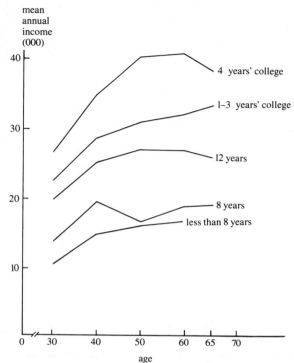

Figure 6.2 Median annual earnings of full-time, full-year male workers in 1985 by education and age (*sources:* U.S. Bureau of the Census, *Money Income of Households, Families and Persons in the United States: 1985,* Current Population Reports P-60, no. 156 [Washington: U.S. Government Printing Office, 1987], Table 35)

So long as the individual continues to gain experience on the job, therefore, the individual's market productivity, w/p, will increase and, with it, annual earnings. Since human capital via experience accumulates with the passage of time, earnings will increase with age. At the point at which the rate of return to experience is driven down to the rate of return on alternative investments, further learning will cease. Past that point the individual will cease to learn more about his or her job and his or her earnings will no longer increase with age. If human capital obsolescence and depreciation becomes important, then the individual's MP will begin to fall and with it earnings.[10]

Formal schooling and experience, then, explain an important part of the age–earnings profiles of individuals. Figures 6.2 and 6.3 illustrate age–earnings profiles by education for males (Figure 6.2) and females (Figure 6.3) for the

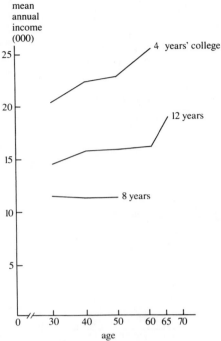

Figure 6.3 Median annual earnings of full-time, full-year female workers in 1985 by education and age (*source:* see Figure 6.2)

year 1985. The figures chart the median annual earnings of full-time, full-year workers. Consequently, the differences must be due to differences in wage rates and not differences in annual hours worked. The shapes of the age–earnings profiles are typical: for males, the higher the level of education, the steeper the rise in earnings with age; for females, annual earnings do not rise much with age. The differences among people in their earnings, therefore, are importantly explained by education and experience (see Mincer 1974).

Much of the difference between the male and female age–earnings profiles is explained by differences in the labor force participation behavior by age between males and females. Males tend to enter the labor force upon completing school and not leave until retirement. The labor market experience of men, therefore, is highly correlated with age. Not so for females. Some females tend to drop out of the labor market when they marry and do not return unless they are divorced or widowed. More drop out to give birth to children and return to the labor market when adequate child day care is found or when their children enter school. Consequently, the labor market experience of females is not as highly correlated with age.

Many analysts have estimated rates of return to education and experience. Willis (1986, Table 10.2, p. 537) surveys the recent literature and reports estimates of the rate of return to higher education (four years of college) of 8–9 percent in the late 1970s and early 1980s and estimates of the rate of return to secondary education of 11 percent for the mid-1970s. Although somewhat dated, Mincer's analysis of experience is the most thorough. He obtained estimates of the rate of return to experience for nonfarm white males in 1960 of between 6 percent and 12 percent (1974, p. 94).

It is very clear that the results of human capital formation activities – formal schooling and experience – are important and explain much of the differences among people in their real wage rates. But the impacts of human capital are not restricted to their effects on the market productivities of men and women. Acquiring human capital is an important household activity in its own right and it has important effects on the conduct of other household activities. Consequently, we must now consider human capital formation as a household activity and in so doing expand the simple view of the household developed in Chapter 5.

Human capital as a household activity

The picture developed in Chapter 5 is of a household in which the individual engages in three major activities: market work, household production, and leisure. The individual's decision as to how much time to spend in each of these three activities was based on the real wage rate that employers would be willing to pay, w/p, the individual's productivity in household production, g^h, and the individual's relative preference for leisure versus goods (whether purchased or homemade), u_l/u_c.

In this picture individuals have no control over the real wage rate at which they can work in the labor market and no control over their productivity in household activities. Although such a view may be correct in the very short run, we now see that it is seriously deficient in the longer run. A more accurate picture would be that individuals have considerable control over their market productivity and, hence, their income. Not only can people control their income by the number of hours they choose to be employed, but they can also control the wage rate at which they are employed by means of the time and other resources invested in human capital formation; the more time and other resources devoted to human capital formation, the higher future wage rates can be. Furthermore, individuals also exercise control over their household productivity – again, by the amount of investment that is made in human capital.

Rather than three possible activities in which people may participate, there are actually four: market work, household production, leisure, and *human capital formation*. Human capital formation is a separate household activity when it takes place via formal schooling. Human capital formation also occurs in conjunction with market work when the investment takes the form of market work experience. Investment in human capital also takes place in conjunction with household production when the formation takes the form of household production experience. Since we have argued that people invest in human capital for the purpose of increasing their capacity to engage in leisure activities (e.g., skiing, swimming, tennis lessons), it finally must be recognized that human capital formation occurs in conjunction with leisure in the form of leisure experience.

The required expansion of the model in Chapter 5 to include human capital formation goes beyond the limits imposed by this text. A complete treatment of human capital in all its guises and dealing with all its effects requires a book. We can explore several applications of the human capital model here, however. We begin with a more detailed discussion of formal education.

Study time, part-time work, and academic performance

College is a time and place where intensive human capital formation occurs. Students come to college to learn a body of knowledge (among other things!). In order to learn they attend classes and study. But the out-of-pocket costs of college are high, and students frequently work part-time in order to help pay tuition and fees and to buy books.[11] Studying and working part-time both require time, and therefore, the student must trade one off against the other.

Implicit in the trade-off between studying and part-time work is the trade-off between academic performance and future consumption: by working part-time during college, students can sacrifice some academic performance in order to reduce the size of their student loans and so reduce their future loan payments after graduation. At all events, there is a presumed link between studying and academic performance on the one hand and, on the other, the very real time constraint in which, if one works part-time, one has less time for other things, including studying. What are the empirical magnitudes of these relationships?

Recent research has been done at Cornell University with respect to Cornell students to estimate the relationships and identify some of the trade-offs. Pappalardo (1986) theorized that, ceteris paribus, the more time students spend studying during a semester, the better their academic performance would be. The productivity of the student's time spent studying in terms of producing academic performance, however, would be conditioned by when during the semester the studying was done (i.e., early or late in the semester), the course load carried by the student, the program in which the student was registered (some programs grade harder than others), and the student's personal characteristics. Consequently, the student's academic performance production function is, according to Pappalardo,

$$GP = a(H_e, H_l, Z_s) \tag{6.7}$$

where GP = academic performance during the semester, H_e = weekly study time early in the semester, H_l = weekly study time late in the semester, and Z_s = a vector of the student's personal characteristics and program characteristics. Academic performance, GP, was measured by the student's total grade point (*not* the average), where the total grade point is the sum over all the courses taken by the student during the semester of the credits earned per course multiplied by the numerical grade earned per course:

$$GP = \sum_{i=1}^{n} c_i g_i \tag{6.8}$$

where c_i = number of credits earned in course i, g_i = numerical grade earned for course i, and n = number of courses taken during the semester. GP automatically takes account of the total number of courses taken, whereas a student's grade point average (GPA) averages out the credit load.

A random sample of Cornell sophomores, juniors, and first-semester seniors during the fall semester of 1984 was used to study three relationships: (1) the students' supply of time to part-time work during the semester, (2) the students' supply of study time (study time includes time spent in classes, recitation sections, and labs as well as the time spent studying outside class) both early and late in the semester, and (3) the students' academic performance production function (i.e., an estimate of equation [6.7]).

With respect to part-time work behavior, the findings were as follows.

1. An increase in the part-time wage rate by $1.00/hr. induces the average Cornell student to reduce the average weekly hours spent working part-time by 0.19 hr./wk. Students' labor supply is backward bending, therefore.

2. An increase of $1,000 in the amount of the student loan possessed by the student lowers the average weekly hours the student spends working part-time by roughly 0.5 hr./wk. Additional income earned over the summer also reduces weekly part-time work. Clearly, part-time work is an inferior good.

With respect to study behavior, the findings were as follows.

1. An increase in the part-time wage rate of $1.00/hr. induces the average student to reduce study time by roughly 5 min./wk. Thus, a wage rate increase induces Cornell students not only to work less but also to study less. The time released from working and studying is spent in leisure activities.

2. An increase of $1,000 in student loans increases the student's weekly

study time by about 12 min./wk. Additional income earned over the summer also increases study time. Studying is, therefore, a normal good. That is, students use summer earnings and student loans "to buy" study time.

3. An increase by 1 hr./wk. in the amount of time the student spends working reduces the amount of time the student spends studying by about 12 min./wk. Students do trade off work against studying but at a rate far below one for one.

With respect to academic performance, time spent studying was broken down into that occurring prior to Thanksgiving ("early" studying) and that occurring after Thanksgiving ("late" studying).

1. An increase in the amount of early studying by 1 hr./wk. increases the average student's total grade point by 0.051 points.

2. An increase in the amount of late studying by 1 hr./wk. decreases the average student's total grade point by 0.5 points.

3. The above two results suggest that students tend to overstudy late in the semester and understudy early in the semester. The average student could increase his or her academic performance by increasing the amount of studying done early in the term and reducing it by a like amount late in the term! The timing of studying during the semester is as important as how much is done in total.

4. A student's academic performance in previous semesters positively affects the student's current academic performance. A student's past performance is an index of the stock of human capital he or she brings to the job of studying in the current semester: the greater the stock of human capital possessed by the student, the more productive the student is in gaining more.

There are several implications of these results when put together.

1. There is a trade-off between academic performance and part-time work: an increase of 1 hr./wk. of part-time work reduces a student's total grade point by 0.09 grade points. This comes about either because the student who does more part-time work must reduce the number of credits taken or because the student obtains lower grades.

2. Just as the timing of study time during the semester is important, so is the timing of part-time work. An hour more part-time work per week early in the semester and an hour less later in the semester turns out to be counterproductive: the average student's grade point will suffer.

3. Student loans do increase academic performance in that students use the money to reduce part-time work, buy study time, and increase their total grade point. Pappalardo estimates that an added $1,000 of student loans translates into an increase in the average student's semester performance of 0.5 grade points. On average, then, the recent policy of the federal government of reducing the amount of student loans tends to lower the academic performance of Cornell students.

The timing of formal schooling and experience

It appears from the Pappalardo study (1986) of Cornell students that a model combining human capital formation with labor supply behavior explains an important part of their behavior during college. Buy why are college students typically young? More generally, why do people tend to invest in human capital, in the form of schooling or experience, when young and to reduce their investments in human capital as they grow older?

The marginal benefit equals marginal cost condition,

$$MB = \sum_{t=1}^{n} (E'_t - E_t)/(1 + i)^t = E_0 + C = MC, \qquad (6.9)$$

that directs human capital investments reveals three reasons.

1. The older the individual, the fewer remaining years left (i.e., the smaller is n in equation [6.9]) for the investment in human capital to pay off in terms of either higher labor market earnings or greater household production of goods and services. Thus, the later in life the investment in human capital is made, the lower the marginal returns and, ceteris paribus, the less likely it will be made.

2. The farther into the future any investment in human capital is postponed, the lower the present value of the returns on the investment and, therefore, the lower the marginal benefits. The lower the marginal benefits from the postponed investment, the less likely it will be postponed. When human capital formation is postponed, say five years, the index, t, begins at $t = 6$ rather than $t = 1$ in equation (6.9). Consequently, the returns to future investments are discounted more than present ones.

A simple example will clarify this point. Suppose a given investment in human capital, such as an added year of school, would increase annual earnings by $500/yr. whether the investment is made immediately or five years hence. At a market rate of interest equal to 10 percent, the present value of the first year's return on the investment when made immediately is $500/(1.10)^2 = $413.22 because the investment takes a year to make plus a year to receive the first annual return of $500. If the investment were to be postponed for five years, the present value of the first year's return on the investment would be $5,700/(1.1)^6 = $282.24. Postponing human capital formation lowers the marginal benefits.

3. The farther into the future an investment in human capital is postponed, the more experience will have been gained in the interim, and the higher the opportunity cost of the investment when it is made. Consequently, the marginal costs of postponed human capital investments rise the more they are postponed, and therefore, the less likely it will be that they will be postponed. In terms of equation (6.9), the farther into the future any human capital investment is postponed, the higher E_0 becomes through experience, raising the marginal cost of the investment.

For these reasons, then, we can expect most people to obtain their formal schooling when young and to accumulate experience at a declining rate as they grow older. For some people past a certain age, depreciation and obsolescence exceed their investments in human capital through experience and, in consequence, their total human capital stock declines with each passing year. This phenomenon is most easily observed in the relationship between age and physical health. Although more difficult to observe, it is present nonetheless with respect to mental acuity.

Expectations and the sex typing of human capital investments

Parents and society at large see to it that children invest in themselves to augment their productivity in the labor market, in the household, and in leisure activities. As children attain a certain degree of social and economic independence, parental and societal pressures to invest in human capital recede, and individuals take over more of the responsibility for making their own human capital investment decisions.

The process is well known. Society enforces school attendance, currently until the age of sixteen. Parents make sure the children engage in certain household and leisure activities in which experience is accumulated. Common examples of learning-by-doing household tasks are making beds, drying dishes, mowing the lawn, looking after pets, and washing the family car. Music, swimming, dancing, and skiing lessons, as well as participation in organized and unorganized sports, are all ways by which investments in leisure activity–specific human capital are made by and on behalf of children.

Expectations about future activities are extremely important in governing how much and what kind of human capital investments individuals make or are made on their behalf. An individual (or a parent on the child's behalf) will invest in human capital that raises his or her labor market productivity, w/p, only if he or she expects to spend much time in the labor market in the future. The more time individuals expect to spend in the labor market over their lifetimes, the higher the marginal benefits to labor market–specific human capital and the greater the investment that will be made. Likewise, the more time one expects to spend over one's lifetime in household or leisure activities, the greater the rate of return to household- or leisure-specific human capital formation and the greater the investments in these kinds of human capital that will be made.

These points arise out of a somewhat-generalized marginal-benefits-equal-to-marginal-costs condition for investment in human capital. The generalization is possible if it is assumed that any investment in human capital has the possibility of increasing the individual's productivity in the labor market, w, his or her household productivity, g_h, or productivity in leisure activities, r_l.[12]

Given this perspective, the equilibrium condition for investment in human capital becomes

$$\sum_{t=1}^{n} w_k(\hat{g}_h H_{gt} + \hat{w}M_t + \hat{r}_l L_t)/(1 + r)^t = MC \qquad (6.10)$$

where $w_t =$ the individual's wage rate in year t in the future; $\hat{g}_h$, $\hat{w}$, and $\hat{r}_l$ are the percentage increases in household productivity, labor market productivity, and leisure activity productivity, respectively, due to a 1 unit investment in human capital; and H_{gt}, M_t, and L_t are the times the individual expects to spend in household production, labor market employment, and leisure activity in year t in the future, respectively.[13]

The left-hand side of equation (6.10) is the marginal benefit of an added unit of human capital. The larger H_{gt} (M_t, L_t), the more time the individual expects to spend in household production (market work, leisure activity) in year t in the future and the greater the marginal benefit from the investment. If H_{gt} (M_t, L_t) = 0, however, the individual expects to spend no time in household production (market work, leisure), and the marginal benefit of the human capital investment will be lower. Alternatively, if $\hat{g}_h(\hat{w}, \hat{r}_l) = 0$, then the contemplated investment in human capital does not augment household productivity (labor market productivity, leisure productivity), and again, the marginal benefit from the contemplated human capital investment is lower.

Sex typing of human capital investments can occur when individuals' expectations, or those of their parents, about their future activities depend upon gender. Historically, females were expected to spend the majority of their lives in household and leisure activities. Consequently, the marginal benefits to labor market–specific human capital investments by or on behalf of females were lower than those for males, reducing the amount of such investments made by females or by society and parents on their behalf.

Although being literate was important for household management and child rearing, higher education for females had a low rate of return because of these expectations and, consequently, few females entered college or graduated. If females entered college, their motives (or those of their parents) were not to amass labor market–specific human capital except as insurance against the possibility of being widowed. Rather, their motives were to invest further in household- and leisure-specific human capital or in some cases to participate in the college "marriage market." As expectations about the future roles of females changed through time, however, rates of return to education of females rose and their high school and college completion rates rose. Tables 6.1 and 6.2 show the trends in years of school completed by level of education for females (Table 6.1) and males (Table 6.2) from 1940 to 1986. The figures in the tables

Table 6.1. *Years of school completed by females 25 years of age and over: 1940–86 (in percentages)*

Year	8 years or less	9–11 years	12 years	13–15 years	16 years or more
1940	69.3	15.7	16.2	6.0	3.7
1950	45.2	17.6	22.6	7.5	5.1
1960	37.8	19.7	27.8	9.0	5.7
1970	26.6	18.0	37.6	9.7	8.2
1980	17.2	14.6	40.5	14.1	13.5
1986	13.1	12.5	41.6	16.7	16.1

Source: U.S. Bureau of the Census, *Statistical Abstract of the United States* (Washington, D.C.: GPO), various volumes.

Table 6.2. *Years of school completed by males 25 years of age and over: 1940–86 (in percentages)*

Year	8 years or less	9–11 years	12 years	13–15 years	16 years or more
1940	61.9	14.2	12.0	4.9	5.4
1950	49.5	16.6	17.8	6.9	6.9
1960	42.2	18.7	21.0	8.6	9.5
1970	28.8	14.8	30.1	10.8	14.1
1980	17.7	13.2	32.8	15.5	20.8
1986	13.5	11.3	34.9	17.1	23.2

Source: U.S. Bureau of the Census, *Statistical Abstract of the United States* (Washington, D.C.: GPO), various volumes.

are percentages of females (males) twenty-five years of age and over who have completed given numbers of years of formal schooling. The rate of increase from 1970 to 1986 in the proportion of females completing 16 yr. of school or more is 96 percent. The rate of increase for males is 64.5 percent. The rates of increase from 1970 to 1986 in the proportions of females and males completing 13–15 yr. of school are 72 percent and 58 percent, respectively. Clearly, the proportion of females who enter and complete college degrees is rapidly catching up with that of males. The more rapid rate of increase stems, in part, from the changed expectations as to how much time females will spend over their life cycle in the labor market.

Another place where altered expectations change investments in human capi-

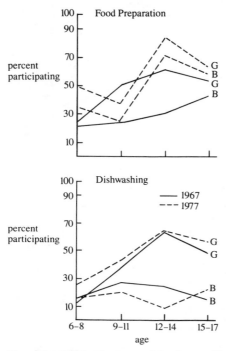

Figure 6.4 Children's age–participation profiles for food preparation and dish-washing in 1967 and 1977 (*source:* O'Neill 1978, Table 5, p. 71)

tal is in activities that increase human capital specific to household production activities. These changes can be observed by comparing the time use patterns of children in two-parent, two-child families in Syracuse, New York, in 1967 and 1977 (O'Neill 1978). In 1967 82.1 percent of all girls aged six to seventeen participated in household production tasks, compared with 78.9 percent of boys. For 1977 the comparable participation rates were 87.7 percent for girls and 88.6 percent for boys. Although the participation in household production activities of both boys and girls increased over the 10-yr. period, the rate of increase for boys was almost double that for girls. Part of this differential increase stems from changed parental expectations about how their children will spend their time in the future.

Age–participation profiles for four specific household tasks for girls and boys in both 1967 and 1977 are shown in Figures 6.4 and 6.5. The figures give more detail than the simple increases in participation rates over the 10-yr. period

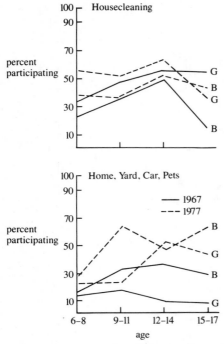

Figure 6.5 Children's age–participation profiles for housecleaning and maintenance of home, yard, car, and pets in 1967 and 1977 (*source:* see Figure 6.4)

discussed above. The age–participation profiles shown are for food preparation, dishwashing, housecleaning, and care of home, yard, car, and pets.

The typical pattern of participation is that a higher proportion of children
participate in given household tasks as they grow older. The increase in children's participation with age levels off or actually falls somewhat in their later
teens as school and other activities command more of their time. Sex typing of
activities was clear in 1967, with higher fractions of girls participating in food
preparation, dishwashing, and housecleaning tasks and higher fractions of boys
engaged in maintenance of home, yard, car, and pets. In all but food preparation the difference in participation between girls and boys grew with age. By
1977 the sex typing of children's participation in household tasks had become
more muted but had not disappeared. And in one case, that of dishwashing, the
sex typing had become more pronounced by 1977. Boys actually decreased

their participation in dishwashing over the 10-yr. period while girls' participation increased somewhat.

Health as a human capital investment

The common view of health has been that one went to a doctor if one was sick or injured. Beyond some simple rules of public health and good nutrition, the rest of the time one's attention was on other things. In a remarkably short period of years, however, this view of health has been radically altered. What was a minor concern over public health has blossomed into an intense concern for the public health implications of the environment and for what humans are doing to the environment. Much more attention is now paid to nutrition. Sports are no longer viewed as idle pursuits for some adults but as crucial for the improvement and maintenance of health. In short, nowadays most people view health as an investment and consciously invest in it.

Theoretically, health is no different from other aspects of human capital in that one will invest in it until the marginal benefits of added investment equal the marginal cost. Thus, the equations equating marginal benefits with marginal costs that we have used to analyze other aspects of human capital apply to investments in health also.

Investments in health, however, also have other important effects. Although an added year of schooling will not increase one's expected life span, investments in health will. Whereas learning-by-doing will not prevent sickness from reducing the number of days of activity per year, proper nutrition and other preventive health measures will.

The effects of such investments are easily illustrated. In Figure 6.6 the usual time use diagram is presented in which the individual allocates his or her time among market work, leisure, and household production activities – but with one difference. The diagram is altered to compare the choices made by an individual who is not sick during the year covered by the diagram (and, therefore, has 365 days to allocate) with the choices made by an individual who is sick and, therefore, has a lower stock of health. The result is that the sick person has fewer days available for market work, household work, and leisure activities.

In Figure 6.6, the individual initially maximizes satisfaction at point P on his "healthy" total budget line, $DEBT$, allocating TH_e days during the year to household production, H_eL_p days during the year to market work, and OL_p days to leisure activity. Now suppose, instead, that he is sick TT' days during the year, leaving OT' days in which to pursue his normal activities. Because he has TT' fewer days, his household production function, AB, is shifted left to $A'B'$. Given that the year has shrunk through ill health but neither his household nor his market productivity have been affected, the point at which $w/p = g_h$ shifts

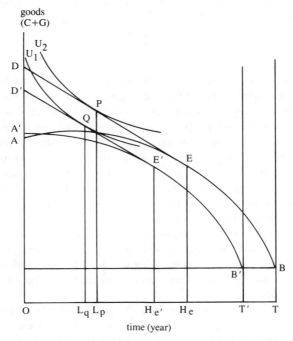

Figure 6.6 The effect on time allocation of lost days per year due to ill health

horizontally from E to E' so that the total budget line is $D'E'B'T'$, given he is sick TT' days per year. Given the individual is incapacitated for TT' days per year, then, he maximizes satisfaction at Q on indifference curve U_1, point P on U_2 no longer being attainable.

The shortened year reduces the time he spends in market work from H_eL_p to H'_eL_q and decreases the time he spends in leisure from OL_p to OL_q. Ill health and the resulting reduction in available days per year represent a diminution of resources or full income equal to DD', with a consequent decline in the demand for leisure. Because the decline in the demand for leisure is less than the number of days lost through ill health, days spent in market work must decline also. Time spent in household production does not decline, because ill health has reduced the number of days available for use and not the productivity of either market work or household work. In reality, ill health may well reduce house-hold productivity somewhat and, therefore, lead to a reallocation of time from household work to market work.[14] In all likelihood, then, the days lost through ill health will result in somewhat less time spent in all three activities.

Using a white, male sample for 1969 Grossman (1976) studied the effect of health status on number of workweeks lost per year through illness. He found that men in good health have 0.2 more workweeks lost per year than men in excellent health, that men in fair health have 0.6 more workweeks lost per year than men in good health, and that men in poor health have 8 more workweeks lost per year than men in fair health (1976, Table 2). The stock of human capital in the form of health does, indeed, make a difference in the amount of market work done. Grossman also relates the number of weeks of schooling lost while individuals were in school to their health status while in school and finds similar results: the better the health of the individual, the fewer weeks of school lost (1976, p. 170). There is no equivalent evidence on the effects of variations in the stock of health on times spent in leisure and household activities.

We have seen that the stock of health does, indeed, affect our time use. But what affects one's current health status; that is, one's stock of health capital? Grossman relates the current health status of white males in 1969 to a number of variables and finds that the individual's age, his own and his wife's education, his past health status, his wage rate, and the absolute value of the difference between the individual's weight and the doctor-determined "ideal weight" given the individual's height all are statistically important (1976, Table 5, p. 176). These variables can be regarded as factors affecting the individual's "demand for health," the demand arising from both the future benefits of investing in one's health today as well as the consumption benefits of enjoying being healthy currently.

One of the interesting elements of these results is that the amount of human capital one has in the form of education has a positive effect on the amount of human capital one has in the form of health. Grossman estimates that an added year of formal schooling increases the likelihood of a white male being in excellent health by 0.011 (1976, Table 11, p. 189). Thus, one's health is affected by one's past schooling. Having more education raises the benefits or lowers the cost of added human capital in the form of health; it is not clear which.

In other work, Edwards and Grossman (1979) have shown that health also positively affects the intellectual development of children. They studied a national sample of children aged six to eleven in 1963–5. They related a set of health-related variables as well as other variables to measures of the children's IQs and to their scores on an achievement test. They found that whether the child was breast-fed, whether it was lighter than 4.4 pounds at birth, whether it was short for its age and sex, whether it had more tooth decay given its age and sex, and whether it had significant abnormalities all affected the child's measured IQ. Holding IQ constant, whether the child was breast-fed, whether it was lighter than 4.4 pounds at birth, whether it had hearing deficiencies or significant abnormalities, and whether the child was short for its age and sex all affected its score on the achievement test (Table 2, p. 287). Whether children are breast-fed, whether they are light at birth, and whether they are shorter than average for their age and sex are all known to be related to nutritional status. These variables may also measure other things.

Human capital in the form of health and in the form of education and intellectual development interact with each other: the more of one increases the stock of the other. Healthy children accomplish more in school. Better educated people are healthier.

Human capital, marriage, and divorce

Human capital formation is an important household activity in both its explicit and implicit forms: explicitly when the activity is primarily motivated as a device to build human capital, as in formal instruction, preventive medicine, exercise, and nutrition; and implicitly when human capital formation accumulates as experience in the activity, regardless of whether the activity is market work, household production, or leisure. Because the human capital formation, especially that gained through experience in household activities, takes place in the context of a household, the type of household affects the returns to investments in human capital and, therefore, the amounts and types of human capital formation. In particular, the sex of the individual, marital status, and household composition (i.e., the number of children) are important.

Because single people can exploit neither the advantages of specialization of function nor economies of size in household production activities, and because their demands for household-produced goods and services are less than a multiperson family's, single people do less household work than multiperson households and, therefore, accumulate little household production–related experience. But since single people also spend less time in paid employment and more time in leisure activities than people in multiperson families, they accumulate more leisure-specific experience. The sex and marital status differences in average times spent in various activities is demonstrated in Table 6.3. Married people and females orient more household work and leisure toward children than do single people and males. Obviously, the more children per family, the more child-oriented the household work and leisure. Consequently, married people, females, and married couples with many children all accumulate more child-specific human capital via experience than unmarried people, males, and couples with no or few children. This is partially shown in Table 6.3, where the average time per week devoted to child care ranges from 0.3 hr. by unmarried men to 4.9 hr. for married women. The sex specificity shows up, too, in the differences in the type of social entertainment in which men and women engage: although religious activities bulk large for both, men spend more time in fraternal organizations and women spend more time in volunteer/help organizations like the Boy Scouts and the PTA (Hill 1985, p. 146).

Table 6.3. *Mean hours spent in various activities per week by sex and marital status: 1975*

Activity	Males		Females	
	Unmarried	Married	Unmarried	Married
Paid employment	32.9	40.2	22.2	16.7
Education	4.0	1.0	2.0	0.4
Household work	12.0	14.3	23.5	34.9
Child care	0.3	1.5	2.2	4.9
Social entertainment	11.8	6.3	10.4	7.8
Active leisure[a]	8.2	4.7	5.7	4.7
Passive leisure[a]	24.2	22.4	23.8	22.0

[a] Active leisure includes sports and hobbies such as woodworking; passive leisure includes reading, TV watching, and conversing.
Source: Hill 1985, Table 7.3, p. 148.

Previously, the concepts of general and specific human capital were introduced in the context of training and experience in the labor market. These concepts have as much cogency with respect to human capital formed through experience in household activities. In this context, the issue is whether and to what extent the human capital accumulated is general human capital that can be transferred to any family or, indeed, to labor market jobs or whether it is specific to the particular marriage in which it was accumulated.

General human capital resulting from marriage

Some of the human relations, child-rearing, management, shopping, and household maintenance skills one learns in a marriage are general to any marriage and, perhaps, to firms as well. The returns to such general human capital are difficult for other family members to capture in the same way the returns to general human capital cannot be easily captured by employers. The reasons are the same. If other family members seek to capture these returns or seek to capture an inordinate share of them, the family member possessing them can remove the human capital from the family, depriving it of the benefits or at least reserving a higher fraction of the benefits for himself or herself.

There are several implications of this fact. Some of the general human capital accumulated through experience in the family is applicable in the labor market and serves to raise the individual's market productivity. One way of removing this general human capital from the family is to increase the proportion of time one spends in paid employment. Here, the returns to the general human capital accrue to the individual through his or her earnings. Depending upon the financial organization of the household, individual family members' labor earnings may not be fully shared with other family members. If not, then the substitution of market for household work may have the effect of reserving for the possessor the returns to general experience gained within the household. This could partly explain the traditional resistance on the part of husbands to the entry of their wives into the labor force. And it could equally be part of the explanation for the rapid increase in the labor force participation rate of married women after 1940.

Another part of the human capital gained within a marriage is general in the sense that it is as productive in any marriage. Faced with the threat of having to share an inordinate fraction of the returns to such general human capital with other family members, an individual may leave the family and form another household, single or married. Such is the stuff of divorce.

Marriage-specific human capital

Marriage-specific human capital yields returns in the context of the marriage within which it is accumulated but in no other marriage or context. The particular knowledge of and skills in handling the personality, capabilities, and failings of one's mate that are gained over time in a marriage are examples of marriage-specific human capital. So, too, are children of the marriage: however charming, likable, and smart, children are "worth" less to others than to their parents. Such capital is carried into another marriage with difficulty and either is not productive or is much less productive than in the marriage in which it was accumulated. This explains, in part, why the remarriage rate of divorced persons with children is lower than the remarriage rate of divorced persons without children. It may also partially explain why the divorce rate among those once divorced and remarried is higher than the divorce rate of people in their first marriage. These issues will be further discussed in Chapter 8.

Human capital and divorce settlements

Finally, human capital formed during a marriage has important implications for divorce settlements. This is most easily and commonly seen in the archetypical case in which one spouse "puts the other spouse through school," and subsequently, there is a divorce. It is argued that a part of the couple's savings was invested in the spouse's schooling and the returns to the investment should be shared by both spouses in the divorce settlement along with the rest of the couple's assets.

Divorce denies to one spouse the subsequent returns to human capital formed within the household that are embodied in the other spouse. If the divorce settlement should recompense the divorced spouse who put his or her mate through school, then consistency demands that the subsequent returns to *all* the human capital investments made during the marriage be shared.

If divorce courts allow such an argument, then it has both narrower and wider application than initially supposed. It is simultaneously narrower and wider than supposed because of the distinction between general and specific human capital. To the extent that the investment in schooling was general human capital, then the schooling yields returns to its possessor outside the marriage and the other spouse has a claim on some of the returns. To the extent that the investment in schooling was specific to the marriage, then its possessor reaps no returns from the investment outside the marriage. Consequently, there are no returns after dissolution to share with the other spouse. In this case there may be a legal case to be made to the effect that the instigator of the divorce denies his or her spouse the returns to marriage-specific human capital and should recompense the spouse for the loss.

These considerations may not be very important in the context of formal schooling, which probably has little or no marriage specificity. But they become very important in the case of human capital formed within the household. To the extent that it is marriage specific, the returns are denied to both spouses. What the settlement does with respect to the marriage-specific human capital is unclear. Women sometimes forgo a larger settlement at divorce in order to have custody of their children. This might be construed to be a payoff at divorce for the fact that the father will be denied his share of the returns to the marriage-specific human capital in the form of his children. The payoff is inequitable, however, since it reduces the woman's financial ability to rear the children.

This very brief discussion of the implications of human capital with respect to marriage and divorce underscores the policy importance of the human capital concept. It has equally important applications with respect to labor market policy, child-care policy, health policy, and education policy. An important hindrance to its widespread application, however, is that empirical work on human capital is in its infancy. Until more empirical work is done, a host of policy problems faced by society, firms, and families will not be adequately understood or solved.

Summary

The model of the household has been broadened in this chapter to include the investment in human capital activities that are properly construed as a special type of household production in which the output is received and consumed in the future. Human capital investment augments not only one's market productivity but one's household productivity as well, thus altering the trade-offs individuals make among household work, market work, and leisure.

CHAPTER SEVEN

The economics of fertility

Introduction

In the United States the birthrate has fallen over the last 185 years from about 55.2 births per 1,000 population in 1820 to 32.2 in 1900 and 15.9 in 1981.[1] Over the long run and with the exception of the post–World War II baby boom, American couples have been having fewer children.

The post–World War baby boom followed by the baby bust of the 1960s and 1970s is the major exception to the long-run trend. Total fertility rates from 1940 to the present tell this tale. The total fertility rate is a better measure of the fertility experience of women than the birthrate because "the total fertility rate is the number of births that 1000 women would have in their lifetime if at each year of age, they experienced the birth rates occurring in the specified year" (U.S. Bureau of the Census 1982. Table 85, p. 60). In 1940–4 the total fertility rate was 2,523 per 1,000 women. It peaked in the 1955–9 period with 3,690 births per 1,000 women, after which birth rates started to fall. In the 1975–9 period the birthrate was 1,810 per 1,000 women. Since over this period the replacement rate (i.e., the birthrate necessary to sustain a constant population) has been 2,110 births per 1,000 women, the birthrate is now below the rate necessary to maintain population at a constant level.

The fertility experience of women has varied widely not only over both the long and the short run but also among women at any point in time. Fertility is negatively related to family income, for instance. Consider the number of women per 1,000 women, aged 18–44 yr., who gave birth in the year preceding June 1980. The number was 94.3 for women in families with incomes of less than $5,000 and 48.5 in families with incomes of $25,000 and over (U.S. Bureau of the Census 1982, Table 91, p. 64). Fertility is also negatively related to women's educational levels. The number of women per 1,000 women, aged 18–44 yr., who gave birth in the year preceding June 1980 and who had less than 12 yr. of school was 91.9, whereas the number for women with 5 or more years of college was 52.1 (U.S. Bureau of the Census 1982, Table 91, p. 64). Although these figures reflect much more than merely the relationships between fertility, family income, and women's education, they do illustrate that

196

the wide variation in the fertility experience of women is related to their socio-economic characteristics.

This brief recital of facts about fertility for the United States indicates that over both the short and the long run Americans have varied their fertility behavior dramatically. How do we explain these changes in behavior? What are the determinants of fertility behavior and how have they changed? More crucially for economics, to what extent are the determinants of fertility economic as opposed to biological, sociological, and psychological? Said differently, what can economics contribute to the explanation of fertility behavior?

For economics to contribute anything at all to the understanding of fertility behavior, three conditions must be present.

(1) Children must yield satisfaction to their parents.
(2) Parents must be able to choose whether to have children, how many to have, and when to have them.
(3) Children must be costly; that is, bearing and rearing children must use scarce resources.

We discuss each of these points in turn.

Currently and historically children have given satisfaction to their parents in at least one of three major ways.[2]

1. Parents love their children and children return that love. Thus, children yield satisfaction directly to their parents.

2. Children are themselves a resource in the production of goods and services either for home consumption or for sale. Wresting America from the wilderness would have taken much longer and would have been harder had it not been for the labor of generations of children on their parent's frontier farms and in their businesses. Likewise, no suburban parent wants to face the summer's lawns or the winter's snows without the assistance of their children. Thus, children yield satisfaction to their parents indirectly through the goods and services they produce for family consumption or sale.

3. Children provide social, psychological, and economic security in a couple's old age. Security for the parents when they are elderly is another indirect way in which children increase their parents' satisfaction. Economic security for their parents was a more cogent reason for couples to have children earlier in our history when Social Security, Medicare, and pensions were not as prevalent. It continues to be quite important for couples in less developed countries.

Despite the fact that having children remains a probabilistic, biological process, couples have always had choice over whether to have children and when to have them. In earlier times choice was controlled by devices like infanticide, sale into slavery,[3] primitive contraception and abortion techniques, and social and religious sanctions surrounding marriage. Today, we have much more sophisticated contraception and abortion techniques and we, too, attempt to control decisions as to whether and when to have children by religious and social sanctions. Moreover, modern medicine and adoption practices allow infertile couples to have children.

Children certainly are costly. Based on data from the 1972–3 Consumer Expenditure Survey, Olson (1983) calculated that "an average two-parent family with no previous children and head aged twenty-five in 1980 can expect to spend a total of $214,956 (in 1982 undiscounted dollars) to raise a son born in 1980 from birth to age twenty-two, assuming that the son is not expected to attend a residential private college" (p. 55). If he attends a residential 4-yr. college, the costs rise to $226,001 (Olson 1983, p. 28). This amounts to 21 percent and 24 percent of the survey's average family's total income, respectively. The average family's total food costs amount to 32.4 percent, housing costs account for 30.2 percent, transportation costs equal 13.5 percent, health care costs take 7 percent, clothing costs total 4.2 percent, and other costs, including education (but not including the 4-yr. residential private college), amount to 12.6 percent. A female child costs somewhat more, because of higher transportation and "other" costs, including education (Olson 1983, p. 28).

These estimates exclude the time costs, which are especially high in the early years of child rearing. Based on a 1975 national study, the average mother with a high school education could be expected to spend 487.1 hr./yr. on direct care of a child 0–2.9 yr. old, 364.9 hr./yr. on direct care of a child 3–4.9 yr. old, 181.1 hr./yr. on direct care of a grade school child, and 110.1 hr./yr. on direct care of a 13–17.9 yr. old (Stafford & Hill 1985, Table 17.2, p. 422). These times do not include the increased time involved in meal preparation, laundry, housecleaning, transportation, and so on that a child occasions. If the estimated values of time for employed mothers from Zick and Bryant (1983) (see Table 5.2) are applied to the mother's time spent in direct care of a child from infancy to 18 yr. old, the result is $17,817.66. Although minor compared with the mother's, the father's time cost is not accounted for in this sum. Obviously, having and rearing children involve large expenditures of both time and money resources by the parents.

It is clear, then, that the three conditions are present that make economics relevant to the explanation of fertility phenomena. However, children have special attributes that prohibit the easy application of the economics of the household to the explanation of fertility behavior. These attributes need to be discussed.

Children have been likened to durable goods because they yield satisfaction and command resources over a long period of time. With a child as with other durable goods the economic focus is on the flow of services to the family through time. Likewise, both durables and children require maintenance through time. In the case of durables the goal is to maintain them in good working order, whereas with children the goal is to encourage their growth and development and their eventual social and economic independence. Thus, the decision to have children takes on the character of an investment–saving decision. In no sense are the decisions similar to current consumption decisions. The implication of the durable-like attributes of children is that an intertemporal model (like the intertemporal model with which we explained consumption–saving choices in Chapter 4 and the model with which we explained investments in human capital in Chapter 6) is probably the most accurate way to clarify parents' fertility choices. Failing this, one must still come to terms with the fact that children yield satisfaction and entail expenditures of resources over long periods.

Children differ from durables in important ways. The patterns of the money and time costs for durables are very different from those for children. In the case of most durables, the ratio of money-to-time cost initially is quite high. As durables age and they require more maintenance, the ratio of money-to-time cost falls somewhat. In contrast, children have modest initial money costs compared with their initial time costs. As children grow up and attain first physical, then sociological, and finally economic independence, the ratio of money-to-time cost rises.

The high initial time cost relative to the initial money cost of children when combined with the division of labor by sex between market and household work means that the decisions to have children and their number and spacing are very mixed up with decisions concerning the amount and pattern by age of the mother's market work. The blending of the mother's work life with the birthing and rearing of children, as well as the fact that children typically come one at a time after a 9-mo. gestation period, means that achieving the desired family size can be a lengthy process. This implies that the characteristics of each child affect the timing and number of subsequent children.

Another way in which children differ markedly from durables is that "used children" markets are very imperfect, whereas used car and housing markets are developed and work rather well by comparison. Used children markets refer to the adoption processes that exist in the United States; that is, the mechanisms by which children are transferred from people who cannot care for them or who do not want them to people who can and do. Adoption agencies run by the state or by religious and charitable organizations are very highly regulated. The regulations along with the supplies of adoptable children available to such agencies have created long waiting lines and elaborate screening procedures. Although the money price of adopting a child through such agencies is low, the time costs are extraordinarily high, involving years of waiting for certain types and ages of children. A private, much less regulated market is run by lawyers who act as brokers between women with unwanted children and couples desiring children. In this segment of the adoption market the money cost of a child is much higher and waiting times much shorter. An illegal market also exists in which regulations safeguarding the parties involved are ignored and the prices charged for children even higher.

Despite the fact that adoption markets exist, they do not work well by whatever criteria are used. The implications are that decisions to have children are much less revocable than are decisions to purchase cars and durables. Being less revocable means that the costs of children are much larger than would be the case if better adoption markets existed.

A simple model of fertility

There are many important questions that could be asked with respect to the fertility choices of people. They include questions about family size (why, for instance, has family size decreased in the United States except for the post–World War II baby boom?), the illegitimate birthrate (why has it increased?), the spacing of children, the timing of children with respect to the age of the mother, the sex of children, the effects of modern contraceptives, the influence (if any) of tax and welfare programs, and on and on. No one model of family behavior can address all of these questions. Here, the goal is to introduce the student to how the tools of economics can shed light on these questions. Thus, it will suffice to build a simple model of fertility choice concentrating on the question of family size.[4]

In order to address the question of family size with the aid of a simple model, we will focus on a few attributes of children and choices involving them and neglect the myriad other attributes that surely impinge on other questions. Here we will focus on five.

1. Since we wish the model to address the question of family size, it makes sense to focus on completed family size. By completed family size is meant the number of children a couple has and rears to adulthood. The number of children a family has by the time the mother is, say, 25 yr. old is irrelevant because she may desire and have several more children during the remaining years she is fecund. The consequence of focusing on completed family size is that the period of analysis is the period of fecundity of the woman. Choosing this as the period of analysis allows us to avoid the complexities of multiperiod models like the ones developed in Chapters 4 and 6 and to benefit from the simplicities of one-period models.

2. Children are a home-produced good requiring combinations of parental time and purchased goods. The parental time involved includes the time spent on prenatal and postnatal child care plus the added time required to perform household tasks when children are present. The purchased goods include the food, clothing, housing, toys, transportation, education, and so on that all must be produced by the family or purchased for children as they grow and develop.

3. Given the historic and current specialization of function within the family, it is the married woman's time rather than the husband's that makes up the majority of the time used in having and rearing children. Consequently, we will focus on the mother's time input and ignore the father's. Furthermore, the model will focus on the woman and neglect the man. This is done not only to focus on the woman's time input but also because most data on fertility are collected relative to women rather than men. This is done partially because it is clear who the mothers of the children are whereas the identities of the fathers are not always apparent.

4. Although the concept is a slippery one, we assume that parents receive satisfaction from "child services." Child services is the flow of services parents consume each year that derives from their children in the same way that people consume flows of car and housing services each year from the cars and houses they possess. The concept of child services is introduced because children are much like durable goods, and economists apply the same concepts to both to the extent possible. That is, we know people consume the flow of services from durable goods, rather than the durables themselves, because durable goods are not entirely consumed in one period. So it is with children.

5. Child services derive from the two components of children: the number of children in the family and the human capital embodied in each child. The distinction is important because we observe that expenditures on children rise with income, holding the number of children in the family constant. Why would parents make such expenditures if the parents' well-being was not being increased? In addition to the number of children parents have, therefore, there must be another attribute of children that is augmented by spending added amounts of time and money on children. The other attribute must be the human capital that children possess. Children have more human capital, the flow of child services is greater, and parents are happier if their children are healthy rather than sick, more rather than less educated, more physically and socially skilled than less, better fed, clothed, and housed rather than less, and so on. Thus, the additional expenditures parents make on their children as income rises augment children's human capital. The demand for children is really a component of the demand for child services and to ignore this fact is to miss an important aspect of fertility behavior.

Finally, as a first approximation it is probably the case that most parents prefer to treat each child equally: that is, to ensure that each of their children is as happy, skilled, healthy, and educated as their other children. Thus, we can avoid having to assume that children within a family differ with regard to the attributes they possess.[5]

We can formalize these notions by defining the quantity of child services produced and consumed by a couple over the expected life of the couple as the

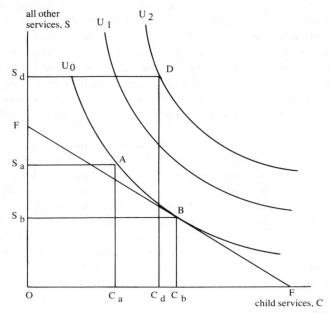

Figure 7.1 The family's preference for child services, C, and parental services, S

product of the number, N, of children they have and the amount of human capital per child, Q, the children possess. Denoting the amount of child services as C, then

$$C = NQ. \tag{7.1}$$

In addition to deriving satisfaction from child services a couple also derives satisfaction from the sum total of all other services they produce and consume over the same period. Here, in contrast to Chapter 5, in which the family was assumed to obtain satisfaction from goods (purchased and produced) and leisure time, we recognize that all activities in the household involve household production whether it is a meal prepared; the laundry washed, pressed, and put away; or a skiing trip planned and executed. All activities require inputs of time and goods. In this simple model of fertility we assume that the couple obtains satisfaction by producing and consuming two goods: child services and all other services, called "parental services," the amount of which is denoted by S.

The preferences of the couple can, therefore, be characterized simply by the utility function

$$U = u(C, S) \tag{7.2}$$

or, alternatively, by the indifference map in Figure 7.1, in which curves $U_0, U_1,$

and U_2 are but three of the myriad of possible indifference curves that could be drawn. Combinations A and B of child services and parental services yield equal satisfaction to the couple, because they are on U_0. Combination D (C_d, S_d) is preferred to either A or B because D is on a higher indifference curve, U_2. The slope of U_0 at B, represented by the slope of the tangent, FF, to U_0 at B, is the marginal rate of substitution of child services for parental services at B, $\text{MRS}_{cs}|_B = MU_c/MU_s$. Given the family consumes C_b of child services and S_b of parental services, $\text{MRS}_{cs}|_B$ is the rate at which the couple would be willing to sacrifice parental services in order to consume one more unit of child services, holding satisfaction constant.

The preferences that are represented by the utility function and by the indifference curves in Figure 7.1 are those possessed by the couple at the beginning of the marriage. It is assumed that the couple plans and makes choices with respect to the desired number of children, N, the desired amount of human capital per child, Q, and the amount of all other services, S, they would like to consume.

Having characterized the couple's desires with respect to children, it remains to characterize the choices open to the couple by means of the budget line. To do this we must define not only the total quantity of resources but also the possible expenditures by the couple. First, define full income as the total possible income the couple could have over its expected lifetime (not each year but in total) as

$$\text{FI} = wT + V \tag{7.3}$$

where FI denotes full income, T is the total time encompassed by the expected lifetime, w represents the market wage rate the woman can command in the labor market, and V represents the sum of the husband's earnings over the period (this can be construed as the present value of the expected stream of his earnings over the lifetime of the couple) plus any unearned income accruing to the couple over the period.[6] FI, therefore, represents the total resources possessed by the couple and which it can devote to "purchases" of C and S.

Second, we denote the expenditures by the couple as

$$Ex = p_c C + p_s S \tag{7.4}$$

where p_c denotes the price per unit of child services purchased, and p_s denotes the price of parental services purchased by the couple.

When we say that the couple purchases child services and parental services what we mean is that the couple combines time and purchased goods and services in the production and subsequent consumption both of child services and of parental services. The price of a unit of child services, therefore, is the sum of the forgone cost of the time used to produce a unit of child services and the money cost of the purchased goods and services going into the production of a unit of child services. Likewise, p_s is the sum of the time and money costs involved in the production and consumption of one unit of parental services.

Thus, we can define the price of child services as

$$p_c = p_{xc} b_c + w t_c \qquad (7.5)$$

where p_{xc} = the index of prices of the market goods and services the couple uses to produce child services, b_c = the quantity of market-purchased goods and services required to produce one unit of child services, w = wife's wage rate, and t_c = amount of the wife's time required to produce one unit of child services. $p_x b_c$, then, represents the money cost of one unit of child services and $w t_c$ represents the forgone time cost of one unit of child services. The money cost of child services includes food, clothing, housing, transportation, education, and health care costs as well as the cost of toys, trips to Disneyland, and any rock concerts paid for by the parents for the children. The time cost of child services includes the value of all the time spent by the mother rearing children either directly in terms of child care or indirectly in terms of the increase in other household work due to the presence of children.

The price of parental services, p_s, is defined similarly:

$$p_s = p_{xs} b_s + w t_s \qquad (7.6)$$

where p_{xs} = the index of prices of the market goods and services the couple buys to produce and consumer parental services, b_s = the quantity of market-purchased goods and services required to produce one unit of parental services, and t_s = amount of the wife's time required to produce one unit of parental services. The money cost of parental services includes the cost of food, clothing, housing, transportation, education, and health care of the parents as well as the cost of parental vacations and the recreation equipment used by parents. The time cost is the value of all the wife's time spent directly and indirectly producing the goods and services consumed by the parents.

Notice that the husband's time inputs into C and S are completely ignored in this formulation. This is because we are here focusing on the woman's time input and the interdependence between the fertility decisions of the family and the mother's career in the labor force.

Notice, also, that b_c and t_c represent the household production technology involved in the production of child services by the family. Likewise, b_s and t_s represent the technology involved in the home production of parental services (see mathematical note 1). In this model these technical constraints on family behavior have been built into the prices of C and S. In the household production model elaborated in Chapter 5 the household production was handled separately (see mathematical note 2).

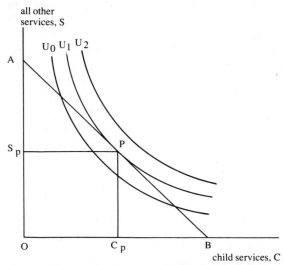

Figure 7.2 The family's budget line, preference map, and equilibrium demands for C and S

The budget constraint, which expresses the alternatives open to the couple, simply maintains that total expenditures equal total resources. Thus,

$$\text{Ex} = \text{FI}$$

or

$$p_c C + p_s S = wT + V. \tag{7.7}$$

The budget constraint is represented geometrically in Figure 7.2 by AB. Point A is the maximum amount of parental services, S^m, the couple could consume if it remained childless. In this case, total resources would be devoted to the production and consumption of parental services and

$$S^m = (wT + V)/p_s = (wT + V)/(p_{xs} b_s + wt_s). \tag{7.8}$$

Likewise, point B represents the maximum amount of child services, C^m, the couple could produce and consume providing it devoted all its resources, FI, to the production and consumption of child services, leaving none for any other purpose. Thus,

$$C^m = (wT + V)/p_c = (wT + V)/(p_{xc} b_c + wt_c). \tag{7.9}$$

Points on AB between A and B, say at P, represent particular combinations of child services C_p, and parental services, S_p, that the couple could produce and consume with its total resources.

As with any other budget line, the slope of AB represents the market rate of exchange between the goods pictured. In this case the slope of AB represents the market rate of exchange of child services for parental services, p_c/p_s; that is, the amount of all other services that must be sacrificed by the couple in order to produce and consume an added unit of child services. This rate of exchange clearly depends upon the technologies involved in the production and consumption of S and C (i.e., b_c, b_s, t_c, and t_s) as well as the prices of purchased goods (i.e., p_{xc} and p_{xs}) and the per hour value of the woman's time (i.e., w).

Family equilibrium

Whereas the indifference curves of Figure 7.2 represent the family's desires, the budget line of Figure 7.2 represents the opportunities open to the family. The two are brought together in Figure 7.2 to determine the equilibrium amounts of child services and parental services.

The family maximizes satisfaction at point P in Figure 7.2, where the budget line is tangent to the highest attainable indifference curve, U_1. Point P represents the combination of child services, C_p, and parental services, S_p, that maximizes the couple's satisfaction given their resources, the prices of C and S, and the couple's preferences. C_p represents the couple's desired amount of child services. C_p is the couple's planned consumption of child services over their marriage. That is, if the couple has been realistic in their assessments of the resources at their disposal ($wT + V$) and of the prices of child services and parental services, p_c and p_s, and if their preferences are unaltered, then C_p is the quantity of child services they plan to consume over the life cycle.

C_p, the desired level of child services, contains within it the couple's desired number of children, N_p, and the desired amount of human capital with which the couple desires to endow each child, Q_p. Provided the couple is fertile and the number of births is controlled by the couple, desired family size will become actual family size. In reality, however, the actual number of children will have some random variation around desired family size. Likewise, there will be random variations in the actual amount of human capital per child around the desired amount, Q_p, since couples know less than everything about how to produce these attributes and children differ in basic genetic capabilities.[7]

Given the complete model, we can then use it to shed light on several major questions with respect to family size. One question is why there is a negative correlation between family income and family size. That family size falls as family income rises has been observed in every society and in every time period for which we have data. Does this mean that children are "inferior goods" or is something else going on that obscures an underlying positive relationship be-

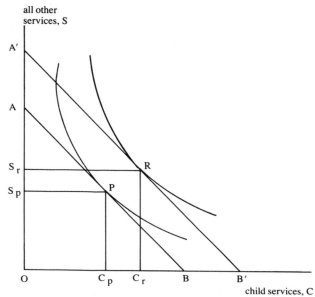

Figure 7.3 The effect of an increase in V on the demand for child services, C

tween income and the number of children, holding prices and preferences constant? Another question relates to the reasons for the negative relationship between the education of married women and the number of children they have; that is, the more educated the woman, the smaller the family size. A third question concerns how contraceptive knowledge operates to affect family size. A fourth and final question: what is the effect of infant mortality on birthrates?

The effect of changes in income

By a change in income we mean a change in full income, holding the prices of child services and all other services constant. Holding p_c and p_s constant implies that neither the married woman's wage rate, w, nor the prices of purchased goods and services, p_{xc} and p_{xs}, change. Thus, only V, the husband's earnings and unearned income, changes.

An increase in V, holding p_c and p_s constant, expands the opportunities open to the couple without changing the relative prices of S or C. If S and C are normal goods, then an increase in V will increase the couple's planned consumption of both. This is shown in Figure 7.3. Point P on AB is the initial equilibrium point, with C_p the initial desired demand for child services. The increase in V shifts the budget line from AB up to $A'B'$. Point R is the new equilibrium point after the increase in V, with C_r the new desired demand for child services. The diagram has been drawn on the assumption that both S and C are normal goods.

Are child services normal goods? Since we do not have empirical measures of either C or Q, the question can only be answered indirectly. Total expenditures on child services are $p_c C$. Since $p_c = p_{xc} b_c + w t_c$, total expenditures can be broken down into total money and total time expenditures:

$$p_c C = (p_{xc} b_c + w t_c)C = p_{xc} b_c C + w t_c C. \tag{7.10}$$

Note that $b_c C = X_c$, the quantity of purchased goods and services spent on children and $t_c C = H_c$ = the amount of time the mother spends on child care (see mathematical notes 1 and 2). Then total expenditures on children can be written

$$p_c C = p_{xc} X_c + w H_c. \tag{7.11}$$

Now, the income elasticity of demand for child services can be decomposed as follows (see mathematical note 3):

$$N_c = s_c N_{xc} + (1 - s_c)N_t \tag{7.12}$$

where N_{xc} = income elasticity of demand for purchased goods and services for children, N_t = income elasticity of demand for child care time, and s_c = the fraction or "share" of total expenditures on child services made up of money expenditures.

To find out whether child services are normal goods (i.e., $N_c > 0$) requires information on N_{xc}, N_t, and s_c. Olson (1983, pp. 55–6 and Table 3.4, p. 22) estimates that money expenditures spent on raising a child to age 22 and on four years of college (i.e., $p_{xc} b_c C = p_{xc} X_c$) as a fraction of total family income in 1972 for the average family (i.e., $p_{xc} X_c / Y$) was 0.24. Since the average family in Olson's 1972 sample had 1.9 children, the cost of raising children as a fraction of total income is $1.9(0.24) = 0.46$. Thus, $Y / p_{xc} X_c = 1/0.46 = 2.17$. Based on the 1972–3 Consumer Expenditure Survey, Olson (1983, Table 3.5, p. 23) estimated that money expenditures on children increase by $0.21 for each $1.00 increase in family income. This results in an income elasticity of demand for purchased goods and services for children of $N_{xc} = 0.46$.[8] The work of Hill and Stafford (1974) on the time married women spend in child care and that of Kooreman and Kapteyn (1987) indicate that time expenditures on child services $(w t_c C)$ are little affected if at all by increases in family income. Thus, $N_t = 0$. Finally, earlier in the chapter total money expenditures on a child to age 22 were estimated to be $226,001 if the child went to a private residential college and the time costs were estimated to be $17,818 for a total of $243,819.[9] Thus, $s_c = 226,001/243,819 = 0.93$.[10] Applying these figures in equation (7.12), then, results in an estimate of the income elasticity of demand for child services of

$$N_c = 0.93(0.46) + (1 - 0.93)0 = 0.43.$$

It appears clear, then, that child services are normal goods and that the demand for child services rises as income rises.

What can be said about N and Q, the components of child services? Do families increase their demand for children, their demand for human capital per child, or both as income increases? The relationship between the income elasticity of demand for child services and the income elasticities of demand for N and Q is

$$N_c = N_n + N_q \tag{7.13}$$

where N_n = the income elasticity of demand for number of children and N_q = the income elasticity of demand for human capital per child (see mathematical note 4).

The evidence we possess on the relationship between family income and family size is misleading. One cannot infer from the negative correlation between family size and family income that children (N) are inferior goods. This is so because p_c and p_s are not typically held constant when such calculations are made. When the major components of p_c and p_s are held constant (i.e., married women's wage rates and the prices of purchased goods), the relationship between income and family size is usually positive but near 0. Mincer's (1963, pp. 75–9) widely quoted results based on a sample of 400 white, urban families in 1950, for instance, indicate that the demand for children is quite unresponsive to increases in income but that N is mildly normal, nonetheless.[11] Moffitt (1984), in his panel study of married women from 1968 to 1979, finds the income elasticity of demand for children to be positive but not statistically different from 0. Dooley (1982), in his cross-section study utilizing data from 1969, finds children to be normal goods or independent of income in white families (the income elasticity of demand for children being 0.04) and usually inferior goods in black families. Fleisher and Rhodes (1979) estimate the income elasticity of demand for children to be 0.22 based on a panel of married white women beginning in 1967. Consequently we must conclude that completed family size, N, is normal or independent. If we use the Dooley or the Fleisher and Rhodes estimate of N_n (0.04 and 0.22, respectively) and the estimate of N_c calculated earlier (0.43), the income elasticity of demand for human capital per child is

$$N_q = N_c - N_n = 0.43 - 0.04 = 0.39$$

or

$$N_q = N_c - N_n = 0.43 - 0.22 = 0.19$$

Clearly, the demand for human capital per child rises as income rises and it rises much more rapidly than the demand for completed family size.

The effect of income on the price of children

That the demand for Q rises with increases in income while the demand for N is relatively unchanged gives us one explanation why rich families have fewer children than poor families. The explanation hinges on the effect of an increase in income on the prices of a child, N (not to be confused with the price of child services), and of human capital per child, Q.

One can divide the expenditures on child services, $p_c C$, by the number of children, N, to obtain the price of children (as opposed to child services); that is,

$$p_n = p_c C / N = p_c N Q / N = p_c Q. \qquad (7.14)$$

The price of a child, therefore, is the unit cost of child services, p_c, times the amount of human capital per child, Q, with which each child is provided.

Likewise, one divides expenditures on child services by Q to obtain the price of human capital per child (i.e., the average cost of human capital). This yields

$$p_q = p_c C / Q = p_c Q N / Q = p_c N. \qquad (7.15)$$

The cost of increasing the human capital of children by one unit, then, is the cost of buying one more unit of child services (p_c) for each of the N children in the family.

Now, consider what happens to p_n and p_q as income increases (see mathematical note 5). Note that here we are interested in what happens to the price of children relative to the price of human capital per child; that is,

$$p_n / p_q = p_c Q / p_c N = Q / N. \qquad (7.16)$$

As income rises, the couple's demand for Q rises relative to the demand for N, as we have seen in the previous section. Consequently, p_n rises relative to p_q with increases in income. As the price of N rises relative to the price of Q, the couple will respond by demanding fewer children and more human capital per child. Accordingly, rich couples will have fewer children than poor couples but spend more on them.

This, then, is one explanation of the negative correlation between family income and family size. As family income rises, the demand for child services rises because the demands for both N and Q rise but the demand for Q rises more rapidly than the demand for N. The rise in the demand for Q relative to N raises the price of children, $p_n = p_c Q$, more than the price of human capital per child,

$p_q = p_c N$, and this causes the family to demand fewer children but to spend more on each of them. Thus, as family income rises, family size falls even though children, per se, are normal goods.

The effects of changes in w on C, Q, and N

One of the most interesting aspects of the economics of fertility is the effect that the rising value of women's time has had on the birthrate. The argument runs as follows. The time cost of having and rearing children is large and is mostly made up of the value of the mother's time that she could have spent in other activities. As the value of mothers' time has increased, as witnessed by the rise in female wage rates,[12] the cost of children has risen and, in consequence, couples have demanded fewer children. This, it is argued, is one of the important factors contributing to the long-run downward trend in family size and to the baby bust since the late 1950s.

Let us consider the argument in greater detail because there is more going on than is apparent. The question is just what effect does a change in the married woman's wage rate have on the budget line facing a couple. Once that is determined, the effects of the change can be ascertained. Her wage rate appears in the couple's full income, $wT + V$, in the price of child services, $p_{xc}b_c + wt_c$, and in the price of all other services, $p_{xs}b_s + wt_s$. When, therefore, her wage rate rises, the couple's full income rises, but the prices of both child services and all other services rise also. These effects can most easily be addressed by thinking geometrically.

In Figure 7.4 line AB represents the budget line facing a couple prior to an increase in the wife's wage rate. Recall that point A is the maximum amount of parental services, S^m, the couple can produce and consume given their full income and the price of all other services. Thus,

$$S^m = (wT + V)/(p_{xs}b_s + wt_s). \tag{7.17}$$

Similarly, point B represents the maximum amount of child services, C^m, the couple can produce and consume given its full income and the price of child services:

$$C^m = (wT + V)/(p_x b_c + wt_c). \tag{7.18}$$

The effect of the increase in w, then, reduces to its effects on S^m and C^m. We deal with each in turn.

An increase in w increases both the numerator and the denominator of C^m but the increase in full income brought about by the increase in w is larger than the increase in p_c. Consequently, an increase in w raises the maximum amount of child services the couple can produce and consume (see mathematical note 6).

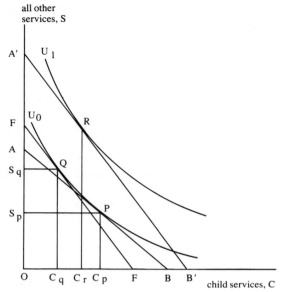

Figure 7.4 The effect of a rise in w on the demand for child services, C

Similarly, an increase in w increases S^m. Thus, the budget line after an increase in the wife's wage rate, $A'B'$, lies to the northeast of AB.

What slope will $A'B'$ have? Will $A'B'$ be parallel to AB or will it have a steeper or a gentler slope? That is, will the increase in w increase, decrease, or leave unaffected the relative price of child services, p_c/p_s? The answer turns on whether child services are more time intensive than all other services. If

$$wt_c/p_c - wt_s/p_s > 0, \tag{7.19}$$

then child services are said to be more time intensive than parental services. The ratio of wt_c to p_c is the ratio of the time cost to the total cost of producing a unit of child services. Likewise, wt_s/p_s is the ratio of the time cost to the total cost of producing a unit of all other services. These ratios measure the time intensity of each good because the more time intensive the good, the larger the ratio of its time cost to its total unit cost. Relative time intensity is measured by whether the ratio for one of the goods is larger than that for the other. If $wt_c/p_c > wt_s/p_s$, then child services are more time intensive than all other services.

A rise in w will increase p_c more than p_s and the slope of $A'B'$ will be steeper than the slope of AB if child services are more time intensive than S (see mathematical note 7). In the preceding section s_c was estimated to be somewhat lower than 0.93, s_c being the money costs of children as a fraction of the total costs, that is, $p_{xc}X_c/p_cC$. Since $X_c = b_cC$, $p_{xc}X_c/p_cC = p_{xc}b_c/p_c$, which is the "goods" intensity of child services. The time intensity of child services is, therefore, somewhat higher than $(1 - s_c) = 0.07$. Although economists do not have an empirical measure of the time intensity of parental services, intuition leads them to believe C is more time intensive than S, the rearing of children being quite time intensive. Figure 7.4 has been drawn on this assumption.

Provided a rise in w increases p_c more than it does p_s, a rise in w not only exerts an income effect on couples' demands for children but also induces a substitution effect. As the value of married women's time has risen, child services have become relatively more expensive and couples have substituted S for C, holding satisfaction constant. This is shown in Figure 7.4 as the move from point P to point Q along indifference curve U_0, involving the decline in the desired amount of child services from C_p to C_q. But since the rising value of women's time has also increased couple's real income, the demands for both C and S have increased. This is shown in Figure 7.4 by the move from Q to R, involving the increase in desired child services from C_q to C_r.

As drawn, the net effect of the rise in w has been to reduce the demand for C. Of course, this need not have happened. The income effect of the increase in w could be large enough to more than counteract its substitution effect, and the demand for child services could increase. Since we are not yet able to measure C, we have not been able to establish whether the net effect of the rise in the value of married women's time has been to increase or decrease the demand for child services.

We are also interested in the effects of rises in w on N, desired family size, and on Q, the amount of human capital per child. Again, however, a combination of measurement and intuition provide some tentative answers. For couples to reduce their demand for C in the face of increases in w by substituting S for Q implies that couples are willing to sacrifice their children's human capital (i.e., their children's health, physical and intellectual skills, etc.) in favor of services that they, the parents, consume. This is very implausible given what we know about the willingness of parents to sacrifice for their children. It is much more likely that couples will substitute S for C as w increases by reducing N and maintaining the expenditures of time and money they make per child.[13]

So much for the intuition: what about the measurement? The measurement pertains to the effect of changes in married women's wage rates on the demand for the number of children. The first to estimate the effect of w on N was Mincer in a study published in 1963 and using data from 1950. For white, urban, married women, age 35–44, Mincer found that an increase of $1,000 per year in their wage rate, holding husbands' annual earnings and education constant, resulted in a decrease in family size by 0.19 children. Subsequently, many studies have been done. In all the studies in which other factors affecting fertility are held constant, there is a strong negative relationship between the value of married women's time (i.e., her wage rate) and her completed family size (Dooley 1982; Fleisher & Rhodes 1979; Moffitt 1984). Fleisher and Rhodes (1979, p. 20), for instance, estimate the wife's wage rate elasticity of demand for number of children to be −0.43.

We conclude that the value of time of married women is an important determinant of couples' demands for child services, for children, and for human capital per child. Any explanation of the fall in the birthrate over the last 185 yr. and of the baby bust since the late 1950s must include the changing time costs of children as the value of women's time has increased.

The effects of contraceptive knowledge, use, and cost

Knowledge of contraceptive techniques is viewed as an important determinant of fertility independent of price and income variables. In the absence of good data on the extent of contraceptive knowledge among women and the effect this variation has on birthrates, women's education has been used as a proxy for contraceptive knowledge and the relationship between education and fertility has been examined.

That highly educated women have fewer children than less well educated women is explained in two ways. First, highly educated females command higher wage rates than poorly educated women and, therefore, the negative association between women's education and their fertility rates is, in part, a consequence of the differences in the values of their time. This was discussed in detail in the previous section and needs no further comment here.

Second, it is argued that highly educated women have better knowledge of the reproductive process and of contraceptive techniques and use this knowledge to keep actual numbers of children in line with desired numbers of children. Consequently, highly educated women have fewer unwanted children. This effect of contraceptive knowledge is demonstrated by the findings of Ryder and Westoff (1971, Table II-1), who found that the difference between expected and intended family size falls as the education of the woman rises. Intended family size indicates the plans women have made and, thus, reflects their demands for children. Expected family size is a woman's prediction of what will actually happen and includes her estimate of unwanted children.

Knowledge of contraceptive techniques is not the only issue, however. Use of birth control techniques is costly monetarily and psychologically and, for those facing religious injunctions against contraception, morally. What effects does the cost of contraceptive use have?

Of course, contraceptives are used when conception is not demanded and are not used when conception is desired. The cost of contraception is, therefore, not incurred when children are desired. Not having to pay the cost of contraceptives (monetarily, psychologically, and, perhaps, morally) when conception is desired constitutes a reduction in the price of a child. The absence of the cost of contraception when children are wanted, therefore, can be viewed as a subsidy for wanting children. That is, if the price of a child from conception onward is p_g, and the per child subsidy of not having to use contraceptives when one wants children is S_c, then the net price of a child (see mathematical note 8) is

$$p_n = p_g - S_c. \tag{7.20}$$

Phrased in this way, it is clear that any reduction in the cost of contraceptives lowers the subsidy, S_c, and, therefore, raises the net price of children, p_n. The introduction of family-planning information or effective contraceptive techniques that are cheaper to use, easier to use, or morally unobjectionable lowers the cost of contraceptive use and raises the net price of children. This, in turn will induce couples to demand fewer children. The same increase in the price of children and reduction in the demand for children results from relaxation of moral injunctions against the use of particular birth control techniques.

Infant mortality

Is there any connection between infant mortality and fertility? This question is more relevant to current policy in more overpopulated, less developed countries than the United States. However, we end this chapter with a discussion of it to emphasize the point that birth and death are part of the seamless web of life in which all human behavior is interconnected.

By infant mortality is meant death prior to the end of the first year of life either through miscarriage during pregnancy or death during the first year of life. Two effects of infant mortality have been identified with the help of the economic framework we have been using.

Recall that the economic framework presumes that couples derive satisfaction from child services as well as from all other goods. Bluntly put, child services can be derived only from live children. The death of an infant destroys the child services and engenders a "replacement" demand for added children to replace the children who die. Said differently, if couples expect a given percentage of all births to end in death before the end of the first year of life, they must give birth to more children than they desire in order to ensure that they have the number of surviving children they want. The higher the infant mortality rate in a country, then, the higher the birthrate can be expected to be.

Infant mortality also affects the cost side of the "market" for children. Miscarriages and death during the child's first year involve heavy monetary and emotional costs. Since couples demand surviving children, not simply conceptions, the cost of those not surviving must be spread over the surviving ones: the higher the infant mortality rate, the higher the costs that must be spread over surviving children. Consequently, the expected price of children, p_n, is higher the higher the infant mortality rate (see mathematical note 9). As the infant mortality rate falls, the expected price per child will fall, and the demand for children will rise and with it the birthrate.

As infant mortality rates fall with better nutrition, better public health measures, and better prenatal and postnatal care, the birthrate will fall as replacement demand falls and rise as the price of children falls. Which effect dominates is an empirical question. The work of Schultz (1973) with Taiwan data suggests that the net effect of a rise in infant mortality is to increase fertility and to do so more for older than for younger women. Presumably, a rise in infant mortality does not raise the fertility of younger women as much as for older women because younger women have plenty of time left to give birth to their desired number of children. For older women, however, the time left to give birth is short and hence their fertility must rise by more if they are to achieve their desired number of children.

Summary

The economics of fertility has been discussed in the context of a very simple two-good, one-period model. It is to be hoped that the power and potential of economics as a tool for understanding fertility has been demonstrated. Questions of the timing of births, the spacing of children, and the desired sex ratios of couples' children are among the myriad of questions not addressed. Some of these can be addressed by more complicated economic models. Others need the light that sociology and biology and the other sciences can shed. Each discipline, including economics, helps us understand human behavior better.

then, results in an estimate of the income elasticity of demand for child services of

$$N_c = 0.93(0.46) + (1 - 0.93)0 = 0.43.$$

It appears clear, then, that child services are normal goods and that the demand for child services rises as income rises.

What can be said about N and Q, the components of child services? Do families increase their demand for children, their demand for human capital per child, or both as income increases? The relationship between the income elasticity of demand for child services and the income elasticities of demand for N and Q is

$$N_c = N_n + N_q \tag{7.13}$$

where N_n = the income elasticity of demand for number of children and N_q = the income elasticity of demand for human capital per child (see mathematical note 4).

The evidence we possess on the relationship between family income and family size is misleading. One cannot infer from the negative correlation between family size and family income that children (N) are inferior goods. This is so because p_c and p_s are not typically held constant when such calculations are made. When the major components of p_c and p_s are held constant (i.e., married women's wage rates and the prices of purchased goods), the relationship between income and family size is usually positive but near 0. Mincer's (1963, pp. 75–9) widely quoted results based on a sample of 400 white, urban families in 1950, for instance, indicate that the demand for children is quite unresponsive to increases in income but that N is mildly normal, nonetheless.[11] Moffitt (1984), in his panel study of married women from 1968 to 1979, finds the income elasticity of demand for children to be positive but not statistically different from 0. Dooley (1982), in his cross-section study utilizing data from 1969, finds children to be normal goods or independent of income in white families (the income elasticity of demand for children being 0.04) and usually inferior goods in black families. Fleisher and Rhodes (1979) estimate the income elasticity of demand for children to be 0.22 based on a panel of married white women beginning in 1967. Consequently we must conclude that completed family size, N, is normal or independent. If we use the Dooley or the Fleisher and Rhodes estimate of N_n (0.04 and 0.22, respectively) and the estimate of N_c calculated earlier (0.43), the income elasticity of demand for human capital per child is

$$N_q = N_c - N_n = 0.43 - 0.04 = 0.39$$

or

$$N_q = N_c - N_n = 0.43 - 0.22 = 0.19$$

Clearly, the demand for human capital per child rises as income rises and it rises much more rapidly than the demand for completed family size.

The effect of income on the price of children

That the demand for Q rises with increases in income while the demand for N is relatively unchanged gives us one explanation why rich families have fewer children than poor families. The explanation hinges on the effect of an increase in income on the prices of a child, N (not to be confused with the price of child services), and of human capital per child, Q.

One can divide the expenditures on child services, p_cC, by the number of children, N, to obtain the price of children (as opposed to child services); that is,

$$p_n = p_cC/N = p_cNQ/N = p_cQ. \tag{7.14}$$

The price of a child, therefore, is the unit cost of child services, p_c, times the amount of human capital per child, Q, with which each child is provided.

Likewise, one divides expenditures on child services by Q to obtain the price of human capital per child (i.e., the average cost of human capital). This yields

$$p_q = p_cC/Q = p_cQN/Q = p_cN. \tag{7.15}$$

The cost of increasing the human capital of children by one unit, then, is the cost of buying one more unit of child services (p_c) for each of the N children in the family.

Now, consider what happens to p_n and p_q as income increases (see mathematical note 5). Note that here we are interested in what happens to the price of children relative to the price of human capital per child; that is,

$$p_n/p_q = p_cQ/p_cN = Q/N. \tag{7.16}$$

As income rises, the couple's demand for Q rises relative to the demand for N, as we have seen in the previous section. Consequently, p_n rises relative to p_q with increases in income. As the price of N rises relative to the price of Q, the couple will respond by demanding fewer children and more human capital per child. Accordingly, rich couples will have fewer children than poor couples but spend more on them.

This, then, is one explanation of the negative correlation between family income and family size. As family income rises, the demand for child services rises because the demands for both N and Q rise but the demand for Q rises more rapidly than the demand for N. The rise in the demand for Q relative to N raises the price of children, $p_n = p_cQ$, more than the price of human capital per child,

Table 8.2. *Marriage and divorce rates by geographic region: 1979*

Region	Marriage rate	Divorce rate
United States	10.6	5.4
New England	8.5	4.0
Middle Atlantic	7.9	3.5
East North Central	9.6	5.2
West North Central	10.0	4.5
South Atlantic	11.5	5.8
East South Central	12.0	6.1
West South Central	12.7	6.7
Mountain	21.3	7.6
Pacific	9.4	6.3

Note: Marriage and divorce rates are calculated as the number per 1,000 population.
Source: U.S. Bureau of the Census 1982, pp. 83 – 4.

At any point in time a smaller fraction of the female population is married, a smaller fraction is single, and a larger fraction is divorced than for males.

Table 8.2 shows the geographic variation in marriage and divorce rates as of 1979. There were 10.6 marriages and 5.4 divorces per 1,000 population in the United States in 1979. Geographically, the Middle Atlantic states had the lowest marriage rate (7.9) and the lowest divorce rate (3.5). The Mountain states had the highest marriage and divorce rates, 21.3 and 7.6, respectively.

It is clear, then, that there are variations in marriage and divorce rates to be explained both through time and across geographic areas. Economic theory is potentially relevant as a (partial) explanation of marriage and divorce only if marriage and divorce can be viewed as economic activities over which the individuals involved have choice. As with fertility, if individuals have no choice over whether they are married or divorced, then economics is irrelevant.[3] Individuals in most countries do have a choice over whether they marry, when and whom they marry, and whether they divorce. Thus, rational decision making with respect to marriage and divorce is possible.

For economics to be relevant, marriage and divorce must also affect individuals' satisfaction or well-being and be costly in that scarce resources are consumed by marriage and divorce. Since marriage and divorce are preeminently affairs of the heart in this country today, saying that they affect individuals' well-being is almost tautological.

Finally, marriage and divorce must be costly for economics to be helpful in explaining the phenomena. Marriage and divorce entails two kinds of costs:

transaction costs and forgone costs. Transaction costs are the costs of marriage licenses, wedding ceremonies, lawyers' fees, court costs, and so on; that is, the costs of transacting the agreement to marry or divorce. Forgone costs are the benefits of the state that one gives up in order to reach another state. That is, the forgone costs of marriage are the benefits of being single that one forsakes in order to become married. Likewise, the forgone costs of divorce are the benefits of continuing the marriage. Although transaction costs can be substantial, it is likely that the forgone costs of marriage and divorce are greater.[4] Either way, marriage and divorce are costly.

Having established that economics may have relevance in the explanation of marriage and divorce, a simple model of the decision to marry will be built. It will provide interpretations of the roles played by such factors as the sex ratio, male and female wage rates, unearned incomes of males and females, and liberal divorce laws in determining marriage rates. The model will be built on the assumption that individuals act on the basis of their expectations about the future benefits and costs of marriage. Once built, the model will be used to draw inferences about the economic determinants of marriage. Several empirical studies of marriage rates will be examined to see if the inferences are correct. Then a model of divorce will be discussed in which divorce is viewed as the reaction to failed marital expectations. The chapter will end with a discussion of some empirical work that sheds light on the model of divorce.

A model of marriage

A model of marriage begins with the idea that individuals will marry if they believe that they will be better off married than single. By being better off married than single is meant that the individuals would be happier (i.e., have greater utility) married than single. Those individuals who remain single are those for whom marriage would not make them any better off. Most individuals would be better off married to several possible mates. Consequently, the individual must choose which of these people to marry. The principle of satisfaction maximization implies that the individual confronted with several possible mates will marry the one who will make him or her "happiest" or "best off." The model formalizes these ideas by focusing on an individual's gain from marriage.

The gain from marriage

Let us focus on two individuals, denoted by M and F, and consider the gains each would obtain by remaining single and by marrying the other.

At this point we need to introduce the concept of household production. We note that individuals use their time along with purchased goods and services in a myriad of activities that yield satisfaction. These activities are household activities, possess all the characteristics of production, and range from preparing a meal, doing the laundry, and cleaning house to going to the theater, skiing, or sleeping. More significantly, when done with another person, the concept of household production encompasses such activities as loving, caring, having and rearing children, and the host of other activities that require the time inputs of two people, typically of the opposite sex.

For the purposes of analysis we can aggregate all the myriad of activities into one aggregate household activity.[5] Denote the output of this single aggregate household activity over the individual's planning period as Z. We can write the relationship between the time and purchased inputs, on the one hand, and the quantity of the aggregate household output, on the other, as

$$Z = z(H_m, H_f, X) \tag{8.1}$$

where H_m = the time input over the planning period of individual M; H_f = the time input over the planning period of individual F; and X = the quantity of purchased inputs used in the single aggregate household activity. X includes both capital equipment like stoves, beds, and dishes and one-use goods and services like food, electricity, theater tickets, and baby-sitters' time.

Now, equation (8.1) has been specified as including the time inputs of both M and F. Clearly, this is correct only if M and F are married to each other. If each is single, then the time input of the other is zero. That is, the output of the household activity of F's single household would be

$$Z_f = z(H_m = 0, H_f, X). \tag{8.2}$$

And the output of M's single household would be what M could produce without F's time input; that is,

$$Z_m = z(H_m, H_f = 0, X) \tag{8.3}$$

Finally, the output of the household they would form if they married would be

$$Z_{mf} = z(H_m, H_f, X) \tag{8.4}$$

In this model, M and F each spend their time in two ways: in household activities, H_i ($i = m, f$), and in market work (i.e., "labor"), L_i ($i = f, m$), where H_i and L_i denote the times spent in household activities and in market work over the planning period, respectively. Thus, if T_i ($i = f, m$) denotes the length of the planning period, each individual's time use is bound by the constraint

$$T_i = H_i + L_f, \qquad \text{for } i = f, m. \tag{8.5}$$

Each individual is assumed to work in the market some time during the planning period and to have some amount of unearned income, denoted by V_i $(i = f, m)$. The individual's total income when single, then, is

$$Y_i = w_i L_i + V_i, \qquad \text{for } i = f, m. \tag{8.6}$$

Of course, each individual seeks to maximize his or her own satisfaction over the planning period. Let the individual's utility be denoted as U_i $(i = m, f)$. It will be dependent on the output of household activities, Z_i, that is,

$$U_i = u_i(Z_i), \qquad \text{for } i = f, m, \tag{8.7}$$

where the greater the Z_i, the larger the U_i; that is, the happier the individual.

Thus, as a single household the individual seeks to maximize U_i over the planning horizon by allocating his or her time between household activity and market work and by using his or her income to buy inputs into household activities. This is no more and no less than the simple model of time use we developed in Chapter 5 and can be written mathematically as follows:

$$\begin{aligned}
&\textit{Maximize } U_i = u_i(Z_i) \\
&\text{subject to } T_i = H_i + L_i \qquad \text{and} \qquad pX + w_i H_i = w_i T_i + V_i, \\
&\text{for } i = f, m.
\end{aligned} \tag{8.8}$$

However, in this case the individual is also faced with deciding whether to marry or to remain single.

Notice that the utility (i.e., the satisfaction) of each individual is a positive function of the quantity of output produced by the aggregate household production activity; the greater the quantity of Z, the more satisfied each individual. Recall that we are concerned only with whether an individual is more or less satisfied in any circumstance compared with any other and not by how much. Consequently, we know that if one situation results in more aggregate household output than other situation, the individual is more satisfied with the former situation. This means that we can neglect completely the individuals' utility functions from this point onward and concentrate on their respective outputs from household activity in married and single states.[6]

Given that we can neglect each individual's utility, the issue of whether any individual will marry depends on the answer to the following question: does the individual's output of Z when single exceed the individual's *share* of the output of Z when married? If the individual's single output, Z_i, exceeds the individual's share, call it S_i, of household output when married, then there is no incentive for individual i to marry. Why? Because, if $S_i < Z_i$, then the satisfaction i obtains from Z_i will exceed the satisfaction i obtains from S_i, i's share of marital output being smaller than i's single output.

Under what conditions will $Z_i > S_i$ and, therefore, marriage be preferred by individual i? First of all, marital output, Z_{mf}, must be at least equal to the sum of the two individuals' outputs when single:

$$Z_{mf} \geq Z_f + Z_m. \tag{8.9}$$

Why? Consider the case in which $Z_{mf} < Z_m + Z_f$. Now suppose that F's share of marital output with M exceeded her single output ($S_f > Z_f$), indicating that it would be in F's best interest to marry M. Since $Z_{mf} < Z_m + Z_f$, however, and $S_f > Z_f$, M's share of marital output with F would be less than his single output ($S_m < Z_m$) and M would have no incentive to marry F: F's love for M will go unrequited! Consequently, marital output must at least equal the sum of the couple's single outputs for marriage to be in the interest of both individuals.

Under what conditions, then, will marital output be at least equal to the sum of the individuals' single outputs and, thus, constitute a reason for marriage? One condition is "economies of household size," which refers to the condition in which household output more than doubles with a doubling of household size. We have argued elsewhere that economies of household size do, indeed, exist. Since adding a member to a single household would more than double household output, then $Z_{mf} > Z_f + Z_m$. But this would occur whenever any two individuals – two males, two females, a male and a female, or an adult and a child – live together. To allow economies of household size to be a sufficient condition for marriage would reduce the theory of marriage to a theory of multimember household formation rather than of marriage per se. Consequently, other reasons why $Z_{mf} > Z_f + Z_m$ have been searched for.

Becker has focused his attention on the question of "complementary inputs" in household production. He argues that there are some types of household output that are produced only by households formed through marriage and not by other means. He considers children and love as the two commodities capable of being produced in households formed through marriage. Given that marital households produce love and children, whereas single households do not because they cannot, then $Z_{mf} > Z_m + Z_f$. And given a distribution of marital output such that $S_f > Z_f$ and $S_m > Z_m$, then the marriage may occur. Critics have pointed out, however, that love and children can and do occur in households of unmarried couples (of the same or opposite sex) and, thus, complementary inputs at most yields a theory of consensual marriage rather than legal marriage.

The decision process to marry as conceived in Becker's theory of marriage, then, is as follows. Each individual behaves as if he or she identifies possible mates. Possible mates are those with whom the individual would be happier married than single. These are the individuals with whom marital output, Z_{mf}, is at least equal to, if not greater than, the sum of their single outputs, $Z_m + Z_f$, and the individual's share of marital output, S_i, would in each case exceed his or her single output, Z_i. From this set of possible mates, the individual selects that mate to marry with whom his or her share of marital output would be the greatest.

This is an elaborate way of saying the following. Ken has Sally, Abby, Beth, Cathy, and Danielle as friends. Through the many social occasions in which he interacts with them he finds he likes Sally, Abby, and Beth much more than either Cathy or Danielle. The former three share his interests and are as romantically interested in him as he is in them. He is not romantically interested in either Cathy or Danielle. They are just good friends. In other words marriage with Sally, Abby, or Beth would produce marital outputs greater than the sums of his single output with each of theirs. The marital outputs if married to either Cathy or Danielle would not equal the sum of his single output with each of theirs. Furthermore, he would be happier married to any of the three women than if he remained single. That is, he estimates that his share of marital output if married to Sally, Abby, or Beth would exceed his single output. Sally, Abby, and Beth, then, are possible mates of Ken and he is a possible mate for each of them.

Through further interaction with the three women, Ken and Abby "fall in love" and decide to marry. In terms of Becker's model of marriage, Ken gets to know the three women well enough (and they him) that Ken determines that he would be happier with Abby than with either Sally or Beth. Happier here means that he estimates that his share of marital output with Abby would be higher than if he married either of the other two women. Thus, marriage with Abby would maximize his satisfaction.

Now each of the women goes through the same process. Each has a set of possible mates and within that set a particular mate with whom she would be happiest if they were married. In Abby's case, this is Ken. Thus, through marriage Abby's and Ken's shares of total marital output are greater than in any other marriage.

To summarize the model then: for an individual to marry at all, two conditions must be met:

1. Total output from the marriage must equal or exceed the sum of the single outputs of the two partners:

$$Z_{mf} \geq Z_m + Z_f.$$

2. The individual's share of marital output must equal or exceed his or her single output:

$$S_i \geq Z_i, \qquad \text{for } i = m, f.$$

This implies, then, that

$$S_m + S_f \leq Z_{mf}. \tag{8.10}$$

The marital shares will sum to marital output in the absence of any transaction cost of marriage. Otherwise, the marital shares will sum to marital output net of transaction costs. Finally, since individuals are assumed to maximize satisfaction, each individual enters into that marriage in which his or her share of marital output is greatest compared with the shares from other possible marriages.

Implications of the model

There are a great number of implications of this theory of marriage. We will pursue only a few of them, leaving the other implications to your own reading. The implications we will pursue will be those that help explain variations in marriage rates through time and among regions in the country.

The ratio of males to females

In the discussion of the presented marriage model, it was implicitly assumed that there were equal numbers of males and females and that the gain from marriage was positive for each person. Therefore, everyone was married and no one was single. But this is not a very accurate picture of the world as we know it. Women outnumber men[7] and there are individuals for whom marriage is inferior to remaining single. Thus, the percentage of males or females married (i.e., the marital status of men and women; see Table 8.1) will never be 100 percent and it will vary through time and geographically. Can we use the theory to begin to understand why? We can, in fact, derive what amounts to supply and demand curves for mates.

Recall that the shares of marital output, S_m and S_f, must sum to total marital output, Z_{mf}. Recall also that an individual, male or female, will not marry unless his or her share of marital output is at least equal to his or her single output. That is, an individual will not marry unless he or she is at least as happy married as single. We can regard an individual's single output, Z_i, as the individual's *reservation price of marriage*, therefore. By the reservation price of marriage is meant that Z_i is the minimum share of marital output individual i will accept in order to be married rather than single. If

$$S_i = Z_i, \qquad \text{for } i = m, f,$$

individual i will be indifferent between being married and single. So long as

$$S_i > Z_i, \qquad \text{for } i = m, f,$$

individual i will be married. Z_i, therefore, is individual i's reservation price of marriage.

Now suppose we know the single outputs, Z_{mi}, for each male in the country or geographic region at time t, where there are $i = 1, \ldots, N_m$ males. Now rank

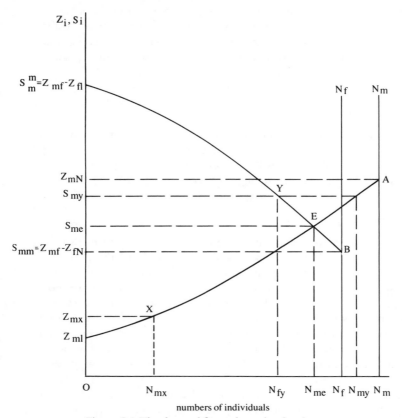

Figure 8.1 The demand for and supply of male mates

the males by their single outputs so that Z_{m1} is the single output of the male with the lowest single output and Z_{mN} is the single output of the male with the highest single output. Prepare a diagram with single output and marital share measured on the vertical axis. The number of males is measured on the horizontal axis ranked so that the males closest to the vertical axis are those with the lowest Z_i's while those farthest to the right from the vertical axis are those with the highest Z_i's. Finally, plot the Z_i for each individual so ranked along the horizontal axis.

Such a diagram is illustrated in Figure 8.1. In Figure 8.1 the vertical line $N_m N_m$ represents the total number, N_m, of males in the country. Z_{m1} is the single output of the male in the country with the lowest single output. Z_{mN} is the single output of the male in the country with the highest single output. The line $Z_{m1} A$ represents the cumulative distribution of males with respect to their single outputs, Z_{mi}. At any point, X, on line $Z_{m1} A$,, N_{mx} males have single outputs equal to or less than Z_{mx}. Put differently, at point X, N_{mx} males would marry if each could have a marital share from their respective marriages at least equal to Z_{mx}.[8] N_{mx}, therefore, is the "supply of male mates" at the "price" of Z_{mx}. Likewise, there is a zero supply of male mates at a price of Z_{m1} and there is a supply of N_m male mates (i.e., all the males in the country) if females "paid" a price of at least Z_{mN}. The curve $Z_{m1}A$, therefore, is the supply curve of male mates.

We are now interested in the demand curve for male mates on the part of females. As with males, females will not marry unless their share of marital output is at least as large as their single output. Thus, the supply of female mates to the marriage market can be derived in exactly the same fashion as the supply of male mates. That is, if women are ranked from the woman with the lowest single output to the woman with the highest, then Z_{f1} is the single output of the woman with the lowest single output and Z_{fN} is the single output of the woman with the highest single output. A curve similar to $Z_{m1}A$ in Figure 8.1 representing the supply curve of female mates could, thus, be drawn.

However, we are interested in the demand curve for male mates on the part of females, not their supply curve. It happens that we can derive the demand for male mates from the supply of female mates. Recall that the sum of the marital shares equal marital output:

$$Z_{mf} = S_m + S_f.$$

Alternatively, we can say that the male's share of marital output is equal to marital output minus the female's share; that is,

$$S_m = Z_{mf} - S_f. \tag{8.11}$$

Now assume for geometric simplicity that marital output is constant across marriages.[9] Then by subtracting the minimum single output for females, Z_{f1}, from marital output, Z_{mf}, one obtains the maximum marital share, S_m^m, a male could obtain if married to the woman with the lowest marital share; that is, her single output. Thus,

$$S_m^m = Z_{mf} - Z_{f1}. \tag{8.12}$$

In other words, no woman could be found who would consent to marry if her husband's marital share was larger than S_m^m. Since in such a marriage she would receive Z_{f1} or lower, she would prefer to remain single and have Z_{f1}. S_m^m, therefore, is the highest price any woman will pay for a male mate. This point is plotted on the vertical axis in Figure 8.1 and constitutes the vertical intercept of the demand for male mates.

Similarly, we can subtract the single output of the woman with the greatest single output, Z_{fN}, from marital output, Z_{mf}, to obtain the minimum marital share any male could obtain; that is,

$$S_{mm} = Z_{mf} - Z_{fN}. \tag{8.13}$$

Recall that Z_{fN} is the minimum marital share that the woman with the maximum single output would accept if she were to marry: all other women would accept less than Z_{fN}. Consequently, all women would marry if each of their marital shares equaled Z_{fN}. S_{mm}, therefore, can be viewed as the price of male mates that would induce all women to marry. If a vertical line, N_fN_f, is erected in Figure 8.1 indicating the number of females in the country or region, then point B on N_fN_f represents S_{mm}. Note that the number of females, N_f, need not equal the number of males, N_m: in the case pictured in Figure 8.1, $N_f < N_m$.

Since females have been ranked from the woman with the lowest Z_f to the woman with the highest Z_f, other points in Figure 8.1 can be found by plotting

$$S_m = Z_{mf} - Z_{fi}, \qquad \text{for } i = 1, \ldots, N_f,$$

against the number of women, N_{fi}, with single output equal to or less than Z_{fi}. The line formed by these points is $S_m^m B$ in Figure 8.1. It represents the demand curve of male mates in the marriage market. Point Y on the demand curve for male mates by women is interpreted as follows: N_{fy} females are willing and able to pay S_{my} in order to have mates. N_{fy}, then, is the number of male mates demanded by females in the marriage market at the price of S_{my}. Recall that N_{fy} females are willing to pay S_{my} for mates in the sense that each of these females requires a marital share at least equal to Z_{fy} in order to be willing to marry. With given marital output, at most S_{my} would remain for the marital share of each of their mates.

Figure 8.1, then, is a diagram of the supply and demand curves for male mates. We could have drawn the supply and demand curves for female mates but the diagram would be symmetrical with Figure 8.1 since one is but a reflection of the other.

Now, consider again point Y. At a price of S_{my}, females demand N_{fy} male mates (i.e., N_{fy} females are willing to marry). But, at $S_{my} = Z_{my}$, N_{my} males are willing to marry. In other words, at a price of S_{my} there is an excess of willing males over willing females. If all the N_{my} willing males are to be married, they must accept lower marital shares than S_{my}. Only some will, however, and they will be the ones with single outputs lower than S_{my} and, thus, require lower marital shares than S_{my}. They will marry women willing to pay lower prices for male mates (i.e., women who have higher single outputs and, thence, require higher marital shares in order to marry).

The willingness of some men to accept a marital share of less than S_{my} will induce more women than N_{fy} to marry. The lower marital share offered by women will reduce the number of men willing to marry. Marriage market

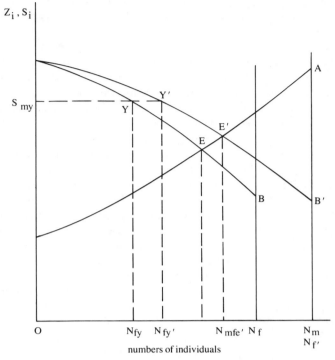

Figure 8.2 The effect of an increase in females on the demand for male mates and the number married

"equilibrium" will occur at point E in Figure 8.1. Point E represents the price at which the number of females demanding males equals the number of males willing to marry. N_{me}, therefore, will be the number of married couples. N_{me}/N_m is the fraction of males who are married, and N_{me}/N_f is the fraction of females who are married (see Table 8.1 on the marital status of the population).

Figure 8.1 shows the marriage market when the number of females is less than the number of males, $N_f < N_m$. What would happen if the number of females increased for some reason so that males equaled females?[10] This is shown in Figure 8.2. Supply curve A and demand curve B and their intersection at E represent the situation in the marriage market in which males exceed females.

Now suppose there is an exogenous increase in the number of females in the country or region so that after the increase $N_m = N_f$. What effects will there be on the demand curve of male mates? So long as the added females are similar to the females previously in the market (i.e., so long as the cumulative distribution of additional females with respect to Z_f is similar to that for the original females), then the demand curve for male mates will shift upward from curve B to curve B'. In other words, at any price, S_{my}, more females will be willing to marry and, thence, demand more males than before the increase in the number of females $(N_{fy} > N_{fx})$. Likewise, given the increased demand for male mates as a result of the increase in females, the demand curve will intersect the (unchanged) supply curve at E' rather than at E and there will be more married couples, $N_{mfe'} > N_{mfe}$. Finally, notice that as the number of females in the population increases relative to men, the fraction of men married increases from N_{mfe}/N_m to $N_{mfe'}/N_m$ and the fraction of married females falls from N_{mfe}/N_f to $N_{mfe'}/N_{f'}$.[11]

The sex ratio of the population (N_m/N_f or its inverse), then, is an important determinant of marital status. The more men there are relative to women, the higher the probability any women has of finding a mate and, therefore, the higher the fraction of females who will be married. Likewise, the more women there are relative to men, the more likely it will be that any man will find a mate and the higher the fraction of men who will be married.

The relationship between the sex ratio and the proportion married has long been observed by demographers and economists. Fredricka Santos (1972), using interstate data on females aged 15–44 yr. for 1950 and 1960, found that a ceteris paribus increase in the sex ratio N_f/N_m by 1 percent induced an increase in the fraction of single females by about 0.05 in both 1950 and 1960. Freidan (1974), in a different analysis of 1960 state data, found that the marriage rate of females per state for each 5-yr. age-group from age 15 to age 39 fell as the sex ratio N_f/N_m rose. For instance, for the age-group 20–24 in 1960, Freidan estimated that as the ratio of females to males rises by 1 percent the fraction of females married falls by 0.20 percent ceteris paribus. Similar relationships were found when intercity data for 1960 were used (Freidan 1974).

Changes in wage rates

The effect of wage rate changes on the gain from marriage importantly depends on the division of labor possibilities open in a marriage that are absent in single households. The division of labor, however, depends on males and females having different market and household productivities.

To see that this is true, suppose that males and females are perfect substitutes in household work and in market work. If they are perfect substitutes in household work, then they are equally productive in household work. That is, if each devoted the same time to household work, each would produce as much household output. Thus, the marginal product of male labor in household work, z_m, equals that of women, z_f. Furthermore, if they are perfect substitutes in market work, each earn the same wage rates: $w_m = w_f$.[12] Suppose further, that males and females have the same single unearned incomes ($V_m = V_f$) and that there are no economies of scale. Under such circumstances, the single outputs of males and females would be equal ($Z_m = Z_f$) and marital output, Z_{mf}, would simply be twice the male or female single output:

$$Z_{mf} = Z_m + Z_f = 2Z_m = 2Z_f,$$

and there would be no gain from marriage.

Now suppose that the ratio of market to home productivity of the two potential partners differ; that is,

$$w_i/z_i > w_j/z_j,$$

where z_i and z_j are the marginal products of the ith and jth individual ($i \neq j$) in household production. Then it will be the case that as a married couple the two individuals will be able to have more household output, Z_{mf}, than twice the sum of their single outputs if individual j specializes in household production and individual i specializes in market work. How so? Suppose, for instance, that $w_i > w_j$ and $z_i = z_j$; that is, that both are equally productive in household production, but individual i has the higher market wage rate. Then, individual j can increase his or her time in household production by 1 hr. and individual i can reduce his or her's by 1 hr. and household production will remain constant. This allows individual i to increase his or her time in market work by 1 hr. and allows individual j to reduce his or hers by 1 hr. Since $w_i > w_j$, family income will increase by $w_i - w_j$, which will then be used to purchase more inputs in household production, X, which will serve to increase total household output, Z_{mf}. Now individual i (with the higher wage rate) works one more hour in the market and one less in the home; individual j does the reverse. This process will continue until individual j is completely specialized in household work and individual i is completely specialized in market work, or until the ratios of the market to household productivities equalize.

This is the theory of comparative advantage as applied to the household: by each partner in a marriage specializing in that activity in which the individual is *relatively* more productive, marital output, Z_{mf}, as well as the gain from marriage, G, can be maximized. The division of labor between spouses is an important incentive to marriage, therefore. Note that the theory *does not* imply that females will specialize in household production while males will specialize in market work. If the female's market productivity *relative* to her household productivity is greater than her husband's, then the wife will specialize in market work while the husband specializes in household work.[13]

To investigate the implications of changes in wage rates, the gain to marriage must be written in a more explicit form. Recall that Z_{mf} is the total marital output that occurs when the household production function,

$$Z = z(X, H_m, H_f),$$

is maximized subject to the total resources constraint,

$$p_x X + w_m H_m + w_f H_f = V_m + V_f + w_m T_m + w_f T_f. \tag{8.14}$$

Similarly, the single output of individual i ($i = m, f$), Z_i, arises from the maximization of the household production function, $Z = z(X, H_m, H_f)$, subject to the total resources constraint,

$$p_x X + w_i H_i = V_i = w_i T_i \qquad (i = m, f) \tag{8.15}$$

and to the constraint that the time of individual j ($i \neq j; j = m, f$) is zero; that is,

$$T_j = 0 \qquad (j \neq i). \tag{8.16}$$

The gain from marriage, then, can be written

$$G = Z_{mf} - Z_m - Z_f; \tag{8.17}$$

that is, the gain from marriage is the difference between total marital output and the sum of the individuals' single outputs. Equation (8.17) is a simple rearrangement of equation (8.9). Unless $G > 0$, marriage will not occur.

Now, we can rephrase G. Let

$$I_{mf} = V_m + V_f + w_m T_m + w_f T_f \tag{8.18}$$

be full income for the married couple whereas

$$I_i = V_i + w_i T_i, \qquad \text{for } i = m, f, \tag{8.19}$$

is the full income for single individual i. Also, let

$$C_{mf} = c_{mf}(p_x, w_m, w_f) = (p_x X + w_m H_m + w_f H_f)/Z_{mf} = I_{mf}/Z_{mf} \tag{8.20}$$

be the average cost function of producing marital output, Z_{mf}, and

$$C_i = c_i(p_x, w_i) = (p_x X + w_i H_i)/Z_i = I_i/Z_i, \qquad \text{for } i = m, f, \tag{8.21}$$

be the average cost function of producing single output, Z_i. Then the gain from marriage can be expressed as (see mathematical note 1)

$$G = I_{mf}/c_{mf}(p_x, w_m, w_f) - [I_m/c_m(p_x, w_m) + I_f/c_f(p_x, w_f)]. \tag{8.22}$$

Equation (8.22) expresses the gain from marriage in terms of prices and wage rates and full income and, in consequence, allows us to examine the effects of changes in these variables.

Now consider an increase in the male wage rate (holding household productivities and female wage rate constant) and its effect on the gain from marriage. Such an increase will increase the real wealth of the couple if married, I_{mf}, and the real wealth of the male if single, I_m. The rise in w_m will also increase both the unit cost of household production if the couple is married, C_{mf}, and the unit cost of household production if the male is single, C_m. The total effects of these diverse changes are summarized in the following formula:

$$\partial G/\partial w_m = (L_m^m/c_{mf}) - (L_m^s/c_m),\qquad(8.23)$$

where $\partial G/\partial w_m$ = effect of a change in w_m on G, L_m^m = time spent by the married male in market work, and L_m^s = time spent by the single male in the market work (see mathematical note 2).

How does one interpret equation (8.23)? Recognize that for the typical American family, at least historically, $w_f/z_f < w_m/z_m$, implying that men have a comparative advantage in market work and females have a comparative advantage in household production. Thus, $L_m^m > L_m^s$; that is, the married male spends more time in market work than if he were single. This is so because specialization of function is not possible as a single male, and in consequence, the single male does more household work than if he were married (see Table 6.3). It is also the case that the average cost of household output when married is smaller than when single; $c_{mf} < c_m$. This is so because average cost is always higher in cases in which an input is fixed than in cases in which inputs are variable.[14] Thus, so long as married men are specialized in market work and married females are relatively specialized in household work,

$$L_m^m/c_{c_{mf}} > L_m^s/c_m \qquad \text{and} \qquad \partial G/\partial w_m > 0,$$

meaning that an increase in male wage rates, holding female wage rates and household productivities constant, will increase the gain from marriage and lead to an increase in the fraction of males who are married.

The argument can be put somewhat more crassly. An increase in w_m, holding income constant, raises the prices of males' time in household activities relative to purchased inputs. In consequence, the single male will spend more time working and substitute purchased inputs for his own time in household activities. One way in which this could be accomplished is by hiring a housekeeper at a wage rate of w_f. But, given the comparative advantage of females in household production $(w_f/z_f < w_m/z_m)$, the same household activities can be produced more cheaply if he were to marry and benefit from division of labor within the household. Santos (1972, p. 21) further argues that the male and female could simply live together but the social stigma of this arrangement raises the "transaction cost" of such a "consensual" arrangement, a cost that could be avoided by legal marriage. It must be remembered that Santos was writing in 1972, when the social stigma of "living together" was much higher than it is today.

Now, suppose that female wage rates rise relative to male wage rates. The effect of a ceteris paribus rise in w_f on the gain to marriage is

$$\partial G/\partial w_f = (L_f^m/c_{mf}) - (L_f^s/c_f),\qquad(8.24)$$

where $\partial G/\partial w_f =$ the effect of a change in w_f on G, L_f^m denotes the time the married woman spends in market work, $L_f^s =$ the time the single woman spends in market work, and c_{mf} and $c_f =$ the average cost of married and single output, respectively.

Clearly, if specialization is complete and married women do no market work, then $L_f^m = 0$,

$$\partial G/\partial w_f = -L_f^s/c_f < 0, \tag{8.25}$$

and a rise in female wage rates increases single female output and reduces the gain to marriage. If specialization of function is not complete, $L_f^m < L_f^s$ (see Table 6.3), the comparative advantage of the female in household production is greatly reduced, and the average cost of marital output, c_{mf}, is not much below the average cost of single female output, c_f. In this case,

$$\partial G/\partial w_f = (L_f^m/c_{mf}) - (L_f^s/c_f) < 0. \tag{8.26}$$

A ceteris paribus rise in w_f, then, reduces the gain from marriage by reducing the increase in household output due to marriage and by raising single output.

Santos (1972, p. 22) argues that a rise in w_f increases the "economic independence" of females (i.e., increases what they can have by remaining single, Z_f) and reduces the complementarity of female with male labor in the context of a marriage. Consequently, female marriage rates would fall as female wage rates rise, ceteris paribus. Underlying the "economic independence" argument is a bargaining model in which the female's single output, Z_f, is the "threat point." That is, the female must get at least Z_f out of a marriage if she is to enter it. And if she is in a marriage that does not yield at least Z_f, she will leave it. This is part and parcel of the alternative marriage model proposed by Manser and Brown (1979 and 1980), but it fits here too.

The arguments made here with respect to changes in relative male and female wage rates are predicated on the assumption that males have a comparative advantage in market work and females have a comparative advantage in household activities, $w_f/z_f < w_m/z_m$. If the reverse were the case, then the predicted wage rate effects would be reversed. Becker argues that women do, in fact, have a comparative advantage in household activities. His argument is that because females, not males, carry and bear children and most mothers have an interest in nurturing them (and, remember, children are an important part of marital output, Z_{mf}), females have a biologically based comparative advantage for household activities. Given that parents expect female children to spend more of their lives in household activities and male children to spend more of theirs in market activities, then the type of human capital investments parents make in their children will accentuate these comparative advantages (see Chapter 6). Even if market wage rates did not differ by sex, different types of human capital investments in boys and girls create and accentuate the comparative advantage females have for household activities and the comparative advantage males have for market activities.

Of course, whether females have a biologically based initial comparative advantage in household activities tends to be irrelevant if market wage rates for men exceed those for women for reasons unconnected to their productivities. Historic sex discrimination in the labor market is sufficient to lead human capital investments in females to differentially augment female household productivity and to lead human capital investments in males to augment their market relative to their household productivities and, in consequence, to give females a comparative advantage in household activities relative to men. As sex discrimination in the labor market has decreased in the twentieth century (see Smith & Ward 1984), the gap between male and female wage rates has diminished, and the comparative advantage of females for household activities based on labor market discrimination has decreased.

It should finally be noted that any biologically based comparative advantage females have historically had for household activities arising out of child bearing and rearing has been and continues to be reduced by market developments and technical change. As high-quality substitutes for maternal (and paternal) care of children become available on the market at reasonable prices, for instance, females' comparative advantage in postbirth household activities vanishes. And medical and public advances in the nineteenth and twentieth centuries have similarly reduced the biological basis for this comparative advantage. For instance, the reduction of infant mortality rates has reduced the expected number of pregnancies needed for one live child (see Chapter 7) and, thus, greatly reduced the amount of time females have to spend in bearing children.

Although female comparative advantage in household activities and male comparative advantage in market activities certainly have been historic facts, they are not immutable. Thus, the sex-specific wage rate effects discussed in this section also are not immutable.

Santos and Freidan have studied the relationship between relative male/female wage rates and marital status. Freidan related the percentage of married females by age per state to male/female wage rate ratios (w_m/w_f), holding the sex ratio and other variables constant. He found that a 1 percent increase in the male/female wage rate ratio increased the percentage of married females aged 20–24 years old in 1960 by state by 0.12 percent (1974, Table 5, p. 365). In contrast, Santos studied the influence of female earnings separately from the influence of male earnings. She found that the proportion of females who were married per state in 1960 rose significantly as male earnings rose, holding female earnings and other variables constant. And the proportion of females who were married in 1960 fell significantly as female earnings rose, holding male earnings and other variables constant (1972, Table 4-26, p. 91).[15] Both studies, therefore, support the theory.

Costs of marriage

In Becker's theory the most prominent cost of being married is the forgone benefit to be gained from remaining single. But this is not the only cost. Other costs impinge on the decision to be married also. We will consider two versions of the same cost: the extent to which marriage is revocable; that is, the ease of getting a divorce once married.

Included in the calculation that rational individuals make in deciding whether to marry is the cost of dissolving a marriage should it turn out to be less than desired. Such a cost was not included in the gain from marriage discussed earlier because the model assumed that the decision was made in the presence of perfect certainty. That is, the individuals knew for certain how the marriage was going to turn out. Of course, that is a caricature of reality. In truth, people do not know with anything like certainty how marriage will turn out. Consequently, the ease or difficulty of dissolving a marriage once made does moderate the gains from marriage: the more difficult is divorce, the lower the gains from marriage and the more likely the individual will remain single.

Two forces impinge on the ease of divorce: the religious faith to which the individual belongs and divorce laws. It is well known that different religious faiths hold different views on whether marriage is revocable. Although it is fair to say that no religious faith common in the United States holds that divorce is an insignificant matter, there is great variance in beliefs regarding divorce. They range from the Roman Catholic belief that regards marriage as well-nigh irrevocable to the belief of some other faiths and the posture taken by most states that divorce is a necessary institution that dissolves bad and destructive marriages. Roman Catholics, therefore, in comparison with people of other faiths would be somewhat less likely to marry, because the extremely high cost of divorce would discourage some from becoming married in the first place. One would expect, then, that after taking into account other factors affecting marriage, the higher the proportion of Roman Catholics in any state, the lower would be the marriage rate.

There is a similar variance in state laws dealing with divorce. Some states make it very difficult to divorce by restricting the allowable causes for divorce or by lengthening the time that divorce takes. In 1960, the year to which the Santos and Freidan studies apply, Nevada and Florida had the least restrictive divorce laws whereas New York and South Carolina had the most restrictive laws (Freidan 1974, Table 2). People in the more restrictive states, then, would be less likely to marry than people in less restrictive states (other factors held constant), because the higher cost of divorce in the more restrictive states would convince the less certain couples not to get married in the first place.

Both Santos and Freidan investigated these hypotheses in their studies of interstate marital status in 1960. Both find strong support for the hypotheses: the higher the percentage of Roman Catholics in the state and the more restrictive the divorce laws, the lower the proportion of married females. Santos finds the same pattern for her 1950 data. However, she finds that the restrictiveness of state laws is less significant a variable than the proportion of the population who are Roman Catholic. This is reasonable since access to easy divorce laws has always been available through temporary residence in states with easy divorce laws. Roman Catholics cannot so easily avoid the injunctions of their faith.

In a study of consensual and legal marriage in Puerto Rico, where data on consensual and legal marriages exist, Nerlove and Schultz (1970) find further support for these conclusions. Puerto Rico is a Roman Catholic commonwealth where marriage is almost irrevocable, certainly among the poor, who have not the resources to pursue divorce. Nerlove and Schulz find that women enter into consensual unions much more frequently than they do legal marriages. Furthermore, it appears that they tend not to become legally married until their spouses gain some job security. Here, the gain from marriage is importantly conditioned by male earnings (see the earlier discussion on the effect of male wage rates). Since legal marriage is irrevocable, females tend to avoid legal marriage, being content with consensual unions until their consensual spouses' incomes become certain.

A model of divorce

With the exception of the discussion of the effect of such factors as divorce laws and religious injunctions against divorce, the model of marriage was phrased as if there were perfect certainty. People knew with certainty what it was going to be like married to each of their potential partners, knew with certainty what it was going to be like remaining single, and could calculate the gain from marriage based on this knowledge.

Of course, reality is not like that. People must make forecasts of what marriage with potential partners and remaining single will be like and these forecasts will be made with considerable uncertainty and so, consequently, will people's estimates of the net gain from marriage. Since divorce dissolves marriages that have not worked, the discrepancy between the actual and the expected gain from any marriage is an important part of the explanation for divorce.

The model of marriage laid out in the first part of this chapter also assumed that people identify and get to know potential mates costlessly and without effort, when, in fact, searching for a mate is a costly business (in terms of time, money, and emotional energy). Costly search reduces the net gain from marriage, inducing some people to remain single and others to enter less attractive marriages than they would have had search costs been zero. Given that the net gain from marriage will be smaller the higher the search costs, there will be a smaller margin for error in choosing a mate. With large expected (i.e., forecasted prior to marriage) gains from marriage, actual gains can be much lower before becoming negative. Search costs reduce this cushion by reducing expected net gains. Search costs, therefore, also figure prominently in any explanation of divorce.

Marriage can, therefore, be likened to an implicit contractual agreement between spouses based on each spouse's expectations as to how the marriage will turn out. To the extent that the expectations are not met, to the same extent the implicit contract is broken. If the reality departs from expectations sufficiently, then divorce ensues.

What constitutes departing from expectations "sufficiently"? If the actual output from a marriage falls below the sum of the outputs of the two partners if they become divorced or, alternatively, falls below the sum of the expected marital shares of the two partners if married to other people, then the marriage fails and divorce ensues.

There are circumstances, however, where this condition is not present yet the marital share of one of the partners is below his or her single output or is below his or her expected marital share if married to someone else. Such an individual wants a divorce whereas his or her partner does not. This implies that the other partner has captured most of the benefits of marriage, leaving too little for the other one. In these circumstances the marriage contract can be renegotiated so as to increase the marital share of the partner with too little and reduce the marital share of the one with too much, and divorce can be forestalled. Such bargaining must be more frequent than one might think given that the profession of marriage counseling has arisen to facilitate and mediate such bargaining. While negotiation is possible, it can be defeated if negotiation costs are high or if one of the partners is obdurate.[16]

Clearly, divorce is more likely the smaller the initial net expected gain from marriage. Given the uncertainty surrounding marriage, actual gains can depart widely (larger or smaller) from what is expected. The lower the expected gain from marriage, the more likely the actual gain will be less than zero, and the higher the probability of divorce. Furthermore, the greater the uncertainty, the wider the distribution of actual net gains around the expected net gains (i.e., the larger the variance in actual net gains), the more likely the actual net gain will fall below zero, and, again, the higher the probability of divorce.

These hypotheses can be illustrated diagrammatically. Consider the panels in Figure 8.3. Panels A and B picture the distribution of possible gains from

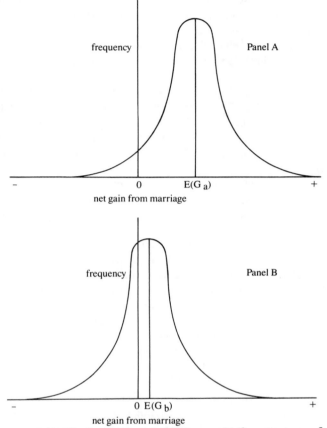

Figure 8.3 The distributions of possible net gains from two types of marriages, each with the same variance but with different expected net gains

different kinds of marriage. Along the horizontal axis of each panel is plotted the possible gains from the two types of marriage: A and B. Marriage A could be, for instance, between two people with equal amounts of education whereas marriage B might be between two people with differing amounts of education. In each case, the marriages could be "made in heaven," and the gains from the marriages would be infinitely large, or they might be "made in hell," with the gains not just negative but infinitely negative. Up the vertical axis is plotted the frequency with which the gains occur in each type of marriage.

The location and spread of the bell-shaped curve in each panel describes the frequency with which marriages with each of the possible net gains occur. In both cases marriages made in heaven and in hell are most infrequent, and consequently, the bell-shaped curves rest on or very near the horizontal axis at these extremes. In both cases marriages with positive net gains are most frequent, and thus, the bell-shaped curves peak in the positive quadrant. But marriages between partners with equal education more frequently have positive net gains than marriages with wide divergences in the partners' educations, and in consequence, the bell-shaped curve in panel A peaks farther to the right than the one in panel B. The average marriage between equally educated partners has a net gain of $E(G_a)$. $E(G_a)$ is the "expected net gain" from marriages of type A. Likewise, $E(G_b)$ is the "expected net gain" from marriages of type B. The locations of the distribution peaks describe the expected net gains from the two types of marriages.

Now, we have argued that an important determinant of whether two people marry is whether they expect the net gain from marriage to be positive. Thus, the higher the expected net gain from marriage, the more likely will two people marry. Given they marry, however, the net gain they actually experience is not $E(G)$ but something else, either higher or lower. The bell-shaped curves show the likelihoods of different outcomes. What is clear from the diagrams is that the smaller the expected net gains, the more likely it is that the actual net gain from the marriage will be negative. This is shown by the area under the bell-shaped curve lying to the left of 0; the greater the area under the curve to the left of 0, the more likely the actual gain from the marriage will be negative. Thus, Figure 8.3 illustrates the hypothesis that it is more likely that marriage between partners with widely disparate levels of education will end in divorce than ones between partners with equal educations because the expected net gain of the latter is greater than the former.

Figure 8.4 illustrates the point that the greater the uncertainty about the net gain from marriage, the higher the probability of divorce. In Figure 8.4 the shape of the distribution of net gains from marriage represents the extent of the uncertainty. Here, the distributions of possible outcomes of marriage for two types of marriage are plotted on the same graph. Both types of marriage, type A and type B, have the same expected net gain, $E(G)$. But the dispersion of possible outcomes (i.e., the variance) is far wider in the case of type A than for type B. Again, the area under the curve to the left of 0 represents the likelihood of divorce. Here, type A has the greater variance in net gains and, therefore, the greater likelihood of divorce.

We can formalize these hypotheses algebraically as follows:

$$P\{D\} = d[E(G), \text{Var}(G)], \tag{8.27}$$

where $P\{D\}$ = the probability of divorce, $E(G)$ = initial expected net gain from marriage, and $\text{Var}(G)$ = variance of actual net gains around the expected net

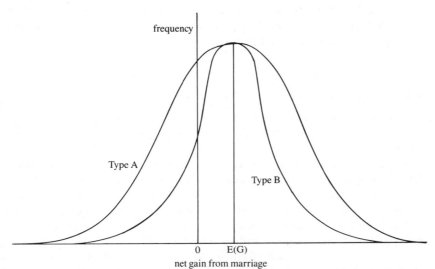

Figure 8.4 The distributions of possible net gains from two types of marriages, each with the same expected net gains but with different variances

gain from marriage. As $E(G)$ increases or $\mathrm{Var}(G)$ decreases, the probability of divorce will decrease;

$$\partial P\{D\}/\partial E(G) < 0, \tag{8.28}$$

$$\partial P\{D\}/\partial \mathrm{Var}(G) > 0. \tag{8.29}$$

Search costs play a role by depressing the net gain from marriage. In consequence, the higher the search costs, the lower the expected gain from marriage:

$$\partial E(G)/\partial C_s < 0, \tag{8.30}$$

where C_s = search costs.

Search costs also increase the variance in actual net gains from marriage around the expected net gain. The greater the search costs, the less search will be undertaken: fewer potential mates will be identified and less will be known about each. Greater search costs increase uncertainty, therefore, and increase the variance of actual net gains from marriage around the expected net gains. Thus,

$$\partial \mathrm{Var}(G)/\partial C_s > 0. \tag{8.31}$$

Under what circumstances will search costs become important in affecting divorce? To find out we have to return to the theory of marriage and discuss positive and negative assortive mating.

Positive and negative assortive mating and divorce

Positive assortive mating is the tendency of people with similar traits to marry. Negative assortive mating is the tendency of people with opposite traits to marry.

Without saying so, we have already discussed negative assortive mating when we discussed the implications of comparative advantage for marriage. That is, the greatest gains from marriage occur when, holding other things constant, individuals with a great comparative advantage in market activities marry individuals with a great comparative advantage in household activities. Thus, the gains from marriage are greater when individuals with high market productivities (i.e., wage rates) marry individuals with low market productivities.[17]

In general, negative assortive mating increases the gains from marriage in productive activities because the principle of comparative advantage will induce specialization of function and make married output larger than otherwise. Thus, we would expect negative assortive mating to occur with respect to traits that affect people's productivities in productive (market and household) activities; for instance, wage rates, labor market experience, and child-rearing abilities.

In contrast, positive assortive mating increases the gains from marriage in consumption activities. Married couples tend to engage in consumption activities together rather than separately. People with similar educational levels, religious preferences, intelligence, and ages will tend to have similar preferences, outlooks on life, and abilities in consumption activities. Thus, they will tend to like the same consumption activities and be similarly adept in their enjoyment, and their shared participation in these activities will increase the total enjoyment (i.e., marital output).[18] In short, people with similar traits are *complements* of each other in consumption activities, and thus, positive assortive mating with respect to these traits will increase the gains from marriage.

According to this principle, then, it is more likely that people with similar educational backgrounds, religious preferences, ages, and so on will marry, because such marriages will tend to maximize the gains from marriage. Furthermore, because of the great expected gains from marriage, such marriages will be less likely to dissolve in divorce due to subsequent divergences between actual and expected gains. In contrast, marriages between people with unlike consumption traits will tend to have small expected gains from marriage and a greater likelihood that the actual gains will be zero for any given amount of uncertainty. For this reason, marriages between people with dissimilar traits will be more likely to dissolve than those between people with similar traits.

People with similar production traits or dissimilar consumption traits will be more likely to marry when search costs are high, making added search for individuals with unlike production traits and like consumption traits too costly. This will happen most often to people with rare traits. Becker et al. (1977) find that people with very high IQs tend to marry people with lower IQs (presumably because mates with very high IQs are too costly to find) and have higher than average divorce rates. Also, Jews living in areas with a low Jewish population tend to intermarry more often than Jews who live in areas where the Jewish population is high (Rosenthal 1963). Being Jewish in areas where there are few other Jews raises the costs of finding a Jewish mate. Divorce rates within the first four years of marriage are much higher among people who have intermarried with respect to religion than among people who marry within the same religion (Becker et al. 1977).

One the strongest correlates of divorce is age at first marriage: the younger the age, the higher the probability of divorce. People who marry young have not searched much, perhaps because they have a very high preference for marriage. For whatever reason, their search has not been extensive, the uncertainty about the gains from marriage is high, and the probability of divorce is likewise high.

Above some age, however, age itself becomes a rare trait. Since search costs also increase with age (i.e., wage rates and, therefore, the cost of the time spent searching rise with age – see Chapter 6), above some age search for the ideal mate becomes increasingly expensive and people settle for marriages with lower expected net gains. Past some age, therefore, expected net gains from marriage will fall and the probability of divorce will rise. Becker et al. (1977, Table 2, p. 1159) present strong evidence that the probability of divorce falls and then rises as age at first marriage rises for a national sample of white men in 1967.

Of the economic factors affecting divorce, income and wage rates have the most pervasive influence. An increase in female wage rates or a decrease in male wage rates reduces the scope for division of labor within marriage and reduces the expected net gains from marriage. Holding the level of uncertainty constant (i.e., the $Var(G)$ in equation [8.27]), a reduction in the expected net gains from marriage increases the likelihood that the actual net gains will be zero or negative and, thence, raises the probability of divorce.

These hypotheses have been borne out by Santos's (1972, Table 4-20, p. 85) analysis of interstate differences in divorce rates in 1960 and by Ross and Sawhill's (1975, Table 12, p. 56) cross-section analysis of a national sample of families from 1968 through 1972. The analysis of 1967 divorce probabilities of white men by Becker et al. (1977, Table 2, p. 1159) also confirms that as men's earnings rise, the probability of divorce falls.

Marriage-specific human capital and divorce

The final influence affecting the gains from marriage and their uncertainty that we will discuss has to do with marriage-specific human capital. Marriage-specific human capital refers to human capital investments made by individuals that increase the net gains from marriage. Two types of such investments are discussed: children and duration of the marriage itself.

As marriages are lived, couples gain experience in the marriage and the experience augments the net gains from marriage. When a couple is first married, the partners know relatively little about each other and how to work and play together in ways that make the marriage more meaningful. As time goes on, however, couples learn a great deal about how to make the marriage work. In the language of economics, experience in the marriage augments the human capital of the partners, raising their productivities in the marriage.

This human capital is marriage-specific in two senses. First, it is specific to marriage as opposed to single status in that couples learn ways to behave that make being married more fulfilling than being single. Second, it is specific to "this" marriage in that the partners learn more and more about how to live with and enjoy marriage to their particular partner. The first kind of experience leads people to benefit more from being married than from being single. The second type of experience leads people to benefit more from their current marriage than either from being single or from being married to someone else.

The likelihood of becoming divorced, therefore, can be expected to fall the longer the duration of marriage. This relationship is a common one found in divorce studies. Becker et al. (1977, Table 2, p. 1159, and Table 4, p. 1165) estimate that other things held constant, the likelihood of becoming divorced fell from .04 for white men or women married less than 5 yr. to .02 for those married 15–20 yr. in 1967.

Children are also very important types of marriage-specific human capital. Children are not only marriage-specific capital but also specific to the marriage into which they are born. In this regard, it is an unpleasant commonplace that someone else's children are less valued than one's own. Own children, therefore, increase the net gain to marriage. Based on these notions, one expects divorce probabilities to fall the more children in the family.

This point, however, refers to *desired* children and not to *unanticipated* children. Unanticipated children, like any other unanticipated occurrence in a marriage, tend to break the marriage contract that was based on a set of expectations. Thus, unanticipated children reduce the net gain from marriage and lead to higher divorce rates. It is well to remember, however, that unanticipated children can be "positive" or negative" in the sense that a couple may desire two children and have either fewer than or more than two. Consequently, having fewer children than desired may be just as destabilizing to the marriage as having too many children.

The timing of children is crucial to the relationship, however. Couples not only want a certain number of children but also plan when to have them. Having more children than planned early in the marriage may not be very destabilizing because planned family size may have been achieved, just faster than anticipated. Similarly, too few children early in the marriage can always be rectified later in the marriage provided the couple is fertile.[19] Having unplanned children late in the marriage will be more destabilizing simply because the mistake cannot be rectified.

The relationship between the number of children in the marriage and the likelihood of divorce, therefore, should be somewhat U- or J-shaped: the probability of divorce should first fall and then rise as the number of children in the family increases. Furthermore, the number of children at which the probability of divorce begins to rise should be lower the longer the marriage.

Becker et al. (1977) present evidence confirming these hypotheses. They find, for instance, that the probability of divorce in the second five years of marriage among white women falls from 6 percent if there were no children born in the first five years to 2.8 percent if there were two children and to 2.4 percent if there were three children born. If there were four children in the first five years of marriage, however, the divorce probability rises again to 2.8 percent. Furthermore, a fourth child born in the second five years of marriage is somewhat more destabilizing to the marriage than a fourth child born in the first five years of marriage.

Finally, we return to the point that children are marriage-specific human capital to the marriage into which they are born but not to subsequent marriages. This point is demonstrated dramatically with the statistics on the probability of remarriage once divorced. Women with no children from previous marriages have much higher probabilities of remarriage than divorced women with children, and each additional child a divorced woman has from previous marriages lowers the likelihood that she will remarry still further.

Summary

Marriage and divorce, then, are economic events in the sense that economics provides insights into and increases our understanding of marriage and divorce rates as well as the probabilities of marriage and divorce that individuals of given characteristics face. Economic variables play important roles in determining marriage and divorce. Furthermore, interpretations of the well-known relationships between marriage and divorce, on the one hand, and variables commonly not thought of as economic variables, on the other, like number of children, religious preference, and education, all have great economic content.

Throughout the course of the book the economic determinants of the organization of households have been discussed. It should now be clear that economic forces mold far more than simply our demands for things like food, clothing, and housing. Economic forces are important in determining the shape and size of the household, its location, the proportion of the household's activities that are market oriented and those that are conducted in the privacy of the household. Only the outlines of the economic organization of the household have been discussed. Additional reading and further courses in the subject are available for those whose appetites have been whetted.

Chapter 1

1. *Webster's Deluxe Unabridged Dictionary,* 2d ed., s.v. "household."
2. Utilizing national data for the United States from 1955 to 1984, I have estimated that for every increase in the population by ten people, the number of households increases by three households. For every $1,000 increase in real personal disposable income, the number of households increases by eighteen households.
3. Becker (1965) laid bare the relationships between the resources of time and income and the household activities in which they are used.
4. A supplement to the *Journal of Political Economy* (vol. 70, no. 5, pt. 2 [1962]) contains the papers given at a conference on "Investment in Human Beings" held by the Universities–National Bureau Committee on Economic Research on December 1 and 2, 1961. These papers represent some of the first modern thinking on the subject.
5. See Mitchell 1912 for a discussion of the lack of an adequate theoretical framework to analyze household behavior. Reid's *The Economics of Household Production* (1934) is an early and classic treatment of the economics of home production. Cairncross (1958) pointed out the firmlike attributes of much household behavior. See Becker 1965; Lancaster 1966a, 1966b; and Muth 1966 for the modern incorporation of the resources–activities–satisfaction schema into the economics of the household.
6. Indeed, much of the developing literature in the economics of crime analyzes the circumstances under which people will knowingly and willingly break the law in pursuit of their own personal well-being.
7. See Bryant 1986; Cowan 1983; and Strasser 1982 for treatments of the effects of technical change on the household.

Chapter 2

1. The terms *price per unit quantity* and *quantity of food* are intentionally vague. For this analysis we cannot add up pounds of beef, oranges, apples, and lettuce to obtain pounds of food. Such a measure is useless because we have added unlike things. Nor can we add the price per pound of beef to the price per pound of lettuce and get a meaningful price of food. Instead, price and quantity *indexes* for food must be developed as well as price and quantity indexes for all other goods and services. Accomplishing this reduces all food items into one composite "good" we call food and all other goods and services into another composite good we will call "all other goods."
2. The composite good "all other goods" includes any saving that the household does and thus really does encompass all the uses to which the household puts its income

other than purchasing food. Expenditures really do equal total family income, then. The price of the composite good "all other goods" is similar in concept and construction to the consumer price index (minus the food component) the U.S. Bureau of Labor Statistics uses to trace the general level of all consumer prices in the economy. Similarly, the price of food, p_f, is similar in concept and construction to the price index of the food component in the consumer price index.

3. Speaking intuitively. It is the case mathematically that each line has an infinite number of points.
4. "Goods" and "bads" have been referred to as *economic goods* and *economic bads* to emphasize the restricted meaning of the two terms. All that is meant by an economic good is something for which more is preferred to less. All that is meant by an economic bad is something for which less is preferred to more. No *ethical* connotations are implied when these terms are used.
5. See Mansfield 1982, chap. 3, or Hirshleifer 1976, chap. 3, for discussions of the history and distinctions between ordinal and cardinal utility.
6. A detailed knowledge of consumer preferences is useful, however, in market research and product development, where products may be tailored to consumers with particular preferences or advertising campaigns may be directed to consumers with particular tastes. Such detailed knowledge of consumer preferences is sought by marketing managers and consumer psychologists. The knowledge is obtained through extremely detailed questionnaires filled out by sample consumers.
7. There are also cases of corner solutions that do not occur at one of the axes and result in a nonzero demand by the household for a particular good. They occur when the budget line is not a straight line but, instead, is "kinked." Kinked budget lines arise for several reasons, one of which is "quantity discount pricing." In such circumstances, the consumer may maximize satisfaction at the kink, where the highest attainable indifference curve intersects the budget line at the kink. In such situations equation (2.6) will not hold. See Chapter 3, where such situations are analyzed.

Mathematical notes to Chapter 2

1. Equation (2.5), $U = u(q_f, q_o)$, is general and represents a very wide class of algebraic forms. Each household's preferences can be represented by a specific algebraic version of equation (2.5). In order to do empirical research on household behavior, economists frequently assume that similar households share the same utility function. This is analogous to the sociologist's assumption that people in the same social class share the same values. One specific functional form for the utility function is

$$U = a_f(\ln q_f - b_f) + a_o(\ln q_o - b_o) \tag{1}$$

where $a_f + a_o = 1$, $a_i > 0$ $(i = o, f)$, and $b_i \geq 0$. The b_i's are interpreted as the subsistence levels of food and other things. This functional form is called a Stone–Geary function after the economists who first used it. From it is derived the Linear Expenditure System, a system of demand equations widely used in empirical research. See Deaton & Muellbauer 1981.
2. Algebraically, the indifference curve can be formed in the following fashion. Set the satisfaction level, U, equal to a constant, say U_c, and substitute U_c for U in equation (2.5). Then, the function

$$U_c = u(q_o, q_f) \tag{2}$$

is the equation for an indifference curve because it gives all the combinations of q_o and q_f that yield the same level, U_c, of satisfaction.

3. What a horizontal (vertical) indifference curve really means is that the good measured along the horizontal (vertical) axis does not affect the household's well-being at all; that is,

$$\partial U / \partial q_x = MU_x = 0 \tag{3}$$

where q_x is the good measured along the horizontal (vertical) axis. If someone says about a particular good, say, cherries: "I can take them or leave them," the person is saying that cherries don't affect his or her well-being at all.

4. The slope of the indifference curve can be found in the following fashion. Take the total differential of the indifference equation, (2):

$$dU_c = (\partial u / \partial q_o)dq_o + (\partial u / \partial q_f)dq_f \tag{4}$$

Now, set dU_c equal to 0 (because movement along the indifference curve keeps the level of utility constant) and solve for dq_o/dq_f to get

$$dq_o/dq_f = -(\partial u / \partial q_f)/(\partial u / \partial q_o) = -(MU_f/MU_o). \tag{5}$$

Equation (5) is the equation for the marginal rate of substitution of food for "all other goods," where MU_f and MU_o are marginal utilities of food and "all other goods," respectively.

5. The calculus of maximizing satisfaction is as follows. Mathematically, maximizing satisfaction amounts to finding values of q_o and q_f for which the utility function $U = u(q_o, q_f)$ is a maximum subject to the budget constraint

$$p_o q_o + p_f q_f = Y. \tag{6}$$

The budget constraint can be solved for q_o (see equation [2.4]) and inserted into the utility function to get

$$U = u([(Y/p_o) - (p_f/p_o)q_f], q_f). \tag{7}$$

The utility function is now a function of q_f only (Y, p_f, and p_o being considered constants).

To maximize utility it remains to differentiate U with respect to q_f, set the derivative equal to 0, and solve the resulting equation for the value of q_f. The resulting equation, called a first-order condition, is

$$\partial u / \partial q_f - (\partial u / \partial q_o)[-(p_f/p_o)] = 0, \tag{8}$$

or

$$(\partial u / \partial q_f)/(\partial u / \partial q_o) = -(p_f/p_o). \tag{9}$$

In these equations $\partial u / \partial q_f$ is interpreted as the marginal utility of food, MU_f; and $\partial u / \partial q_o$ is interpreted as the marginal utility of "all other goods," MU_o. The ratio of these two marginal utilities is clearly the marginal rate of substitution of food for "all other goods" (equation [5]). Thus, this equation says no more than is said by the tangency between the highest attainable indifference curve and the budget line. Both specify the equilibrium combination of food and "all other goods" given household income and market prices for the two goods.

Equation (8) can be rephrased in still another useful way:

$$MU_f/p_f = MU_o/p_o. \tag{10}$$

This is the form of the equation interpreted in the text.

6. The calculus of corner solutions is as follows. The consumer maximizes

$$U = u(q_v, q_o)$$

subject to the budget constraint

$$p_o q_o + p_v q_v = Y$$

and the provisos $q_o \geq 0$ and $q_v \geq 0$. Form the expression

$$L = u(q_v, q_o) - \lambda_y(p_o q_o + p_v q_v - Y) + \lambda_o(q_o \geq 0) + \lambda_v(q_v \geq 0) \tag{11}$$

where $\lambda_i = 0$ if $q_i > 0$ ($i = o, v$); otherwise $\lambda_i > 0$; and $\lambda_y > 0$ when $p_o q_o + p_v q_v - Y = 0$, otherwise $\lambda_y = 0$. L is a function of q_o, q_v, λ_y, λ_o, and λ_v. To find the maximum of L and, thence, maximum satisfaction, differentiate L successively by q_o, q_v, λ_y, λ_o, and λ_v, setting each partial derivative to 0. This yields

$$u_o - \lambda_y p_o + \lambda_o = 0, \tag{12}$$

$$u_v - \lambda_y p_v + \lambda_v = 0, \tag{13}$$

$$-p_o q_o - p_v q_v + Y = 0, \tag{14}$$

$$q_o \geq 0, \tag{15}$$

$$q_v \geq 0. \tag{16}$$

If $q_v = 0$ and $q_o > 0$, then equations (12) and (13) become

$$u_o - \lambda_y p_o = 0 \quad \text{and} \tag{17}$$

$$u_v - \lambda_y p_v + \lambda_v = 0. \tag{18}$$

Solving equations (17) and (18) each for λ_y and equating yields

$$(u_v + \lambda_v)/p_v = u_o/p_o, \tag{19}$$

or

$$(u_v + \lambda_v)/u_o = p_v/p_o. \tag{20}$$

Since $q_v = 0$, $\lambda_v > 0$ and

$$u_v/u_o < p_v/p_o; \tag{21}$$

that is, the price the household is willing to pay for VCRs, u_v/u_o, is less than the market price, p_v/p_o, and therefore, no VCRs will be purchased.

The price at which the household is indifferent to buying or not buying a good (VCRs in this case), $(u_v/u_o)|_{q_{v--}}$, is called the household's *reservation price* for the good. Retailers must charge prices somewhat lower than households' reservation prices for goods in order to induce them to buy.

Chapter 3

1. The assertion that changes in income alter household consumption alternatives but do not change their preferences is different from the hypothesis typically made in sociology and anthropology. To sociology and anthropology income represents an important component of "social class." As such, an increase in income not only expands the alternatives open to a household, it also tends to put the household into the next higher social class. Once in the new social class, the household's consumption preferences are altered; the household tends to adopt the preferences of the new class and cast off the preferences of the old class. The hypothesis of "stable preferences," then, marks an important difference between economics on the one hand and sociology and anthropology on the other. Note that to test the hypothesis of changing preferences it is necessary to know the household's preferences and to observe whether they change in the face of changes in income. Furthermore, the change in income must be large enough to ensure that the household enters the next higher "social class," as operationally defined by sociology.

2. This point illustrates the difference between demand and need. Demand is defined as the quantity of a good the household *is willing and able* to purchase and consume, whereas the concept of need is independent of the ability to purchase. Certainly, a household needs both food and "all other goods" in order to survive and prosper. But with no income, it has no demand because it is unable to make any purchases.

3. Recall Figure 2.11, which depicted a corner solution in which the household maximized satisfaction by demanding no VCRs and devoting all its income to the purchase of "all other goods."

4. The income elasticity of demand for food consumed away from home comes from Tyrell & Mount 1987. The estimate of the income elasticity of demand for motor vehicles and parts comes from Bryant & Wang 1990a. It is higher than other estimates of the income elasticity of demand for motor vehicles and parts in the literature because it is a "permanent income" elasticity. See Chapter 4 for a discussion of permanent income.

5. Goods for which people demand more as the price rises and less as the price falls are called Giffen goods, after a nineteenth-century Englishman who believed he observed the poor in London increase their demand for potatoes when the price of potatoes rose. The logic is as follows. Potatoes bulked large in the diet of London's poor, and being poor, they spent most of their meager incomes on food. Hence, when the price of potatoes fell, their real incomes rose substantially and allowed them to substitute a higher quality food for potatoes. Thus, the demand for potatoes fell. This means that potatoes must have been a very inferior good to London's poor. That Giffen actually observed this behavior is now disputed. See Stigler, 1965.

6. Equation (3.15) is an approximation to the Slutsky equation (Slutsky 1915) expressed in terms of first derivatives. See mathematical note 3 for its derivation. The Slutsky equation is the fundamental equation in demand theory and was first published in 1915. It and the economics of the household are, therefore, not new.

7. One must be careful with this implication of Proposition 3. The implication applies to own-price effects but not to own-price elasticities. Just because the rich demand more of a good than the poor does not imply that the rich's demand for the good will be more own-price elastic than the poor's. See mathematical note 4 for a demonstration of this fact.

8. In a study of unit price differences by package size, Walker and Cude (1983) concluded that the largest sizes of packages had the highest unit prices for four of nineteen products in two stores polled and for one of nineteen products in another store polled.
9. Recall Figure 2.11 and the accompanying discussion.
10. The adjective *real* is used to modify both the price the consumer is willing to pay and the market price because they are phrased in terms of the goods (i.e., the consumer's "real" resources) that must be given up in order to get good X.
11. Although the tied sale has been phrased in terms of breakfast cereal and the junk toys cereal companies include with the cereal, the principle is the same as that used by the car salesperson who "throws in" a stereo sound system rather than lowering the price as an inducement to have you buy the car.
12. The definitions given in the text are for gross cross-price effects. Substitutes and complements are also defined in terms of cross-substitution effects. See mathematical note 6.

Mathematical notes to Chapter 3

1. The income effect is derived by the calculus in the following way. Find the conditions for maximizing the utility function,

$$U = u(q_x, q_o), \tag{1}$$

subject to the budget constraint,

$$p_x q_x + p_o q_o = Y, \tag{2}$$

by forming the Lagrangean expression

$$L_g = u(q_x, q_o) - \lambda(p_x q_x + p_o q_o - Y) \tag{3}$$

(where λ = the Lagrangean multiplier); differentiating equation (3) with respect to q_x, q_o, and λ; and setting the first derivatives to 0. This yields the following first-order conditions for a maximum:

$$u_x - \lambda p_x = 0, \tag{4}$$

$$u_o - \lambda p_o = 0, \tag{5}$$

$$-p_x q_x - p_o q_o + Y = 0. \tag{6}$$

Now, taking the total differential of equations (4)–(6) yields

$$u_{xx} dq_x + u_{xo} dq_o - p_x d\lambda = \lambda dp_x, \tag{7}$$

$$u_{ox} dq_x + u_{oo} dq_o - p_o d\lambda = \lambda dp_o, \tag{8}$$

$$-p_x dq_x - p_o dq_o - Od\lambda = q_x dp_x + q_o dp_o - dY. \tag{9}$$

Equations (7)–(9) can be solved for dq_x in terms of dp_x, dp_o, and dY by employing matrix algebra to get

$$dq_x = \lambda(D_{xx}/D)dp_x + \lambda(D_{xo}/D)dp_o + (D_{x\lambda}/D)(q_x dp_x + q_o dp_o - dY) \tag{10}$$

where D_{xi} $(i = x, o, \lambda)$ is the cofactor of the xi^{th} element of the matrix

$$\begin{bmatrix} u_{xx} & u_{xo} & -p_x \\ u_{ox} & u_{oo} & -p_o \\ -p_x & -p_o & 0 \end{bmatrix}$$

and D is the determinant of the above matrix.

Equation (10) is the general form for the demand function for X expressed as a differential equation. That is, equation (10) tells us by how much the demand for X will change (i.e., dq_x) given small changes in p_x, p_o, and Y when they all occur at the same time.

The income effect on the demand for X, however, is the change in the demand for X when Y changes, holding p_x and p_o constant. To find the income effect on the demand for X, it remains to set dp_x and dp_o both equal to 0 (because prices are being held constant), divide through by dY, and change the "d" notation to the "∂" notation (in recognition of the fact that holding prices constant while income changes is a partial, not a total, derivative). Thus,

$$\partial q_x / \partial Y = -D_{x\lambda}/D. \tag{11}$$

From the second-order conditions for a maximum (see Henderson & Quandt 1958, chap. 2, for a discussion of the second-order conditions), we know that $D > 0$, but we know nothing about the sign of $D_{x\lambda}$. Consequently, the income effect can be positive (a normal good), negative (an inferior good), or zero (income independent).

2. The equation

$$\Delta(p_x q_x) = p_x \Delta q_x + q_x \Delta p_x \tag{3.10}$$

actually holds only for small changes. The exact relation is the total differential of expenditures,

$$d(p_x q_x) = p_x dq_x + q_x dp_x,$$

where the "d" notation stands for "small change."

3. The Slutsky equation is derived from equation (10) in mathematical note 1. Recall that equation (10) is the total differential of q_x, showing the change in the demand for X given small changes in p_x, p_o, and Y all occurring simultaneously. To derive the own-price effect from equation (10), set dY and dp_o equal to 0 (because income and other prices are held constant), divide through equation (10) by dp_x, and change the "d" notation to "∂" in recognition of the fact that holding Y and p_o constant while changing p_x is a partial derivative. Thus,

$$\partial q_x / \partial p_x = \lambda(D_{xx}/D) + q_x(D_{x\lambda}/D). \tag{12}$$

How is equation (12) to be interpreted? Consider the second term on the right-hand side first. Since $\partial q_x/\partial Y = -D_{x\lambda}/D$ (see equation [11]), equation (12) can be rewritten as

$$\partial q_x/\partial p_x = \lambda(D_{xx}/D) - q_x(\partial q_x/\partial Y).$$ (13)

Clearly, the second term on the right-hand side of equation (13) is the "income effect" of the price change. As p_x falls, real income rises and the household increases its demand for X if X is normal. The more X the consumer purchased prior to the fall in p_x, the more income is saved at the lower price that can be spent on yet more X or other things. This is the explanation for the $-q_x$ term in the income effect part of equation (13). Furthermore, the more responsive the household is to any change in income (brought about in this case by a fall in p_x), the greater the income effect of the price change will be. Hence, the $\partial q_x/\partial Y$ term in equation (13).

Now consider the interpretation of the $\lambda(D_{xx}/D)$ term. One way of looking at $\lambda(D_{xx}/D)$ is to view it as the change in the demand for X due to a change in p_x, holding p_o constant and when $q_x dp_x + q_o dp_o - dY = 0$ in equation (10). Thus, we must find the conditions under which

$$q_x dp_x + q_o dp_o - dY = 0.$$ (14)

Along with the change in p_x, suppose income is (hypothetically) changed so that the household is neither better off nor worse off than before the price change. If so, household utility will not have changed and any change in utility brought about by price-induced changes in X must be exactly offset by changes in utility brought about by price-induced changes in other things, O. Thus,

$$dU = u_x dq_x + u_o dq_o = O.$$ (15)

But, since the household remains in equilibrium, equations (4) and (5) in mathematical note 1 still hold true. We can solve (4) for u_x and (5) for u_o and insert the results into equation (15) to get

$$\lambda p_x dq_x + \lambda p_o dq_o = O$$

or, dividing through by $-\lambda$,

$$-p_x dq_x - p_o dq_o = O.$$ (16)

Now, the total differential of the budget constraint is

$$-p_x dq_x - p_o dq_o = q_x dp_x + q_o dp_o - dY.$$ (17)

Since the left-hand side of equation (17) equals 0 according to equation (16), so must the right-hand side. Consequently, it must be the case that $\lambda(D_{xx}/D)$ is the change in the demand for X given a change in p_x, holding satisfaction (i.e., utility) constant. Thus,

$$\partial q_x/\partial p_x|_{u=c} = \lambda(D_{xx}/D).$$ (18)

The notation $\partial q_x/\partial p_x|_{u=c}$ is to be read as "the change in the demand for X due to a change in p_x, holding satisfaction (i.e., utility) constant." Clearly, then, equation (18) is the own-substitution effect.

Substituting (18) into (13) yields

$$\partial q_x/\partial p_x = \partial q_x/\partial p_x|_{u=c} - q_x(\partial q_x/\partial Y), \tag{19}$$

which is the Slutsky equation. This presentaiton is an elaboration of the discussion in Henderson and Quandt 1958, p. 25.

4. To express the Slutsky equation in elasticity terms multiply equation (19) through by p_x/q_x and multiply the second term on the right-hand side by Y/Y to get

$$(\partial q_x/\partial p_x)(p_x/q_x) = (\partial q_x/\partial p_x)|_{u=c}(p_x/q_x) - (p_x q_x/Y)(\partial q_x/\partial Y)(Y/q_x),$$

or

$$E_x = E_x^* - \alpha_x N_x, \tag{20}$$

where $E_x = (\partial q_x/\partial p_x)(p_x/q_x)$, $E_x^* = (\partial q_x/\partial p_x)|_{u=c}(p_x/q_x)$, $\alpha_x = (p_x q_x/Y)$, and $N_x = (\partial q_x/\partial Y)(Y/q_x)$.

The question is how X's budget share, α_x, changes as income changes. To find out in which direction, differentiate α_x by Y:

$$\partial \alpha_x/\partial Y = [Yp_x(\partial q_x/\partial Y) - p_x q_x(\partial Y/\partial Y)]/Y^2, \tag{21}$$

or after manipulation,

$$\partial \alpha_x/\partial Y = \alpha_x(N_x - 1)/Y. \tag{22}$$

Since the denominator of (22) is positive, $\partial \alpha_x/\partial Y$ will be positive (negative) if the numerator is positive (negative). $\alpha_x > 0$, and $N_x - 1$ will be positive (negative) if N_x is greater than 1 (less than 1). Thus,

$$\partial \alpha_x/\partial Y \gtreqless 0 \quad \text{as} \quad N_x \gtreqless 1. \tag{23}$$

As income rises, then, X's budget share will rise (fall) if the income elasticity of demand for X is elastic (inelastic). Thus, rich people's own-price elasticity of demand will be greater than poor people's for income elastic goods and will be less than poor people's for income inelastic goods, ceteris paribus.

5. The tied sale way of raising consumers' reservation prices above the market price can be modeled as follows. Suppose the consumer's utility function is

$$U = u(q_1, q_2, q_3) \tag{24}$$

where q_1 is breakfast cereal, q_2 is magic decoder rings, and q_3 is all other goods. Suppose, further, that the breakfast cereal firm creates a new good, q_z, by packaging magic decoder rings with the breakfast cereal such that one ring is packaged with each unit of cereal. Thus,

$$q_1 = q_z \quad \text{and} \quad q_2 = q_z. \tag{25}$$

Suppose, finally, the firm charges a price for the cereal plus the ring, p_z, equal to the price of the cereal, p_1. Form the budget constraint

$$p_1 q_1 + p_3 q_3 = Y. \tag{26}$$

Substitute (25) into (24) and (26) to get

$$U = u(q_z, q_z, q_3) \tag{27}$$

and

$$p_1 q_z + p_3 q_3 = Y. \tag{28}$$

Maximizing (27) subject to (28) yields the following equilibrium conditions:

$$(u_1 + u_2)/u_3 = p_1/p_3, \quad \text{for} \quad q_z > 0 \quad \text{and} \quad q_3 > 0; \tag{29}$$

$$(u_1 + u_2)/u_3 < p_1/p_3, \quad \text{for} \quad q_z = 0 \quad \text{and} \quad q_3 > 0. \tag{30}$$

The reservation price of good z is $(u_1 + u_2)/u_3|_{q_z=0}$. The addition of the ring to the cereal raises the reservation price of cereal by u_2, thus raising the likelihood that more consumers will purchase the cereal than in the absence of the tied sale.

6. The definitions of substitutes and complements given in the text are for *gross substitutes* and *gross complements;* that is, the definitions are in terms of the *total cross-price effects.* However, total cross-price effects can be decomposed into *cross-substitution and income effects* by means of a Slutsky equation just as *own-price effects* can be decomposed into *substitution and income effects.*

The Slutsky equation for the cross-price effect is derived from equation (10) by setting $dp_x = dY = 0$, dividing through by dp_o, and changing the "d" notation to the "∂" notation to signify a partial derivative. This yields

$$\partial q_x/\partial p_o = \lambda(D_{xo}/D) + q_o(D_{x\lambda}/D), \tag{31}$$

where $\lambda(D_{xo}/D) = \partial q_x/\partial p_o|_{u=0}$ and is called the cross-substitution effect, and $-(D_{x\lambda}/D) = \partial q_x/\partial Y$ and is called the income effect (see equation [11]). Consequently, the cross-price Slutsky equation is

$$\partial q_x/\partial p_o = \partial q_x/\partial p_o|_{u=0} - q_o \partial q_x/\partial Y. \tag{32}$$

Even though equation (32) was derived from a two-good model, the Slutsky equation for the cross-price effect when there are more than two goods has the identical form.

Net substitutes and *net complements* are defined in terms of the cross-substitution effect. Two goods are net substitutes if the cross-substitution effect of a change in the price of one of the goods on the demand for the other is positive. Two goods are net complements if the cross-substitution effect of a change in the price of one of the goods on the demand for the other is negative. Unless otherwise stated in the text, the terms *substitutes* and *complements* will refer to gross complements and substitutes.

Chapter 4

1. The U.S. government classifies cars, furniture, and household equipment as durables and includes them in personal consumption expenditures (see Table 3.1). Clothing and cassette tapes are judged to have lives of less than three years and are classified as nondurables but are also included in personal consumption expenditures (U.S. Bureau of Economic Analysis 1986). In reality, then, government statistics overestimate consumption and underestimate saving.
2. The price of consumption goods and services, p_c, is assumed not to change between year one and year two. This assumption allows us to postpone discussing questions of inflation and deflation until later in the chapter.
3. Another motive, that of saving so as to leave bequests to one's heirs, has been excluded previously by assuming that families leave no bequests and exhaust their lifetime resources by consuming everything before death. The motive of saving for the future as a hedge against uncertainty is also excluded because our model assumes perfect knowledge.
4. Note that we discussed the ratios of aggregate consumption to aggregate income in the United States at the beginning of this chapter when we discussed Table 4.1. In

Table 4.1 the sum of personal consumption expenditures plus interest paid by consumers is analogous to current consumption as defined here. Thus, the consumption/income ratio in 1987 was 96.7 percent and the saving/income ratio was 3.2 percent.

5. When first offered, the permanent income and the life-cycle income hypotheses were viewed as quite different. In the interim the essential similarities have been identified so that the two have become almost one. The permanent income hypothesis is due to Milton Friedman and is found in his *A Theory of the Consumption Function* (1957). The life-cycle income hypothesis was put forward by Franco Modigliani, and a version can be found in Ando & Modigliani 1963.

6. Remember, these hypotheses do not take into account changing prices, interest rates, and family size through time. Certainly, as we saw at the end of the last chapter, an increase in family size will alter the total demand for goods and services and, thus, can be expected to affect the fraction of income saved. Thus, as families have children and as the children grow up, become independent, and leave home, one can expect the fraction of income saved first to fall and then to increase. Furthermore, in Chapter 5 we will see that the systematic changes in the price of people's time (i.e., their wage rates) over the life cycle affects the consumption pattern over the life cycle. But here we ignore these phenomena and concentrate on the relationship between total resources and consumption.

7. If the timing of income as well as total resources is important in people's consumption and saving decisions, then families with income patterns like that pictured in panel A of Figure 4.8 can be expected to save in year one. Families faced with income patterns like that pictured in panel B can be expected to be net borrowers in year one.

8. In Friedman's framework transitory consumption appears as a random disturbance term and not as part of the systematic model. Since we are dealing here with only the nonstochastic elements of the hypothesis, the distinction between permanent and transitory consumption is neglected: C_1 is permanent consumption.

9. See Duncan 1984 for data showing the remarkably large fraction of the poor in any year who are temporarily poor.

10. See Duesenberry 1967. This hypothesis has recently been revived by Frank (1985).

11. See Sadan & Tropp 1973. This research, besides providing evidence for the importance of the permanent and relative income hypotheses in explaining kibbutz consumption behavior, demonstrates the power of the economic theory of the household. Not only is the theory applicable in explaining the behavior of "conventional" households, it is also applicable to the explanation of the behavior of "unconventional" households.

12. This analysis is correct in a market environment in which saving and borrowing are refinanced each year; that is, where there are no fixed-rate securities or loans. The relative price and real income effects of interest rate changes apply only to new saving and new loans if old saving and loans were made at fixed rates on long-term contracts. Examples are twenty-five-year mortgages at a fixed rate of interest, say at 12 percent, and five-year saving certificates at a fixed interest rate set at, say 10 percent.

   The situation is somewhat more complicated with fixed-rate bonds for which there is a market. Suppose a bond were bought at 10 percent and subsequently interest rates rose. If the consumer owning the bond were to sell it, the selling price would be lower than the price at which it was originally bought in order to compensate the buyer for the lower rate of interest it carries. Consequently, interest rate changes do, indirectly, have both relative price and real income effects in such markets. The change in the interest rate is reflected in an opposite change in bond prices with consequent capital gains or losses to the original bond holders.

Currently, money markets are characterized by adjustable-rate loan instruments and fixed-rate instruments with short terms. Thus, the current situation is much closer to the theory than conditions before 1980.

13. Obviously, regardless of what the interest rate is, the family can always be at point P by neither borrowing nor lending. Consequently, point P is on both budget lines.

Mathematical notes to Chapter 4

1. $Y_2/(1 + r)$ is the present value of Y_2 valued at the beginning of year one. This can be generalized to many periods quite easily. Suppose Y_3 is the expected income in year three. Then, the present value of Y_3, valued at the beginning of year one, is the sum that, if invested at an interest rate of r, would total Y_3 in year three. Call the sum PV_3, then

$$PV_3 + rPV_3 + r(PV_3 + rPV_3) = Y_3,$$

or, when factored out,

$$PV_3(1 + r)^2 = Y_3.$$

Dividing through by $(1 + r)^2$ yields

$$PV_3 = Y_3/(1 + r)^2.$$

Generalizing to the present value of income in year n, Y_n, yields

$$PV_n = Y_n/(1 + r)^{n-1}.$$

Finally, the present value of an income stream beginning in year one and ending in year n is

$$PV = PV_1 + PV_2 + \cdots + PV_n,$$

or

$$PV = Y_1 + [Y_2/(1 + r)] + \cdots + [Y_n/(1 + r)^{n-1}].$$

If income is constant through time and equal to Y, then

$$PV = Y \sum_{t=1}^{n} [1/(1 + r)^{t-1}].$$

2. The calculus solution to this maximization problem is as follows.

To maximize the intertemporal utility function,

$$U = u(C_1, C_2), \tag{1}$$

subject to the intertemporal budget constraint,

$$p_c C_1 + \left(\frac{p_c}{1 + r} C_2\right) = A_1 + Y_1 + \frac{Y_2}{1 + r}, \tag{2}$$

form the Lagrangean expression

$$\text{Lg} = u(C_1, C_2) - \lambda \left[p_c C_1 + \left(\frac{p_c}{1 + r} C_2\right) - A_1 - Y_1 - \frac{Y_2}{1 + r} \right] \tag{3}$$

differentiate with respect to C_1, C_2, and λ, and set each partial derivative equal to 0. This yields the equilibrium conditions

$$u_1 - \lambda p_c = 0, \tag{4}$$

$$u_2 - \lambda \left(\frac{p_c}{1+r} \right) = 0,\tag{5}$$

$$-p_c C_1 - \left(\frac{p_c}{1+r} C_2 \right) + A_1 + Y_1 + \frac{Y_2}{1+r} = 0.\tag{6}$$

Solving (4) and (5) each for λ, equating, and rearranging yields

$$u_1/u_2 = 1+r\tag{7}$$

where $u_1/u_2 =$ the marginal rate of substitution of consumption in year one for consumption in year two; and $1+r =$ the rate at which consumers can exchange a dollar in year two for a dollar in year one. $u_1/u_2 =$ the slope of the indifference curve at E in Figure 4.4, whereas $1+r =$ the slope of the budget line, AB.

3. If the permanent consumption/permanent income ratio, C_p/Y_p, is constant over time despite large increases in income, then the marginal propensity to consume out of permanent income, $\Delta C_p/\Delta Y_p$, must be equal to C_p/Y_p. To see this, consider the contrary. If $\Delta C_p/\Delta Y_p > C_p/Y_p$, then as permanent income rises, C_p/Y_p must rise. C_p/Y_p must fall with increases in income if $\Delta C_p/\Delta Y_p < C_p/Y_p$. Consequently, a constant C_p/Y_p implies that $C_p/Y_p = \Delta C_p/\Delta Y_p$. But, since $N_p = (\Delta C_p/\Delta Y_p)/(C_p/Y_p)$, $N_p = 1$.

4. To show that

$$N_p = \frac{(C_1^1 - C_1^0)/C_1^0}{Y_1^1 - Y_1^0/[Y_1^0 + (Y_2^0/(1+r))]} = 1,\tag{8}$$

substitute $R_i^1(1+r)/(2+r) = Y_p^i$ (for $i = 0, 1$) into equation (4.18) to get

$$N_p = \frac{(C_1^1 - C_1^0)/C_1^0}{(R_1^1 - R_1^0)/R_1^0}.\tag{9}$$

Then, substitute $R_1^i = Y_1^i + [Y_2^i/(1+r)]$ (for $i = 0, 1$) to get

$$N_p = \frac{C_1^1 - C_1^0}{C_1^0} \left/ \frac{Y_1^1 + [Y_2^1/(1+r)] - Y_1^0 - [Y_2^0/(1+r)]}{Y_1^0 + [Y_2^0/(1+r)]} \right.\tag{10}$$

or

$$N_p = \frac{C_1^1 - C_1^0}{C_1^0} \left/ \frac{Y_1^1 - Y_1^0}{Y_1^0 + [Y_2^0/(1+r)]} \right. = 1.\tag{11}$$

5. If one takes the total differential of equations (4)–(6) and solves the resulting system of equations for dC_1, one obtains

$$dC_1 = \frac{\lambda D_{11}}{D} dp_c + \frac{1}{1+r} \frac{\lambda D_{12}}{D} dp_c - \frac{p_c}{(1+r)^2} \frac{\lambda D_{12}}{D} dr$$

$$+ \left\{ D_{1\lambda}/D \left[C_1 dp_c + \frac{1}{1+r} C_2 dp_c - \frac{p_c}{(1+r)^2} C_2 dr \right. \right.$$

$$\left. \left. - dR_1 + \frac{Y_2}{(1+r)^2} dr \right] \right\}\tag{12}$$

where $R_1 = A_1 + Y_1 + [Y_2/(1+r)]$ and D is the determinant and D_{ij} ($i, j = 1, 2, \lambda$) is the cofactor of the ijth element of the bordered Hessian

$$\begin{bmatrix} u_{11} & u_{12} & -p_c \\ u_{21} & u_{22} & -p_c/(1+r) \\ p_c & -p_c/(1+r) & 0 \end{bmatrix}.$$

Now set $dp_c = dr = 0$, divide by dR_1, and change the d notation to ∂ notation to reflect the fact that we are considering a partial derivative. This yields

$$\partial C_1/\partial R_1 = -D_{1\lambda}/D, \tag{14}$$

which is the net wealth effect on consumption. The net wealth effect is analogous to the income effect in a one-period model.

To find the interest rate effect, set $dp_c = dR_1 = 0$, divide through by dr, and change the d notation to ∂ notation to obtain

$$\frac{\partial C_1}{\partial r} = \frac{p_c}{(1+r)^2} \frac{\lambda D_{12}}{D} - \frac{p_c}{(1+r)^2} \frac{C_2 D_{1\lambda}}{D} + \frac{Y_2}{(1+r)^2} \frac{D_{1\lambda}}{D}. \tag{15}$$

Substituting (14) into (15) yields

$$\frac{\partial C_1}{\partial r} = -\frac{p_c}{(1+r)^2} \frac{\lambda D_{12}}{D} + \frac{1}{(1+r)^2} \frac{(p_c C_2 - Y_2)\partial C_1}{\partial R}. \tag{16}$$

The first term on the right-hand side is the substitution effect of a change in the interest rate; the second term on the right-hand side is the income effect. Assume that $p_c = \$1.00/\text{unit}$ for simplicity. If $C_2 > Y_2$, then saving in year one must have been positive and the income effect of the interest rate change is positive. However, if $C_2 < Y_2$, saving in year one must have been negative (i.e., the consumer is a borrower in year one) and the income effect of the interest rate change is negative.

Chapter 5

1. If we were interested in building a model to explain occupation choice, however, the job satisfaction each occupation renders becomes much more important and would have to be taken into account explicitly.
2. A sad iron was a very heavy iron (made of iron) that was heated on the top of a stove. Several were used and rotated from stove to ironing board and back as they cooled down and needed reheating.
3. Note that the slope of the post-injury production function, BT, is less for any given amount of time spent than the slope of the pre-injury production function, AT, indicating that Crusoe's marginal productivity has fallen as a result of the injury; that is, $g_h'|R < g_h|_P$ where $g_h'|_R$ is the post-injury marginal product of labor at R and $g_h|_P$ is the pre-injury marginal product of labor at P.
4. See, for instance, Singh, Squire, & Strauss 1986. In the peasant household case the family uses its time either in leisure or on the land to produce a crop, say rice. It consumes some of the rice and sells the rest to obtain the money required to purchase other needed consumption goods and, perhaps, agricultural inputs like fertilizer. See mathematical note 2.
5. Leisure time and household work time can be aggregated because both ways of spending time have the same price, w, the wage rate. When aggregated, $H + L$ is called a Hick's composite good (see Hicks 1946, mathematical appendix).

6. The notation $|_Q$ reminds us that the equality occurs at point Q.

7. See Pencavel 1986 and Killingsworth & Heckman 1986 for extensive surveys of the empirical cross-section literature.

8. One should note that there is disagreement about the relevance of any aggregate analysis for individual behavior. One of the criticisms of aggregate work is that unless specific algebraic forms are used for the labor supply functions, one cannot say that the elasticities obtained pertain to the underlying individual behavior. Also, aggregate analyses mix the decision to work with the decision about the number of hours to work, given that the decision to work is in the affirmative. Consequently, the elasticities estimated from aggregate data pertain to neither decision.

9. See Gronau 1977; Cochrane & Logan 1975; and Kooreman & Kapteyn 1987. Graham and Green's study (1984) deals only with employed married women and *assumes (rather than tests)* that the nonlabor income effect on household work time is zero. Although an interesting article, it is of little use in this context.

10. Recall that since p is the price of purchased goods, an hour of his market work can buy w_m/p units of goods and services.

11. See Becker 1981, chap. 2, for an extensive discussion of this topic. See mathematical note 6 for an outline of a two-person model with specialization of function.

12. Becker (1981, chap. 2) argues that a division of labor by sex in which the wife is specialized in household work is more economically efficient. Owen (1987) presents the contrary view. See Bryant and Wang 1990b for an empirical analysis confirming that in two-parent, two-child families, the amounts of time males and females spend on household work and leisure activities together are perfect complements rather than the substitutes required for specialization of function.

13. Note that Kooreman and Kapteyn (1987) find that the total time wives spend in household work changes as their husbands' wage rates change. But we argued above that her household work time would *not* change when his wage rate changes because his wage rate changes neither her household productivity nor her market wage rate and, consequently, the trade-off between market and household work would not change for her. Kooreman and Kapteyn's results do not support the simple model presented in this chapter.

Is the model too simple, then? Yes and no. The findings of Kooreman and Kapteyn suggest that one or the other of two simplifying assumptions that were made is incorrect. To be able to use two-dimensional diagrams we assumed that (1) market-purchased goods are perfect substitutes for homemade goods (see equation [5.2]) and (2) household production is a function of the time spent in household production of only one household member (see equation [5.5]). If, for instance, purchased goods and homemade goods are not perfect substitutes, then an increase in his wage rate changes the trade-off between his leisure and homemade goods and leads to a change in the time the wife spends making them. Alternatively, if homemade goods are produced by both spouses, a change in his wage rate alters the trade-off between his and her household work time and leads to a change in the time she spends in household work.

The model of household time allocation we are discussing, then, may be too simple if the behavior analyzed is disaggregated as in the Kooreman and Kapteyn study. It is quite adequate if the behavior is aggregate, as in the Gronau study (1977) (which distinguishes only among total leisure, total household work, and market work), or in the studies of labor market behavior (which distinguish only between market work and nonmarket time). Note that the same economic principles underlie both the simple model and the more complicated model. The model is simply adapted to suit the complexity of the problem.

14. Typically, the sum D depends on family size.
15. Notice that the greater the benefit reduction rate, the flatter the FV portion of the budget line. In the limit when $b = 1$, the budget line facing recipients becomes horizontal. This is the case in programs that reduce the monthly welfare payment by $1.00 for each dollar earned. The Aid to Families with Dependent Children Program currently has a benefit reduction rate equal to 1 if the recipient receives benefits under the program for more than four months. A benefit reduction rate of 1 is the equivalent of an income tax rate of 100 percent.

Mathematical notes to Chapter 5

1. The slope of the household production function is the first derivative of the household production function with respect to H; that is,

$$\partial G/\partial H = g_h > 0.$$

It is positive, indicating that more is produced if additional time is used. Under conditions discussed in the text, it can become negative. That the slope of the production function becomes shallower as more time is used refers to the second derivative:

$$\partial(\partial G/\partial H)/\partial H = g_{hh} < 0.$$

It is assumed to be negative in accordance with the principle of diminishing marginal productivity; that is, each added unit of an input yields less added output than the one before when other inputs in the production process are held constant.

2. A simple peasant model is as follows. Let

$$u = u(C, G_c, L) \tag{1}$$

be the peasant's utility function where C = purchased consumption goods, G_c = that portion of farm output (say, rice) that the peasant consumes, L = the peasant's leisure. The peasant divides his time between farm production, H, and leisure, L so that

$$T = H + L. \tag{2}$$

The production function representing the peasant's rice production is

$$G = g(H; X) \tag{3}$$

where X is the quantity of land on which the rice is planted. Rice output is divided between the quantity he consumes, G_c, and the quantity he sells, G_s. Therefore,

$$G = G_s + G_c. \tag{4}$$

The peasant sells G_s of his rice crop at a price of p_g for a total income, Y, of

$$Y = p_g G_s. \tag{5}$$

The receipts from selling G_s of his rice are used to purchase consumption goods, C. Thus,

$$p_c C = Y = p_g G_s. \tag{6}$$

The equilibrium conditions governing the time the peasant spends in rice production, the time left over for leisure, total rice output, the portion sold, and purchased goods consumed are found by substituting equation (2) into (3) and (3) into (6) and forming the expression

$$Lg = u(C, G_c, L) - \lambda_y[p_cC - p_gg(T - L; X)], \qquad (7)$$

where λ_y is the Lagrangean multiplier and equals the marginal utility of income. Differentiating (7) with respect to C, G_c, and L and setting each equal to 0 yields

$$u_c - \lambda_y p_c = 0, \qquad (8)$$

$$u_g - \lambda_y p_g = 0, \qquad (9)$$

$$u_1 - \lambda_y p_g g_h = 0. \qquad (10)$$

Solving (9) for λ_y and substituting into (10) yields

$$u_1/u_g = g_h. \qquad (11)$$

Interpreted, this means that when the peasant is maximizing satisfaction, his marginal rate of substitution of time for rice in consumption equals his marginal product of time spent producing rice. This is analogous to point P in Figure 5.3.

Solving (8) and (9) for λ_y, equating, and rearranging yields

$$u_c/u_g = p_c/p_g. \qquad (12)$$

Interpreted, this means that in equilibrium the peasant's marginal rate of substitution of rice for purchased consumption goods must equal the rate at which rice can be exchanged for purchased goods in the market. This is the same equilibrium condition discussed so extensively in Chapter 2.

The peasant agricultural model, therefore, combines elements of both the Robinson Crusoe model and the conventional demand model.

3. These conditions are found in the following way. Form the Lagrangean expression

$$Lg = u[C + g(H; X), L] - \lambda(pC + wH + wL - wT - V) \qquad (13)$$

by substituting the household production function into the utility function for G and by substituting the time constraint for M in the budget constraint, $p_cC = wM + V$. λ is the Lagrangean multiplier, a positive number.

The equilibrium conditions are found by differentiating the Lagrangean expression by H, C, L, and λ in turn and equating each first derivative to 0. These are

$$\partial Lg/\partial H = u_g g_h - \lambda w = 0, \qquad (14)$$

$$\partial Lg/\partial C = u_g - \lambda p = 0, \qquad (15)$$

$$\partial Lg/\partial L = u_l - \lambda w = 0, \qquad (16)$$

$$\partial Lg/\partial \lambda = -pC - wH - wL + wT + V = 0, \qquad (17)$$

where u_g = marginal utility of goods (either C-goods or G-goods), u_l = marginal utility of leisure, g_h = marginal product of labor in household production, and λ = Lagrangean multiplier, which equals the marginal utility of income. Solving (14) and (16) each for λw and equating yields

$$u_l/u_g = g_h;\tag{18}$$

that is, the marginal rate of substitution of leisure for goods equals the marginal product of labor in household production in equilibrium. Solving (14) and (15) each for λ and equating yields

$$g_h = w/p;\tag{19}$$

that is, the marginal product of labor in household production equals the real wage rate in equilibrium. And, from (18) and (19) comes

$$u_l/u_g = g_h = w/p,\tag{20}$$

which is the equilibrium condition for individual S.

Since individual R does no market work,

$$u_l/u_g = g_h > w/p\tag{21}$$

in equilibrium.

4. In a more complete model, the household is seen as deriving satisfaction from goods, from the wife's leisure, and from the husband's leisure. Thus, the utility function would be

$$U = u(C + G, L_f, L_m)\tag{22}$$

where L_f is the wife's leisure hours and L_m is the husband's. The household production function would be specified as

$$G = g(H_f, H_m; X)\tag{23}$$

where H_f and H_m are the times spent in household work by the wife and husband, respectively. The budget constraint would be

$$pC + w_f H_f + w_f L_f + w_m H_m + w_m L_m = w_f T_f + w_m T_m + V\tag{24}$$

where T_f and T_m are the total times available for each spouse.

In this larger model the household decides how much time each spouse has for leisure activities and how much each spouse devotes to household work and to market work. Thus, the equilibrium conditions derivable by maximizing the Lagrangean expression

$$\begin{aligned}\text{Lg} = \; &u[C + g(H_f, H_m; X), L_f, L_m] \\ &- \lambda[pC + w_f L_f + w_f H_f + w_m H_m + w_m L_m - (w_f + w_m)T - V]\end{aligned}\tag{25}$$

are

$$u_c - \lambda p = 0,\tag{26}$$

$$u_g g_f - \lambda w_f = 0,\tag{27}$$

$$u_g g_m - \lambda w_m = 0,\tag{28}$$

$$u_f - \lambda w_f = 0,\tag{29}$$

$$u_m - \lambda w_m = 0,\tag{30}$$

where u_i ($i = f, m$) is the marginal utility of spouse i's leisure, g_i is the marginal product of spouse i's time in household production, and w_i is the market wage rate commanded by spouse i. From (27) and (28), for instance, one obtains

$$g_f/g_m = w_f/w_m;$$ (31)

that is, in equilibrium, the marginal rate of technical substitution of spouse f's time for spouse m's time in household production will equal the ratio of their wage rates. This implies that the proportion in which the two spouses combine their time in household production activities depends on the opportunity costs of time and not upon their preferences.

The effect of change in one spouse's wage rate on the other's time allocation appears as a cross-wage effect in such models and will be discussed later in the chapter.

5. The conclusions about the effect of nonlabor income on the household work time of those who are also employed in market work are altered if market goods and home-produced goods are not perfect substitutes. In this case the household's utility function is

$$U = u(C, G, L).$$ (32)

Maximizing this utility function subject to

$$pC + wH + wL = wT + V$$ (33)

yields the following first-order conditions:

$$u_c - \lambda p = 0,$$ (34)

$$u_g g_h - \lambda w = 0,$$ (35)

$$u_l - \lambda w = 0,$$ (36)

where u_c is the marginal utility of market goods and u_g is the marginal utility of home-produced goods. These marginal utilities will not be the same, because C-goods and G-goods in this model are not perfect substitutes. From equations (35)–(36) it is seen that

$$u_l/u_c = w/p = (u_g/u_c)g_h,$$ (37)

rather than the simpler version,

$$u_l/u_g = w/p = g_h,$$ (20)

that results from assuming that C-goods and G-goods are perfect substitutes.

When an increase in nonlabor income increases the options open to the household, the demands for C, G, and L will each increase so long as each is normal. In order to obtain the increase in G-goods demanded, the household must increase the time spent in their production. Put differently, the increase in nonlabor income will alter the marginal rate of substitution of G-goods for C-goods, (u_g/u_c) in (37), and the household will adjust its household productivity, g_h, by changing H to compensate.

6. The two-person model outlined in mathematical note 4 can be altered to illustrate the specialization of function and division of labor between spouses. In contrast to mathematical note 4, assume that the wife's and husband's household work times, H_f and H_m, are perfect substitutes. That is, the wife and the husband can do household work equally well. Thus, the household production function becomes

$$G = g(H_f + H_m; X). \tag{23a}$$

This implies that the marginal products of his and her household work times are equal: $g_f = g_m = g_h$. As in the text, assume also that $w_m < w_f$.

The couple has the incentive to produce any given level of household-produced goods as cheaply as possible. The marginal cost of producing G using H_f is w_f/g_h and the marginal cost of G using H_m is w_m/g_h. Since $w_f > w_m$, it is cheaper to use the husband's time in household production and none of the wife's. Consequently, there are two possible situations in which the couple maximizes satisfaction. One is expressed by the Lagrangean

$$\text{Lg} = u(C + G, L_f, L_m) - \lambda(pC + w_f L_f + w_m L_m + w_m H_m - w_f T_f - w_m T_m - V), \tag{38}$$

which, when maximized, yields

$$u_c - \lambda p = 0, \tag{39}$$

$$u_g g_h - \lambda w_m = 0, \tag{40}$$

$$u_f - \lambda w_f = 0, \tag{41}$$

$$u_m - \lambda w_m = 0. \tag{42}$$

Recognizing that $u_c = u_g$ (because C and G are perfect substitutes) and solving for λ yields

$$u_m/u_c = w_m/p = g_h, \tag{43}$$

$$u_f/u_c = w_f/p > g_h. \tag{44}$$

The marginal rate of substitution of his leisure for goods equals his real wage rate and his household productivity, in equilibrium. Her marginal rate of substitution of leisure for goods equals her real wage rate and both exceed her household productivity. In this situation the couple has a large enough demand for goods and services relative to his leisure that she specializes completely in market work and he does both market and household work.

The other possible situation is expressed by the Lagrangean

$$\text{Lg} = u(C + G; L_f, L_m) - \lambda_y(pC + w_f L_f - w_f T_f - V) - \lambda_m(H_m - L_m - T_m), \tag{45}$$

which, when maximized, yields

$$u_c - \lambda_y p = 0, \tag{46}$$

$$u_g g_h - \lambda_m = 0, \tag{47}$$

$$u_m - \lambda_m = 0, \tag{48}$$

$$u_f - \lambda_y w_f = 0. \tag{49}$$

Thus,

$$u_f/u_c = w_f/p, \tag{50}$$

and since $g_h > w_m/p$, because the husband is specialized in household work,

$$u_m/u_c = g_h > w_m/p. \tag{51}$$

Here, the wife is completely specialized in market work and her husband is completely specialized in household work. The marginal rate of substitution of her leisure for goods equals her real wage rate. The marginal rate of substitution of his leisure for goods equals his household productivity, and both exceed his real wage rate. In this situation, the couple's demand for goods and services relative to his leisure is low enough that he is not induced to work both at home and in the labor market.

Chapter 6

1. Total wealth really represents the total amount of resources available to the household. Total wealth in this chapter is the analogue to the full income concept used in Chapter 5.
2. The rate of return is the only investment criterion for a wealth-maximizing household with perfect foresight, the case under discussion. There are other criteria, like the certainty of the rate of return if, in the more realistic case, the future is not foreseen perfectly. These added criteria are a major focus in standard finance theory texts.
3. Be clear about what has been said here. As MC in equation (6.3) becomes larger, holding the stream of benefits, $E'_t - E_t$, constant, the rate of return, i, must fall in order to maintain the equality between marginal benefits and marginal costs.
4. The term *student* comes from the Latin verb *studere*, "to be zealous."
5. Demand curve $D_s D_s$ can also represent the demand curve for education in the case in which education not only raises market productivity, w/p, but also household productivity, g_h. This will be discussed in greater detail later.
6. Our word *pupil* comes from Latin *pupillus* (feminine, *pupilla*), "orphan" or "ward." The pupil is, then, the ward of the teacher and, like most orphans in fiction, an unwilling one!
7. This statement ignores monopsonistic labor markets, discriminatory wage differentials, and wage differentials that compensate workers for working in unsafe or distasteful occupations and for working at unpleasant locations and times. See Ehrenberg & Smith 1982, chaps. 5 and 8, for a treatment of these issues.
8. In reality, there is a continuum from general experience to specific experience rather than two discrete and mutually exclusive categories. The student who learns to use the university's computer, for instance, learns how to program and use any computer as well as the idiosyncrasies of the university's computer system.
9. See Becker 1975, chap. 2, for a more detailed discussion of general and specific human capital.
10. Another reason annual earnings begin to fall past middle age is that as the wage rate rises, individuals faced with the work–leisure trade-off discussed in Chapter 5 will increase their demand for leisure, reducing the number of hours they work annually. With the reduction in annual work time comes a decline in annual earnings. This partially explains why annual vacations tend to increase with job seniority.
11. We exclude room and board as costs of college since one must be housed and fed regardless of whether one is in college.
12. Suppose the output of leisure activities is denoted by R, where R stands for recreation. The output, R, can be viewed as an index of the music made or listened to, vacations taken, books read, TV programs watched, chess games played, etc. Suppose, further, that the output of recreation activities increases with the time, L, spent

in leisure activities and with the amount of other inputs that are used with the leisure time, X, (e.g., books, beer, TVs, musical instruments, theater tickets, chess sets, skiing equipment). Then the recreation activity can be written as $R = r(L, X,)$ where $r_l = \partial R/\partial L$ = the marginal product of time in leisure activities; that is, the added amount of recreation output obtainable by increasing the amount of time spent in leisure activities by 1 hr.

13. This expression is a generalization of expression (1.25) in Becker 1981, pp. 9–12. I have assumed that $\partial H_t/\partial Q_{t-1} = 1$ in Becker's expression (1.25).

14. Any reduction in household productivity would be represented by a counterclockwise rotation of $A'B'$ around B', lowering the slope of $A'B'$ in exactly the same way that Robinson Crusoe's injury sustained while bodysurfing rotated at AT to BT in Figure 5.3.

Chapter 7

1. U.S. Bureau of the Census 1982, Table 84, p. 60; and 1960, Table B, 19–30, p. 23. The white birthrate declined from 55 per 1,000 population in 1800 to 17.6 in 1933, increased to 24 in 1956 (the peak year of the baby boom), and decreased to 14.8 in 1979. The nonwhite birthrate declined from 35 in 1920 (the first year for which data exist) to 25.5 in 1933, rose to 35.4 in 1956, and declined to 22.8 in 1979.

2. Sociobiologists remind us that from an evolutionary perspective ensuring that one's gene pool survives and continues into future generations is a powerful drive, whether for iguanas or for humans. Success and happiness, therefore, derive from the number of progeny. Here is a fourth way in which children yield satisfaction to their parents.

3. Among the ancient Romans, "infanticide remained an accepted practice, widespread among the poor, occasional among their betters. Roman Law also sanctioned . . . the custom of selling surplus children" (Gies & Gies 1987, p. 27).

4. The basic model is that developed by Becker and Lewis (1974).

5. It is obvious that the children in any family differ in their education, health, physical and social prowess, and psychological well-being, even if parents endeavor to endow each of their children equally. For a discussion of family models in which our assumption of equality of treatment among children is dropped, see Pollak 1988.

6. The woman's wage rate, w, comes very close to being the woman's permanent wage rate over the couple's expected life. The term *permanent* is used in the same sense as in *permanent income* in Chapter 4. This is because, by necessity, it ignores the year-to-year variations in her wage rate throughout the period. These year-to-year variations can be interpreted as transitory variations around a permanent level.

7. Again, it is to be noted that this is a simple model. In reality, couples' plans change over time as they learn more about their own biology and preferences, their resources, and the prices of the things they demand. Furthermore, it may be that having the first child alters plans for subsequent ones. This model neglects these changes, which may be one other reason actual family size can differ from initial (i.e., at the beginning of the marriage), desired family size.

8. The income elasticity of demand for money expenditures on children is $N_{xc} = p_{xc}(\partial X_c/\partial Y)(Y/p_{xc}X_c)$. Since $p_{xc}(\partial X_c/\partial Y) = 0.21$ and $Y/p_{xc}X_c = 2.17$, $N_{xc} = 0.21(2.17) = 0.46$.

9. Since the time costs are from birth to 18 yr. of age, it is assumed that the mother spends no time rearing the child from age 18 to age 22. Furthermore, it should be recalled that the estimated time cost includes direct child care and excludes the

increased time spent in food preparation, laundry, and housecleaning as a result of the child. The time costs are somewhat underestimated, therefore.

10. The underestimated time costs of raising a child lead to an overestimate in the fraction of the total costs made up of money costs.

11. Mincer (1963) regresses number of children per family in a sample of urban, white, two-spouse families in which the wife is 35–44 yr. old against the annual wage rate of the wife, the husband's annual earnings, and the husband's education. He finds that the number of children per family increases by .01 child given a $1,000 increase in the husband's earnings, holding the wife's wage rate and the husband's education constant.

12. Female wage rates rose at the rate of 6.5 percent per year between 1955 and 1984, whereas consumer prices rose at the rate of 4.8 percent per year (see Bryant & Wang 1990a).

13. This is really part of a larger question concerning how and by what means the family allocates its resources among family members as family resources and prices change. This is a crucial question for economic development in the Third World. For instance, if one is interested in raising the nutritional status of peasant children, is it more effective to raise the wage rates of men or of women? See Rosenzweig 1986 for a survey of the issues involved in modeling the intrahousehold allocation of resources. See Lazear & Michael 1988 for an empirical study based on American data.

Mathematical notes to Chapter 7

1. The type of household production function used in this chapter is called the fixed coefficient function and can be expressed as follows:

$$b_c C = X_c \quad \text{and} \quad t_c C = H_c. \tag{1}$$

Thus, $b_c = X_c/C =$ the purchased goods required to produce a unit of C, and $t_c = H_c/C =$ the time required to produce a unit of C.

The function is called a fixed coefficient function because b_c and t_c are fixed and do not change with increases in X_c or H_c. Using the notation for the household production function introduced in Chapter 5, we could express the child services household production function more generally as

$$C = c(H_c, X_c). \tag{2}$$

In this formulation $\partial C/\partial H_c = c_h$ is the marginal product of the woman's time in the production of child services and C/H_c is the average product of the woman's time in the production of child services. Likewise, $\partial C/\partial X_c = c_x$ and C/X_c are the marginal and average products of purchased inputs in the production of child services, respectively. Note that $1/t_c = \partial C/\partial H_c = C/H_c$ and $1/b_c = \partial C/\partial X_c = C/X_c$ are the marginal and average products of the woman's time and purchased inputs in the production of child services in the fixed coefficient production function. It is because the average and marginal products are equal that the function is termed "fixed coefficient."

It should also be noted that the fixed coefficient production function implies that X_c and H_c are perfect complements. That is, both purchased inputs, X_d, and time, H_c, are required to produce C, and they are required in fixed proportions. We know this because

$$X_c/H_c = b_c C/t_c C = b_c/t_c.$$

Since b_c and t_c are both fixed, so too is their ratio.

2. The choice has to do with whether one is interested in answering questions about the household's behavior with respect to the inputs into household activities or the household activities themselves. Suppose the time constraint is

$$T = H_c + H_s + M \tag{3}$$

where $T =$ the duration of the marriage, $H_c =$ the married woman's time spent in child birthing and rearing, $H_s =$ her time spent in producing parental services, and $M =$ her time in paid employment. Given that the couple exhausts its income over the life of the marriage on the purchases of X_c and X_s, then

$$p_{xc}X_c + p_{xs}X_s = Y \tag{4}$$

where p_{xc} and p_{xs} are the prices of purchased inputs into C and S, respectively, and $Y =$ total expected family income over the life of the marriage. Furthermore,

$$Y = wM + V \tag{5}$$

where $w =$ the wife's wage rate and $V =$ the husband's earnings plus the couple's unearned income.

Combining (3), (4), and (5) yields the couple's total budget line:

$$p_{xc}X_c + wH_c + p_{xs}X_s + wH_s = wT + V. \tag{6}$$

Note that (6) is expressed in input space and, therefore, is useful only if the analysis pertains to the inputs into the production and consumption of child or parental services.

To transform (6) into the form useful for analyzing behavior with respect to C or S (i.e., output space), substitute the fixed coefficient production function for child services, equation (1), and its analogue for parental services into (6) to get

$$p_{xc}b_cC + wt_cC + p_{xs}b_sS + wt_sS = wT + V.$$

Factoring out C and S and letting $p_{xc}b_c + wt_c = p_c$ and $p_{xs}b_s + wt_s = p_s$ yields

$$p_cC + p_sS = wT + V, \tag{7}$$

which is the budget constraint in output space and the one used in the text of the chapter.

3. The income effect on total expenditures on child services is

$$\partial(p_cC)/\partial Y = p_{xc}\partial X_c/\partial Y + w\partial H_c/\partial Y.$$

Multiplying through by Y/p_cC yields

$$N_c = (p_{xc}/p_cC)(\partial X_c/\partial Y)Y + (w/p_cC)(\partial H_c/\partial Y)Y.$$

Mutliplying the first term on the right-hand side by X_c/X_c and the second term on the right-hand side by H_c/H_c, defining $p_{xc}X_c/p_cC = s_c$ and $wH_c/p_cC = 1 - s_c$, yields

$$N_c = s_cN_{xc} + (1 - s_c)N_t \tag{7.12}$$

where $N_{xc} =$ income elasticity of demand for purchased goods and services for children, $N_t =$ income elasticity of demand for child care time, and $s_c =$ the fraction or "share" of total expenditures on child services made up of money expenditures.

4. The income effect on child services can be decomposed as follows:

$$\partial C/\partial Y = \partial(NQ)/\partial Y = Q\partial N/\partial Y + N\partial Q/\partial Y.$$

Multiplying through by $Y/C = Y/NQ$ yields

$$(\partial C/\partial Y)(Y/C) = (\partial N/\partial Y)(Y/N) + (\partial Q/\partial Y)(Q/Y)$$

or

$$N_c = N_n + N_q.$$

5. The mathematical issue here is the effect of a change in V on the price of children relative to the price of human capital:

$$\frac{\partial(p_n/p_q)}{\partial V} = \frac{\partial(p_cQ/p_cN)}{\partial V} = \frac{\partial(Q/N)}{\partial V} = \frac{(N\partial Q/\partial V) - (Q\partial N/\partial V)}{N^2}$$

Multiplying through by VN/Q expresses the result in terms of income elasticities:

$$N_{(q/n)} = N_q - N_n$$

where $N_{(q/n)}$ is the percentage change in the price of children relative to human capital per child given a 1 percent change in income. Thus, if the income elasticity of demand for human capital per child is larger than the income elasticity of demand for numbers of children, then an increase in unearned income will increase the price of the number of children relative to the price of human capital per child.

6. The issue can be addressed by differentiating C^m with respect to w as follows:

$$\frac{\partial C^m}{\partial w} = \frac{\partial[(wT + V)/(p_x b_c + wt_c)]}{\partial w} = \frac{p_c T - FYt_c}{p_c^2} = \frac{T - C^m t_c}{p_c}.$$

Since t_c = the time required to produce and consume one unit of child service, $C^m t_c = H_c^m$ = the time required to produce and consume C^m units of child services. But since $T \geq H_c^m$, $\partial C^m/\partial w \geq 0$.

7. The issue is whether $\partial(p_c/p_s)/\partial w$ is positive, negative, or 0. Differentiating p_c/p_s with respect to w yields

$$\partial(p_c/p_s)/\partial w = (p_s t_c - p_c t_s)/p_s^2. \qquad (8)$$

Since $p_s^2 > 0$, the sign of (8) depends on the sign of the numerator; that is,

$$p_s t_c - p_c t_s. \qquad (9)$$

Thus,

$$\partial(p_c/p_s)/\partial w \gtreqless 0 \quad \text{if} \quad p_s t_c - p_c t_s \gtreqless 0.$$

Adding $p_c t_s$ to both sides of (9) and multiplying by $w/p_c p_s$ yields

$$wt_c/p_c > wt_s/p_s, \qquad (10)$$

the expression used in the text.

8. The price per child including the subsidy is derived as follows. Focusing on children rather than child services, let the couple derive satisfaction from intercourse without

contraception, I_o, intercourse with contraception, I_w, children, N, and all other goods, A; that is,

$$U = u(I_w, I_o, N, A). \tag{11}$$

Suppose that the average number of times intercourse must occur without contraception for one conception to occur is b. Then,

$$bN = I_o. \tag{12}$$

Clearly, b varies with the couple's biology and with contraceptive technique. The couple's budget constraint is

$$p_w I_w + p_o I_o + p_g N + p_a A = Y \tag{13}$$

where p_w = the cost of coitus with contraception, p_o = cost of coitus without contraception (where $p_o < p_w$), p_g = cost per child from conception onward (i.e., excluding the cost of intercourse), and p_a = price index of other goods and services.

The couple maximizes satisfaction, (11), subject to its budget constraint, (13). The equilibrium conditions are derived by differentiating the Lagrangean expression

$$\text{Lg} = u(I_w, bN, N, A) - \lambda[p_w I_w + (p_o b + p_g)N + p_a A - Y] \tag{14}$$

with respect to I_w, N, and A and setting each derivative equal to 0; that is,

$$u_w - \lambda p_w = 0, \tag{15}$$

$$u_o b + u_n - \lambda(p_o b + p_g) = 0, \tag{16}$$

$$u_a - \lambda p_a = 0, \tag{17}$$

where u_w = the marginal utility of intercourse with contraception, u_o = marginal utility of intercourse without contraception, u_n = the marginal utility of children, u_a = marginal utility of all other goods and services, and λ = marginal utility of income.

Solving (16) for u_n and dividing through by λ yields

$$u_n/\lambda = p_o b + p_g - bu_o/\lambda. \tag{18}$$

Substituting u_w/p_w for λ on the right-hand side of (18) yields

$$u_n/\lambda = p_g - b(p_w u_o/u_w - p_o). \tag{19}$$

Equation (19) says that when the couple is in equilibrium, the satisfaction they would receive from an additional dollar spent "purchasing" a child, u_n/λ, must equal the price of an added child, where the price per child is

$$p_n = p_g - b(p_w u_o/u_w - p_o). \tag{20}$$

But p_g is the cost of a child from conception onward and

$$S_c = b(p_w u_o/u_w - p_o) \tag{21}$$

is the per child subsidy received by the couple from not having to use contraceptives during intercourse when children are wanted. In particular, the subsidy is the difference between the cost of contracepted intercouse weighted by the marginal rate of substitution of intercourse without contraception for contracepted intercourse and the cost of intercourse without contraception all multiplied by the average number of times uncontracepted intercourse must occur for conception to occur. This is the amount saved per child by being able to have intercourse without, rather than with, contraception.

Any change in contraceptive technology that lowers the cost of contraceptive use will lower p_w and, thus, lower the subsidy granted to couples seeking to have children and will raise the price of children. The introduction of family planning will lower the cost of contraceptive knowledge and also lower p_w. Also, the relaxation of moral injunctions against contraception will raise u_w, induce couples to use more effective contraceptive methods, and lower the subsidy and raise the price of children.

9. This can be shown algebraically. Let β = the probability that any conception will end in death before the end of the first year of life. $1 - \beta$, therefore, is the probability that any foetus will survive beyond the first year. Let V = the total number of conceptions, N = the number of children who survive the first year, and D = the number of conceptions terminating in death prior to the end of the first year.

Based on the probability of infant mortality, β, the expected number of children surviving past the first year is

$$E(N) = (1 - \beta)V. \tag{22}$$

The expected number of infant deaths is

$$E(D) = \beta V. \tag{23}$$

Define p_n as the actual cost of a child through the first year. The couple must pay p_n whether the child survives or not. Then the expected total cost (ETC) of a couple's children through the first year will be

$$ETC = p_n E(D) + p_n E(N) = p_n \beta V + p_n (1 - \beta)V \tag{24}$$

where $p_n E(D)$ is the expected cost of those not surviving and $p_n E(N)$ is the expected cost of those who survive. Since the expected total cost of children is spread over the surviving children, we can divide the expected total cost by the expected number of surviving children to obtain the expected cost per surviving child. Denoting the expected cost per surviving child as p_n^*, then

$$p_n^* = \frac{p_n \beta V + p_n(1 - \beta)V}{(1 - \beta)V} = \frac{p_n(\beta + 1 - \beta)V}{(1 - \beta)V} = \frac{p_n V}{(1 - \beta)V} \tag{25}$$

or

$$p_n^* = p_n[1/(1 - \beta)]. \tag{26}$$

Since $0 < \beta < 1, p_n^* > p_n$. Thus, the higher β, the higher the expected price of surviving children.

$1/(1 - \beta)$ can be viewed as the insurance premium per dollar cost of a child that one must pay in order to be compensated for the cost of a child should it die.

Chapter 8

1. A more complete treatment may be found in Becker 1981.

2. Two individuals "cooperatively bargain" to form a marriage when they maximize the product $U_f U_m$, of their respective utilities (where U_f = the female's utility when married and U_m = the male's) subject to the budget and time constraints and subject to the proviso that the marriage provides each mate at least as much satisfaction as each would have had by remaining single.

3. Even if individuals have no choice over whether and whom they marry or divorce, an economic theory of marriage is still possible if focused on the parties that do have choice; for example, their parents in those societies in which marriage is arranged by parents on behalf of their children.

4. Furthermore, at least for marriage it is frequently the parents of the principals that pay for much, if not all, of the monetary transaction case. In the case of divorce, however, the couple pays the transaction costs.

5. The mathematical conditions under which one can aggregate all the different house-hold activities into one global household activity are stringent. Consequently, this is one of the foci for criticism of this particular model. See Manser & Brown 1979.

6. Notice that this amounts to a lot of hand waving. By aggregating all household activities into one global activity on which individuals' well-being depends, the prob-lem of making interpersonal utility comparisons is finessed. But every finesse comes at a cost. The cost in this case is the stringent conditions that must be met in order to aggregate all household activities into one global activity. Indeed, some economists count the cost too high and opt for alternative formulations. See, for instance, Manser & Brown 1979.

7. Women outnumber men primarily because of the higher mortality rate among men.

8. Actually, the N_{m-1} males with single outputs below Z_{mx} would marry because each of them would receive Z_{mx} as his marital share, which would exceed his single output. The N_{mx}th male would be indifferent between marriage and remaining single because Z_{mx} would equal his single output.

9. The qualitative conclusions from the demand curve derived using this simplification are the same if Z_{mf} varies among marriages.

10. This would happen, for instance, if medical research reduced female-specific diseases by more than male-specific diseases; say, if breast and uterine cancers were reduced but prostate cancer was not. An exogenous increase in the number of women did occur in colonial French Canada when, in response to the dearth of women in the colony, the French authorities recruited French women willing to emigrate to Can-ada and marry there (McInnis 1959, p. 54). Today, advertising and publicity achieve the same end. Currently, there is an excess of men in Alaska, and a magazine pub-lished in Anchorage and entitled *Alaska Men* advertises the marriage virtues of men in Alaska.

11. The fall in the fraction of females married as the number of females in the population increases occurs so long as the supply curve of male mates is positively sloped. When the supply curve is positively sloped, $N_{mfe'} - N_{mfe} < N_{f'} - N_f$ and, in consequence, the fraction of females married will fall.

12. Even if males and females are perfect substitutes in market work, their wage rates may differ because of discrimination. Thus, discrimination is ruled out here.

13. A more complete discussion of specialization of function and division of labor as it applies to the household can be found in Chapter 5 and in Becker 1981, chap. 2.

14. When H_f is fixed at 0 for a single male household, $c_m = w_m/z_m > w_f/z_f$, indicating that if H_f were increased to some positive amount and H_m were reduced below H_m^*, total cost would fall for the same output. But, if this were done, then the household would no longer be a single male household and the average cost would be denoted by c_{mf}. Since total cost would fall for the same output, $c_{mf} < c_m$.

15. It should be noted here that Santos (1972) used annual earnings of married females with spouse present. Annual earnings are the product of wage rates and annual hours worked. To the extent that annual hours worked varied among states, annual earnings do not reflect interstate variations in wage rates. Freidan (1974) solved this problem by using the annual earnings of females and males who worked full-time, full-year. Consequently, interstate variations in Freidan's male/female ratio variable did constitute variations in wage rates rather than in hours of work. Therefore, Freidan's results are of somewhat higher quality than Santos's results. However, one should not completely dismiss Santos's findings on this count.
16. See Peters 1986 for an elaboration of this argument and empirical evidence bearing on it.
17. The applicability of the principle of comparative advantage to marriage is much greater than this. In general, the gains from marriage are also greater if one spouse has comparative advantage in some household activities while the other spouse has comparative advantage in other household activities. If so, then further specialization of function and division of labor can occur. For instance, one spouse may specialize in yard work, car maintenance, and laundry while the other may specialize in financial planning and management, meal preparation, and housecleaning.
18. For an analysis of the extent to which spouses share household activities see Bryant & Wang 1990b.
19. Of course, other strategies, like adoption, surrogate mothers, or artificial insemination, can also be utilized to rectify too few children early in the marriage caused by the infertility of either or both of the partners.

Mathematical notes to Chapter 8

1. Equation (8.22) is derived as follows. Begin with equation (8.17), $G = Z_{mf} - Z_m - Z_f$, and multiply Z_{mf} by I_{mf}/I_{mf}, Z_m by I_m/I_m and Z_f by I_f/I_f to get

$$G = I_{mf}/(I_{mf}/Z_{mf}) - I_m/(I_m/Z_m) - I_f/(I_f/Z_f). \qquad (1)$$

Since $I_{mf} = w_m H_m + w_f H_f + p_x X$ from equation (8.14) and $I_i = w_w H_i + p_x X$ $(i = m, f)$ from equation (8.15), the I_{mf}, I_m, and I_f in the denominators of equation (1) can be replaced to get

$$G = \frac{I_{mf}}{(w_m H_m + w_f H_f + p_x X)/Z_{mf}} - \frac{I_m}{(w_m H_m + p_x X)/Z_m} - \frac{I_f}{(w_f H_f + p_x X)/Z_f}. \qquad (2)$$

However, $(w_m H_m + w_f H_f + p_x X)/Z_{mf} = C_{mf}$ from equation (8.20) and $(w_i H_i + p_x X)/Z_i = C_i$ $(i = m, f)$ from equation (8.21). Thus,

$$G = (I_{mf}/C_{mf}) - [(I_m/C_m) + (I_f/C_f)].$$

2. Equation (8.23) is derived as follows:

$$\frac{\partial G}{\partial w_i} = \left[\left(\frac{c_{mf}\partial I_{mf}}{\partial w_i} - \frac{I_{mf}\partial c_{mf}}{\partial w_i} \right) \Big/ c_{mf}^2 \right] - \left[\left(\frac{c_i \partial I_i}{\partial w_i} - \frac{I_i \partial c_i}{\partial w_i} \right) \Big/ c_i^2 \right], \qquad \text{for } i = m, f,$$

$$= \left[T_i - \frac{(I_{mf}/c_{mf})\partial c_{mf}}{\partial w_i} \Big/ c_{mf} \right] - \left[T_i - \frac{(I_i/c_i)\partial c_i}{\partial w_i} \Big/ c_i \right]. \qquad (3)$$

Since $I_{mf}/c_{mf} = Z_{mf}$ and $I_i/c_i = Z_i$ (equations [8.20] and [8.21]),

$$\frac{\partial G}{\partial w_i} = \left[T_i - \frac{Z_{mf}\partial c_{mf}}{\partial w_i} \Big/ c_{mf} \right] - \left[T_i - \frac{Z_i \partial c_i}{\partial w_i} \Big/ c_i \right]. \tag{4}$$

But

$$\frac{\partial c_{mf}}{\partial w_i} = \frac{\partial[(p_x X + w_m H_m + w_f H_f)/Z_{mf}]}{\partial w_i} = \frac{H_i^m}{Z_{mf}} \tag{5}$$

where H_i^m = the time individual i spends in household production if married. Similarly,

$$\frac{\partial c_i}{\partial w_i} = \frac{[(p_x X + w_i H_i)/Z_i]}{\partial w_i} = \frac{H_i^s}{Z_i} \tag{6}$$

where H_i^s = the time individual i spends in household production if single. Substituting (5) and (6) into (4) yields

$$\frac{\partial G}{\partial w_i} = \frac{T_i - H_i^m}{c_{mf}} - \frac{T_i - H_i^s}{c_i}. \tag{7}$$

Since $T_i - H_i^m = L_i^m$ (the time the individual spends in market work if married) and $T_i - H_i^s = L_i^s$ (the time the individual spends in market work if single),

$$\frac{\partial G}{\partial w_i} = \frac{L_m^m}{c_{mf}} - \frac{L_i^s}{c_i}, \qquad \text{for } i = m, f.$$

Note that this formula applies to either sex.

Adrian, J., & R. Daniel. 1976. "Impact of Socioeconomic Factors on Consumption of Selected Food Nutrients in the United States." *American Journal of Agricultural Economics* 58:31–8.

Ando, A., & F. Modigliani. 1963. "The Life-Cycle Hypothesis of Saving: Aggregate Implications and Tests." *American Economic Review* 53:55–84.

Becker, G. S. 1965. "A Theory of the Allocation of Time." *Economic Journal* 75(299):493–517.

1973–4. "A Theory of Marriage: Parts I and II." *Journal of Political Economy* 81(4):813–46; 82(2):S11–S26.

1975. *Human Capital.* 2d ed. New York: Columbia University Press for the NBER.

1981. *A Treatise on the Family.* Cambridge: Harvard University Press.

Becker, G. S., & G. Lewis. 1974. "Interaction between Quantity and Quality of Children." In T. W. Schultz (ed.), *Economics of the Family: Marriage, Children and Human Capital,* pp. 81–90. Chicago: University of Chicago Press for the NBER.

Becker, G. S., R. T. Michael, & E. M. Landes. 1977. "An Economic Analysis of Marital Instability." *Journal of Political Economy* 85(6):1153–89.

Beierlein, J. G., J. W. Dunn, & J. C. McCornon, Jr. 1981. "The Demand for Electricity in the Northeastern United States." *Review of Economics and Statistics* 58(3):403–8.

Bergstrom, T. C. 1989. "A Fresh Look at the Rotten Kid Theorem and Other Household Mysteries." *Journal of Political Economy* 97(5):1138–55.

Bloom, D. 1986. "Women and Work." *American Demographics.* September, pp. 25–30.

Bryant, W. K. 1986. "Technical Change and the Family: An Initial Foray." In R. E. Deacon & W. E. Huffman (eds.), *Human Resources Research, 1887–1987: Proceedings.* pp. 117–26. College of Home Economics, Iowa State University.

Bryant, W. K., & Y. Wang. 1990. "American Consumption Patterns and the Price of Time: A Time-Series Analysis." *Journal of Consumer Affairs* 24(2):280–306.

Bryant, W. K., & Y. Wang. 1990. "Time Together, Time Apart: An Economic Analysis of Wives' Solitary Time and Time Shared with Spouses." *Lifestyles.* 11(1):87–117.

Burkhauser, R. V., & J. A. Turner. 1978. "A Time-Series Analysis on Social Security and Its Effects on the Market Work Decision of Men at Younger Ages." *Journal of Political Economy* 86(4):701–16.

Cairncross, A. K. 1958. "Economic Schizophrenia." *Scottish Journal of Political Economy* 5:15–21.

Campbell, C. R., & J. M. Lovati. 1979. "Inflation and Personal Saving: An Update." *Federal Reserve Bank of St. Louis Review* 61(8):3–9.

Capps, O., Jr., & J. Havlicek, Jr. 1987. "Analysis of Household Demand for Meat, Poultry, and Seafood Using the S_1-Branch System." In R. Raunikar and C.-L.

Huang, (eds.), *Food Demand Analysis: Problems, Issues, and Empirical Evidence*, pp. 128–42. Ames: Iowa State University Press.

Cochrane, S. H., & S. P. Logan. 1975. "The Demand for Wife's Nonmarket Time: A Comparison of Results from Surveys of Chicago School Teachers and South Carolina College Graduates." *Southern Economic Journal* 42:285–93.

Cogan, J. 1980. "Labor Supply with Fixed Costs of Labor Market Entry." In J. P. Smith (ed.), *Female Labor Supply*, pp. 327–64. Princeton, N.J.: Princeton University Press.

Cowan, R. S. 1983. *More Work for Mother: The Ironies of Household Technology from the Open Hearth to the Microwave*. New York: Basic Books.

Danziger, S., R. Haveman, & R. Plotnick. 1981. "How Income Transfer Programs Affect Work, Savings, and the Income Distribution: A Critical Review." *Journal of Economic Literature* 19(1):975–1028.

Deaton, A., and J. Muellbauer. 1981. *Economics and Consumer Behavior*. New York: Cambridge University Press.

Dooley, M. D. 1982. "Labor Supply and Fertility of Married Women: An Analysis with Grouped and Ungrouped Data from the 1970 U.S. Census." *Journal of Human Resources* 17:499–532.

Duesenberry, J. 1967. *Income, Saving, and the Theory of Consumer Behavior*. New York: Oxford University Press.

Duncan, G. 1984. *Times of Poverty, Years of Plenty*. Ann Arbor: Survey Research Center, Institute for Social Research, University of Michigan.

Eastwood, D. B., & J. A. Craven. 1981. "Food Demand and Savings in a Complete Extended Linear Expenditure System." *American Journal of Agricultural Economics* 63(3):544–9.

Edwards, L. N., & M. Grossman. 1979. "The Relationship between Children's Health and Intellectual Development." In S. J. Mushkin & D. W. Dunlop (eds.), *Health: What Is It Worth? Measures of Health Benefits*, Chap. 12. New York: Pergamon Press.

Ehrenberg, R. G., & R. S. Smith. 1982. *Modern Labor Economics*. Glenview, Ill.: Scott, Foresman & Co.

Evenson, R. E. 1978. "Time Allocation in Rural Philippine Households." *American Journal of Agricultural Economics* 60(2):323–30.

Fleisher, B. M., & G. F. Rhodes. 1979. "Fertility, Women's Wage Rates, and Labor Supply." *American Economic Review* 69(1):14–24.

Frank, R. 1985. "The Demand for Unobservable and Other Nonpositional Goods." *American Economic Review* 75(1):101–16.

Freidan, A. 1974. "The U.S. Marriage Market." In T. W. Schultz (ed.), *Economics of the Family: Marriage, Children and Human Capital*, pp. 352–71. Chicago: University of Chicago Press for the NBER.

Friedman, M. 1957. *A Theory of the Consumption Function*. Princeton: Princeton University Press for the NBER.

Gerner, J. L., & C. D. Zick. 1983. "Time Allocation Decisions in Two-Parent Families." *Home Economics Research Journal* 12(2):145–58.

Ghez, G. R., & G. S. Becker. 1975. *The Allocation of Time and Goods over the Lifecycle*. New York: Columbia University Press for the NBER.

Gies, F., & J. Gies. 1987. *Marriage and the Family in the Middle Ages*. New York: Harper & Row Publishers.

Goldsmith, R. W. 1955. *A Study of Saving in the US*, Volume I. Princeton, N.J.: Princeton University Press.

Graham, J. W., & C. A. Green. 1984. "Estimating the Parameters of a Household Production Function with Joint Products." *Review of Economics and Statistics* 66(2):277–82.

Gramm, W. L. 1974. "The Demand for the Wife's Nonmarket Time." *Southern Economic Journal* 41:124–33.

Gronau, R. 1977. "Leisure, Home Production, and Work–The Theory of the Allocation of Time Revisited." *Journal of Political Economy* 85(6):1099–123.

Grossman, M. 1976. "The Correlation between Health and Schooling." In N. Terleckj (ed.), *Household Production and Consumption*, pp. 147–211. Studies in Income and Wealth, vol. 40. New York: Columbia University Press for the NBER.

Hager, C. J., & W. K. Bryant. 1977. "Clothing Expenditures of Low Income Rural Families." *Journal of Consumer Affairs* 11(2):127–32.

Hall, R. E. 1988. "Intertemporal Substitution in Consumption." *Journal of Political Economy* 96(2):339–57.

Henderson, J. M., & R. E. Quandt. 1958. *Microeconomic Theory*. New York: McGraw-Hill Book Co.

Hicks, J. R. 1946. *Value and Capital*. 2d ed. Oxford: Clarendon Press.

Hill, C. R., & F. P. Stafford. 1985. "Parental Care of Children: Time Diary Estimates of Quantity, Predictability, and Variety." In F. T. Juster & F. P. Stafford (eds.), *Time, Goods, and Well-Being*, Chap. 17. Ann Arbor: Survey Research Center, Institute for Social Research, University of Michigan.

Hill, M. S. 1985. "Patterns of Time Use." In F. T. Juster & F. P. Stafford (eds.), *Time, Goods, and Well-Being*, Chap. 7. Ann Arbor: Survey Research Center, Institute for Social Research, University of Michigan.

Hill, R., & F. Stafford. 1974. "Allocation of Time to Preschool Children and Educational Opportunity." *Journal of Human Resources* 9(3):323–41.

Hirshleifer, J. 1976. *Price Theory and Applications*. Englewood Cliffs, N.J.: Prentice-Hall.

Houthakker, H., & L. Taylor. 1970. *Consumer Demand in the United States*. Cambridge: Harvard University Press.

Juster, F. T., et al. 1978. "Time Use in Economic and Social Accounts." Ann Arbor Survey Research Center, University of Michigan, Manuscript.

Keynes, J. M. 1936. *The General Theory of Employment, Interest and Money*. London: Macmillan.

Kiefer, N. M. 1977. "A Bayesian Analysis of Commodity Demand and Labor Supply." *International Economic Review* 18(1):209–18.

Killingsworth, M. R., & J. J. Heckman. 1986. "Female Labor Supply: A Survey." In O. C. Ashenfelter & R. Layard (eds.), *Handbook of Labor Economics*, vol. 1, pp. 103–98. New York: North-Holland Publishing Co.

Kooreman, P., & A. Kapteyn. 1987. "A Disaggregated Analysis of the Allocation of Time within the Household." *Journal of Political Economy* 95(2):223–49.

Kuznets, S. S. 1942. *Uses of National Income in Peace and War*. New York: NBER.

Lancaster, K. J. 1966a. "Change and Innovation in the Technology of Consumption." *American Economic Review* 56:14–23.

——— 1966b. "A New Approach to Consumer Theory." *Journal of Political Economy* 74:132–57.

Lange, M. D. 1979. "Economic Analysis of Time Allocation and Capital–Labor Ratios in Household Production of Farm Families in Iowa." Ph.D. diss., Iowa State University.

Lazear, E. P., & R. T. Michael. 1988. *Allocation of Income within the Household*. Chicago: University of Chicago Press.

Lebergott, S. 1968. "Labor Force and Employment Trends." In E. Sheldon and W. E. Moore (eds.), *Indicators of Social Change: Concepts and Measurement*. chap. 4. New York: Russell Sage Foundation.

McInnis, E. 1959. *Canada: A Political and Social History*. Rev. ed. New York: Rinehart & Co.

Mann, J. S., & G. E. St. George. 1978. *Estimates of Elasticities for Food Demand in the United States*. Economics, Statistics, and Cooperative Service Technical Bulletin 1580. Washington, D.C.: U.S. Department of Agriculture.

Manser, M., & M. Brown. 1979. "Bargaining Analyses of Household Decisions." In C. B. Lloyd, E. S. Andrews, & C. L. Gilroy (eds.), *Women in the Labor Market*, chap. 1. New York: Columbia University Press.

1980. "Marriage and Household Decision-Making: A Bargaining Analysis." *International Economic Review* 21(1):31–44.

Mansfield, E. 1982. *Microeconomics: Theory and Applications*. 4th ed. New York: W. W. Norton Co.

Mayer, T. 1972. *Permanent Income, Wealth and Consumption*. Berkeley and Los Angeles: University of California Press.

Mincer, J. 1963. "Market Prices, Opportunity Costs, and Income Effects." In C. Christ et al., (eds.), *Measurement in Economics: Studies in Mathematical Economics and Econometrics in Memory of Yehuda Grunfeld*, pp. 75–9. Stanford, Calif.: Stanford University Press.

1974. *Schooling, Experience, and Earnings*. New York: Columbia University Press for NBER.

Mitchell, W. C. 1912. "The Backward Art of Spending Money," *American Economic Review* 2:269–81.

Moffitt, R. 1984. "The Estimation of Fertility Equations on Panel Data." *Journal of Human Resources* 19(1):22–34.

Muth, R. F. 1966. "Household Production and Consumer Demand Functions." *Econometrica* 34:699–708.

Nerlove, M., & T. P. Schultz. 1970. *Love and Life between the Censuses: A Model of Family Decision Making in Puerto Rico, 1950–1960*. RM-6322-AID. Santa Monica, Calif. Rand Corp.

Olson, L. 1983. *Cost of Children*. Lexington, Mass.: Lexington Books.

O'Neill, B. M. 1978. "Time-Use Patterns of School-Age Children in Household Tasks: A Comparison of 1967–68 Data and 1977 Data." M.S. thesis, Cornell University.

Owen, J. D. 1971. "The Demand for Leisure." *Journal of Political Economy* 79(1): 56–76.

Owen, S. J. 1987. "Household Production and Economic Efficiency: Arguments for and against Domestic Specialization." *Work, Employment & Society* 1(2):157–78.

Pappalardo, J. 1986. "Financial Aid, Labor Supply–Study Time Trade-offs, and Academic Performance Production: An Economic Analysis of Student Resource Allocation." Ph.D. diss., Cornell University.

Pencavel, J. 1986. "Labor Supply of Men: A Survey." In O. C. Ashenfelter & R. Layard (eds.), *Handbook of Labor Economics*, vol. 1, pp. 3–102. New York: North-Holland Publishing Co.

Peters, H. E. 1986. "Marriage and Divorce: Informational Constraints and Private Contracting." *American Economic Review* 76(3):437–54.

Pollak, R. A. 1988. "Tied Transfers and Paternalistic Preferences." *American Economic Review* 78(2):240–4.

Reid, M. 1934. *The Economics of Household Production*. New York: John Wiley & Sons.

Reisman, D. 1950. *The Lonely Crowd: A Study of the Changing American Character*. New Haven: Yale University Press.

Rosenthal, E. 1963. "Studies of Jewish Intermarriage in the United States." *American Jewish Yearbook* 64:3–53.

Rosenzweig, M. R. 1986. "Program Interventions, Intrahousehold Distribution and the

Welfare of Individuals: Modeling Household Behavior." *World Development* 14(2):233–43.

Ross, H. D., & I. V. Sawhill. 1975. *Time of Transition: The Growth of Families Headed by Women*. Washington, D.C.: Urban Institute.

Ryder, N. B., & C. F. Westoff. 1971. *Reproduction in the United States*. Princeton: Princeton University Press.

Sadan, E., & E. Tropp. 1973. "Consumption Function Analysis in a Communal Household: Cross-section and Time Series," *Review of Economics and Statistics* 55(4):475–81.

Sanik, M. M. 1983. "Repeated Measure Design: A Time Use Application." *Home Economics Research Journal* 12(2):122–6.

Santos, F. P. 1972. "Some Economic Determinants of Marital Status." Ph.D. diss., Columbia University.

Schultz, T. P. 1973. "Economic Facts Affecting Population Growth: A Preliminary Survey of Economic Analysis of Fertility." *American Economic Review* 68(2):71–8.

Schultz, T. W. (ed.). 1974. *Economics of the Family*. Chicago: University of Chicago Press for the NBER.

Singh, I., L. Squire, & J. Strauss. 1986. *Agricultural Household Models: Extensions, Applications, and Policy*. Baltimore: Johns Hopkins University Press.

Slutsky, E. 1915. "Sulla Teoria del Bilancio del Consumatore." *Giornale degli Economisti* 51:19–23.

Smith, J. P. 1977. "Family Labor Supply over the Life Cycle." *Explorations in Economic Research* 4(2):205–78.

Smith, J. P., & M. Ward. 1984. *Women's Wages and Work in the Twentieth Century*. R-3119-NICHD. Santa Monica, Calif.: Rand Corp.

Stafford, F. P., & G. Duncan. 1985. "The Use of Time and Technology by Households in the United States." In T. F. Juster & F. P. Stafford (eds.), *Time, Goods, and Well-Being*, chap. 10. Ann Arbor: Survey Research Center, Institute for Social Research, University of Michigan.

Stigler, G. J. 1965. "Notes on the History of the Giffen Paradox." In G. J. Stigler, *Essays in the History of Economics*, pp. 374–85. Chicago: University of Chicago Press.

Strasser, S. 1982. *Never Done: A History of American Housework*. New York: Pantheon Books.

Taylor, L. D. 1975. "The Demand for Electricity: A Survey." *Bell Journal of Economics* 6(1):74–110.

Tyrrell, T. J., & T. D. Mount. 1987. "Analysis of Food and Other Expenditures Using a Linear Logit Model." In R. Raunikar & C.-L. Huang (eds.), *Food Demand Analysis: Problems, Issues, and Empirical Evidence*, pp. 143–53. Ames: Iowa State University Press.

U.S. Bureau of the Census. 1960. *Historical Statistics of the United States: Colonial Times to 1957*. Washington, D.C.: GPO.

    1982. *Statistical Abstract of the United States: 1982–83*. 103d ed. Washington, D.C.: GPO.

    1989. *Statistical Abstract of the United States: 1989*. 109th ed. Washington, D.C.: GPO.

U.S. Bureau of Economic Analysis, U.S. Department of Commerce. 1986. *The National Income and Product Accounts of the United States, 1929–82*. Washington, D.C.: GPO.

Wachtel, P. 1977. "Inflation, Uncertainty and Saving Behavior since the Mid-1950s," *Explorations in Economic Research*, fall, pp. 558–78.

Walker, R., & B. Cude. 1983. "In-Store Shopping Strategies: Time and Money Costs in the Supermarket." *Journal of Consumer Affairs* 17(2):356–69.

282   References

Weber, W. E. 1975. "Interest Rates, Inflation and Consumer Expenditures." *American Economic Review* 65(5):843–58.

Willis, R. J. 1986. "Wage Determinants: A Survey and Reinterpretation of Human Capital Earnings Functions." In O. C. Ashenfelter & R. Layard (eds.), *Handbook of Labor Economics,* vol. 1, chap. 10. Amsterdam: North-Holland Publishing Co.

Wright, C. 1969. "Saving and the Rate of Interest." In A. C. Harberger & M. J. Bailey (eds.), *The Taxation of Income from Capital,* pp. 275–300. Studies of Government Finance. Washington, D.C.: Brookings Institution.

Zick, C. D., & W. K. Bryant. 1983. "Alternative Strategies for Pricing Home Work Time." *Home Economics Research Journal* 12(2):145–58.